Hidden Treasure

Also by F. Aster Barnwell

Meditations on the Apocalypse

The Pilgrim's Companion

www.AsterBarnwell.com

Hidden Treasure

Jesus's Message of
Transformation

F. Aster Barnwell

iUniverse, Inc.
Bloomington

Hidden Treasure
Jesus's Message of Transformation

iUniverse books may be ordered through booksellers or by contacting:

iUniverse
1663 Liberty Drive
Bloomington, IN 47403
www.iuniverse.com
1-800-Authors (1-800-288-4677)

Cover Art: The cover depicts the Heart Chakra, reproduced from The Chakras, by C. W. Leadbeater; Published by The Theosophical Publishing House, Adyar, Chennai, India; http://www.adyarbooks. com/ & http://www.ts-adyar.org.

Cover Design: Aster Barnwell / Cindy Cake
Text Design: Heidy Lawrance
Typeset: Heidy Lawrance / Beth Crane

ISBN: 978-1-4620-4333-0 (sc)
ISBN: 978-1-4620-4334-7 (hc)
ISBN: 978-1-4620-4335-4 (ebk)

Library of Congress Control Number: 2011913962

Printed in the United States of America

iUniverse rev. date: 10/28/2011

For my granddaughter,
Sia

CONTENTS

ACKNOWLEDGMENTS

As any author would attest, getting a book ready for publication is not the easiest of tasks, even in the best of circumstances, and self-publishing increases the order of difficulty by several magnitudes. What you see as a final product contains the contributions of many individuals besides the person whose name appears on the cover, and *Hidden Treasure* is no exception. Accordingly, I would like to express my appreciation to all those who have facilitated this effort.

I'm profoundly indebted to Simone Gabbay for bringing her consummate editorial skills to the process. Although she joined this project at a later stage than she would have preferred, she was still able to make a significant contribution and vastly lifted the quality of the writing. Whatever flaws of grammar and style that remain are entirely mine, due in part to my stubborn insistence on retaining my own authentic, though imperfect, grammatical "accent" in places.

My heartfelt thanks are extended to Heidy Lawrance and Beth Crane of WeMakeBooks.ca for piloting this book through the text and page design stages to produce a print-ready document. It is due to their esthetic sense, professionalism, and commitment to this project that the vision I've held for *Hidden Treasure* has been shaped into the reality of the book you're holding.

I would also like to offer my appreciation to Cam McNaughton for reading the manuscript and offering valuable feedback, as well as for his friendship and encouragement over the last few years.

My sincere thanks as well to Cherry Noel, my iUniverse Publishing Services Associate, for her patience and her advocacy on my behalf as we sought out solutions within her organization that best suited *Hidden Treasure*.

And to Gar, who assisted me with property maintenance as I cloistered myself away at my computer over the past months, a heartfelt thank-you for being a terrific and helpful neighbor.

Last, but not least, I'm forever and immeasurably grateful to Providence for the many seeming setbacks I encountered as I worked at getting *Hidden Treasure* ready for publication. What appeared to be impediments at different moments in time turned out eventually not to be such, but necessary pauses for reflection, resulting in a much more rounded, and hopefully better, product.

PREFACE

I'm delighted to offer this new, substantially reworked version of my earlier book *The Meaning of Christ for Our Age* (subsequently referred to as *MOC*). After a small print run in 1984, it went out of print a few years later and remained so for the majority of the intervening quarter century. Why? For one, it was likely ahead of its time twenty-five years ago. And it didn't help that its presentation might have scared off those in a position to benefit most from its message—namely Christians. None of the Christian publishers that my agent contacted were interested, and, in fact, the only interest came from a publisher established in the occult genre.

This meant two things. First, the message didn't reach those who, like me, had been molded by lessons from the Bible. Second, it meant the book attracted its share of detractors. One self-proclaimed anti–New Age crusader cited me as a "New Age authority" and labeled the contents of *MOC* "hideous." His assessment of the book's threat has now been upgraded to "sinister," and in recent Web postings, he has even seen fit to induct me into the ranks of some nefarious group referred to as The Illuminati. To round out his demonization, he has attributed statements and philosophical positions to me that are the complete opposite of what's contained in *MOC*, not to mention diametrically opposed to everything I have ever stood for or written.

Despite these difficulties, *MOC* did reach some readers who were appreciative of its message. As well, I received endorsements from Christian ministers, both Catholic and Protestant, along with some well-known experts in the field of Consciousness exploration. So, with a new title and focus, and with greater accessibility, I believe *MOC*-reborn can offer its message at a time when the world is a bit more ready.

In addition to getting a new title, this edition has been substantially rewritten with the goal of making its writing style more accessible. To this end, all Bible quotations have been changed from the King James Version to the English Standard Version (ESV). I also have put much effort into explaining concepts that may be unfamiliar to many readers and, for many of these concepts, added accompanying illustrations.

Finally, a significant part of this renovation effort has gone into presenting the information in a way that readers can make practical use of it. The Appendix section has been thoroughly overhauled, with an emphasis on placing some of the insights presented in the main chapters into a usable format. The appendices provide readers with material they can use in study groups or for individual meditation and contemplation exercises.

- Appendix I, *A Meditation on the Unforgivable Sin*, can be read as a stand-alone essay, and is a good place to start the more intensive spiritual work the reader is invited to undertake in Appendices II, III, and IV.

- Appendix II presents insights on the Beatitudes in a manner that can be useful in workshop settings.

- Appendix III shows how the insights garnered from the seven Parables of the Kingdom in Matthew 13 can be used as spiritual exercises to help the reader become more receptive to the higher energies of Consciousness.

- Appendix IV shares practical insights for utilizing the Lord's Prayer to facilitate spiritual attunement.

- Appendix V elaborates on the zodiacal linkage in the relationship between Jesus and his twelve named disciples in the Gospels.

I've also made the effort, where relevant, to share more of my own religious background, so that readers can get a better sense of where I am coming from. For, apart from the transformational experience I shared in the introduction to the previous edition, my efforts then were pretty much focused on the task of disseminating the information I had discovered about the "hidden" teachings in the Gospels directed at the awakening of a higher state of consciousness in us all. I did not make a substantive-enough effort to establish my credentials as a messenger who did not have an axe to grind, as the saying goes, nor did I share how I actually became the possessor of this knowledge. I now see that not providing enough of my personal background information in MOC may have enticed some readers to impute their own motivations to me, as did the aforementioned "crusader" who placed me in Satan's camp. I believe I have remedied this oversight in this edition by providing more personal sharing at relevant points in the book.

HIDDEN TREASURE'S KEY MESSAGE

Quite simply, the message of *Hidden Treasure* is that there is a "treasure" hidden in the well-trodden field of the New Testament Gospels. This treasure exists as a well-defined psychology of transformation, geared toward leading its practitioner to a state of higher consciousness. This psychology is designed on a template of the subtle energy network of the human body-mind. The presence of this template is detectable most prominently in the Gospel of Matthew. As this energy is awakened through the application of this psychology, we become more spiritually attuned and thus connected to one another, and life around us. Continued application of the psychology encoded in the Gospel message eventually leads to enlightenment—a radical awakening of consciousness.

Even without explicit knowledge of the transformational psychology embedded in the Gospels, those who apply themselves to the teachings inherent in these documents can undergo changes in consciousness that bring them to the realization that the "plan of salvation" is really a plan of transformation. Each of the spiritual reference points relating to salvation would take on a newer and more immediate meaning as one's understanding deepens. Thus, salvation would be understood as the process of the transformation of personal consciousness itself, which does not have a definite endpoint.

For individuals who treat the Christian message as something to be "believed" only, rather than something to be practiced, they would miss out on the opportunity to take advantage of the power of the message to transform consciousness. In turn, since a higher level of consciousness is the key to discerning the symbolic from the Real, they also miss out on the depths of understanding that come with a changed consciousness. The consequence? "Believers" who do not grow in much-needed understanding, and in its absence, are left to cling ever more tightly to a literal reading of the symbolic messages in scriptures.

At one level, it's obvious that burying the transformational message of the Gospels is unfortunate, particularly for those who make the mistake of thinking that the objective of Christian teachings is a salvation that comes simply by believing in Jesus. However, at another level, this "device" of burying the real message is unavoidable. To attract adherents, enticements are provided in the form of "proxy entitlements." Proxy entitlements are promises that are made to people in terms relevant to their levels of consciousness and understanding. Many doctrinal teachings fall under this category. They are meant to sustain the believer just enough until a sufficiently higher level of consciousness is attained, at which point the proxy entitlement can be exchanged for the real article.

Here's an example: At one level of consciousness, one might need an incentive to behave ethically; hence, the promise of an afterlife reward, such as the Kingdom of Heaven. At a higher level of consciousness, however, one can see that ethical behavior is its own reward, since as we advance in consciousness, we experience fewer things as relating to "other" or "not-self," and more as relating to "Self." To grow in consciousness, then, is to grow in the experience of our unity. As it says in the Bhagavad Gita, " … when a man sees that the God in himself is the same God in all that is, he hurts not himself by hurting others; then he goes indeed to the highest path." [1]

Another good example of proxy entitlement can be found in the fable of Aesop about a dying farmer and his lazy sons. The ill farmer called his sons to his deathbed and told them a treasure was hidden in their field, but failed to give a specific location. In their hope of gaining instant wealth, the sons dug up the entire field, and finding no treasure, cultivated the field, as the plowing was already done. The thoroughly ploughed field brought in a bumper harvest, from which the accidental farmers made a substantial profit.

We might argue as to whether the farmer was justified in inventing a story of a hidden treasure for his sons, technically lying to them. But one might also argue that this is a moot point, for in the end, the sons found their treasure—just not in the way they had expected. It simply required them to apply their effort and labor. Indeed, knowing his sons, the farmer found the key to accessing their wills. Had he lectured them about the virtues of hard work, they would likely have ignored him as they would have done at most other times in their lives. The promise of a treasure was a proxy entitlement. Proxies are stand-ins for something else, and in this case, the notion of a hidden treasure was a proxy for the rewards of honest labor.

NEW DEVELOPMENTS IN THE FIELD

Since *Hidden Treasure's* predecessor was published in 1984, a significant body of literature has come to light questioning the historical accuracy of the Gospels' accounts of Jesus. The works of Bart Ehrman, which document many of the numerous errors and potential forgeries that constitute the canonical New Testament, stand out as the most thorough and thought-provoking.[2] Apart from such works of conventional scholarship, there's a field of research making the case that many of the attributes ascribed to Jesus have borrowed heavily from Egyptian mythology. Works in this vein include those of Ahmed Osman,[3] D. M. Murdock, writing under the pen name of Acharya S,[4] Gerald Massey,[5] Alvin Boyd Kuhn,[6] Timothy Freke and Peter Gandy,[7] and Tom Harpur.[8] At this point, the question might be asked as to what the relevance is for *Hidden Treasure* if, as contended by the authors just mentioned, the Jesus of the Gospels was either a partially or fully fictional character, composed from mythological and other diverse biographies. The answer is that there is no relevance whatsoever. The transformational psychology demonstrated in *Hidden Treasure* is independent of any historical case that can be made for or against Jesus. That's because the validity of the psychology that is embedded in the Gospels does not depend on the authentication of Jesus's historical reality.

Instead, the drama surrounding Jesus—whether taken literally or figuratively—merely serves as a scaffold, or container, for the psychology. This is true in the same sense that the curative properties of a chemical compound inside a medicinal capsule are not dependent on the method of delivery for their efficacy. In other words, encapsulated or not, it's the compound itself that promotes the cure; the medicine would be just as efficacious if delivered by other means, for example, intravenously. So it is for the psychology of transformation contained within the Gospels—and for which *Hidden Treasure* provides both a map and a plan for its utilization.

INTRODUCTION

A Transformational Experience

Toward the close of 1976, at the age of twenty-nine, I had several unexpected spiritual experiences. These experiences transformed, over the course of half a year, my understanding of my own religion—Christianity—as well as of religions that I had, until then, neither the interest nor the time to investigate.

These experiences began at the same time that the emotional and material security that I had been working hard to build also started to crumble around me. I went through a family breakup, and lost my social standing, friends, property, and professional status. Not having anywhere to turn, I reached for and clung to the memory of an earlier period of life when my religious faith, which I had long neglected, provided a sense of purpose and inner security. And in short order, I made the decision to recapture this faith.

The purpose of my quest was to discover God's will for my life; to know with certainty and confidence that I was on the right track. Over a period of six months, I methodically dismantled every philosophical tenet and religious belief I held, thoroughly examining each one with almost childlike curiosity. Everything was subjected to a simple test: "Can I *really* make sense of this?" And I was not aiming at theoretical knowledge, but intuitive understanding.

During this period, I digested the core books in the school of psychology known as Transactional Analysis. I also studied astrology, read up on mysticism, and began practicing meditation. In the process, the emptiness inside me began to be filled, and the theological and philosophical questions of a lifetime began to find resolution, one by one.

For many years prior to this time, every theological and philosophical problem I could not find an answer to was mentally filed away. In numerous moments of philosophical reflection, I would tell myself that someday I would devote time to the quest for answers. I'd always think, "Such things are better left for a more convenient day"— a day when the responsibilities of building a career, earning a living, and raising a family were safely behind me.

My own design for my life notwithstanding, the chaos and accompanying emotional turmoil in my twenty-ninth year brought the "convenient day" to the fore. In the ensuing struggle to rise above the difficulties, I took refuge in the thought that there was some hidden significance to my trials that I was just not aware of; I even compared my experiences to those of Job in the Old Testament. But what was most important about this period in my life was that I felt challenged to justify my existence as a human being. In a tangible way, this was my "Judgment Day," in which I had to justify my life by calling upon my inner resources.

After the first six months of intense study and self-inquiry, I felt that not only had I regained lost ground, but I also had grown closer to God. For the very first time in my life, I felt God loved and cared for me as an individual.

Around that time, one of my new acquaintances invited me to a conference on spiritual healing, which I gladly accepted, as I felt that a pilgrimage of sorts was in order. The conference was held in Virginia Beach under the auspices of the Edgar Cayce Foundation, also known as The Association for Research and Enlightenment (A.R.E.). The organization had been formed to preserve and disseminate the information provided in some fourteen thousand psychic readings given by the late "sleeping prophet," Edgar Cayce.* I was interested because I had recently read *There*

---

* Edgar Cayce (1877-1945) has been described as "the sleeping prophet," and the "father of holistic medicine," in reference to the thousands of psychic "readings" he gave while in an unconscious state. The majority of these readings dealt with diagnosing illnesses and revealing past lives of those seeking his counsel, while many others dealt with prophecies concerning future world events. The website of the A.R.E. (now retitled Edgar Cayce's A.R.E.) describes Cayce as " the most documented psychic of the 20th century."

Is a River,[1] the life story of Cayce as told by Thomas Sugrue, and it had supplied a few of the missing pieces of knowledge in my quest for religious understanding.

The atmosphere at Virginia Beach was friendly and open. There were lectures, workshops, and mealtime discussions, all of which contributed to making this a rewarding spiritual adventure. Over the course of the week-long conference, all my personal problems drifted far, far away. It was as if life had neither past nor future; all time ceased, depositing me in the Eternal Present. Indeed, the whole experience was so remarkable that, years later, I look back on it as a major turning point in my life.

The crowning point of the conference came on the second-to-last day. That evening, I was determined to make progress in the practice of meditation, which, at the time, I had been doing as recommended by the Cayce material. In the Cayce method, you hold one particular thought—a principle of your choosing—while rejecting all others. The aim is to program this principle into your mind. For example, you might dwell on the meaning of patience until you come to a deeper emotional understanding of how to give this quality fuller expression in your life.

In this form of meditation, you can also use a command called an *affirmation*. For example, one of the affirmations recommended in the Cayce material is "Be still and know that I am God" (Psalm 46:10). This command is supposed to bring the mind to a state in which it is receptive to divine inspiration. In many ways, affirmation is equivalent to the Eastern (Hindu and Buddhist) concept of a *mantra*. The main difference is that with a mantra, the individual tries to waken the mind's hidden powers. With affirmation, the conscious mind programs the subconscious with higher values so that they become as spontaneous in expression as something instinctual.

Up to this point, I'd had little experience at meditation. After listening to others who claimed to be experts in the practice, I felt woefully far from attaining a meditative state. On this particular night, I approached the whole exercise with my usual anticipation of going deeper in my practice.

As was my custom, I was lying in bed, on my back, silently repeating my affirmation, when I drifted into a state of altered consciousness. My first impression was that I had fallen asleep and had reawakened.

As I took stock of this new experience, I became aware of several sensations that were new to me. I felt extremely heavy, as if in a deep sleep, but my mind was alert. As I continued to explore this new state, I became aware of the beating of my heart and then my breathing. The breath originated deep inside me, yet was noiseless. Exhalations and inhalations merged into one another to give the sensation of the rotation of a water wheel. Then, as I focused on my breathing, another strange thing happened: my breath stopped, and then restarted at a pace so strong that my sternum was moving up and down, in much the same manner as a set of bellows.

But as suddenly as these sensations had taken over, they shifted and were replaced by others. First, I felt a numbing sensation spread all over my body, starting at my feet and working its way up. Wave after wave of sensation arose, each leaving the body in a deeper state of numbness. The thought that I was dying crossed my mind. I remembered a story I had heard in my youth about a woman who had methodically reported on the progression of death's pall on her as it moved from her feet to her head. At the same time, I felt no fear of dying; I had lost the fear of both death and the unknown in general as a result of my intense spiritual study and inquiry over the preceding half-year.

Then, amid these new sensations and thoughts, my attention was drawn to another phenomenon: I "heard" a noise very much like thunder, although I realized the sound was internal, because I had heard it before while meditating. This time, though, it was more prolonged, and I was able to locate its source. It came from the region around the base of my spine. Drawing my attention there, I then "saw" a column of luminous something—I will refer to it as liquid light—rise up like water from an artesian well, and progress toward my head. The perspective was one of looking down upon it, and as it rose, it was as if I became absorbed in it.

The most notable aspect of this whole experience was that it was accompanied by intense pleasure, or better, ecstasy, the likes of which I had not known before. The closest earthly comparison I could make is the climax of sexual union.

When the column of light reached the base of my brain, it "exploded" in a flash, filling my head with light that seemed many times brighter than direct sunlight. The light seemed to obliterate everything around me, such that I became the light and the experience of it at the same time. Then, as the light extinguished itself, I felt another sensation emerging from deep inside the frontal lobe of the brain, directly behind the spot between the eyebrows. This sensation flowed like water, bathing my head, face, torso, arms, and legs, as it descended and tranquillized both my mind and body, leaving me in a state of blissful peace. I instinctively recognized this as the "peace which surpasses all understanding."* At the time, I understood that expression to mean a peace that could not be made the successful object of human grasping. It was the gift of God. In fact, so powerful was this peace that its biological effects did not wear off for several weeks. It made my body feel alive and acutely sensitive, and when the effects did wear off, it was not sudden, but gradual and intermittent.

Psychological changes also occurred as a result of this experience. For one, meditation came quite easily after that; to be transported upon the wings of peace and love I needed only to close my eyes, as my mind was continually drawn towards contemplation on spiritual matters. On the flip side, it was almost impossible for me to engage in the activities of ordinary life for some time. I could not watch television or listen to popular music on the radio, so I gave away my TV set and my records. I began to listen to classical music. I became so sensitive to various kinds of violence that when I went to the supermarket, I found it too emotionally painful to visit the meat section. The biggest challenge, however, was to meet the intellectually demanding requirements of my job as an economist. I found

---

*"And the peace of God, which surpasses all understanding, will guard your hearts and your minds in Christ Jesus." (Philippians 4:7).

it impossible to concentrate on my work. I kept a Bible in my desk and found myself dipping into Proverbs, Ecclesiastes, and the Gospel of John several times a day. Fortunately, my bosses and colleagues tolerated my drop-off in performance, attributing it to the recent breakup of my marriage; and owing to my previous high productivity, they were prepared to cut me considerable slack. But it took a great deal of effort to master this constant pull toward meditation and spiritual contemplation sufficiently to carry on the responsibilities of ordinary life.

My Search for Context

Returning to the night of this experience, my most immediate concern was to place what had happened into some general framework. My first attempt at doing so was inadvertently hilarious: *So this is what meditation is about!*" I thought. So the morning after, I conferred with the friend who had suggested the conference to me to begin with. I wanted to find out if he, too, had had such an experience. He had not, however, and did not know how to help me put it into context. Other "experienced meditators" I approached were also unable to help. One person suggested that I slow down, that I had been trying to "open up" too fast. Of course, I could not relate to this idea as I had not been trying to open up to anything.

Next, I took my search to the bookstore at the A.R.E., browsing through books dealing with meditation and mysticism. This exploration also proved fruitless. In fact, the only thing I had read that came anywhere close to my experience was the story of the Apostle Paul, formerly Saul of Tarsus. The report, recorded in *Acts of the Apostles* in the New Testament, documents the adventure of Saul, who, bent on persecuting the early followers of Jesus Christ for heresy, was on his way to Damascus to bind Christians and deliver them to the Jewish Council. On his journey, a spiritual presence that identified itself as Jesus of Nazareth intercepted him, at which point Saul was blinded by a light he described to be brighter than the noonday sun, and heard a voice rebuking him for playing adversary to the Christians. Accounts of this incident vary slightly. In Acts 9:7, those with Saul were reported to have heard the voice, but no mention was made of them seeing a light. In Acts 22:7 and 26:13, they were reported to have seen the light, but there was no mention made of the voice. Regardless, the experience became the turning point for Saul's life. He remained without sight for three days. His name was changed to Paul, and he left his former life of persecuting Christians to become the most devoted, effective ambassador for the newly emerging church in the non-Jewish world.

Still, I was reluctant to see a complete parallel between my experience and Paul's for three reasons: First, I regarded the New Testament world too far removed, both in time and context. Second, I was of the belief that experiences such as Paul's were one of a kind. Third, my inbred bigger-than-life regard for biblical characters discouraged any personal identification with them. Consequently, I was left with no option but to continue my search, believing that some logical, methodical explanation existed for what had happened to me that night.

As Providence would have it, my first clue came from reading a book someone had recommended for a totally different reason. I learned about something referred to as "arousal of *Kundalini*" in the terminology of the Eastern discipline of Yoga. And my subsequent readings on the subject confirmed that this was indeed what I had experienced. In addition to discovering the psychological significance of what had taken place, I also found that there was an entire tradition built around the solicitation of this "enlightenment" experience and the beneficence it was supposed to bestow upon the one having it. In fact, Kundalini was the objective of almost every Eastern religious discipline—Yoga, contemplation, austerities, religious devotion in its many forms, meditation, and various secret rites and rituals.

What puzzled me was that I had no previous knowledge of the Kundalini phenomenon. I had not practiced any Eastern disciplines and had not been in association with anyone who had. Ironically, this answer to my earlier search only made way for more questions and more searches.

I took time to prepare a written account of my Kundalini experience shortly after I returned home from the conference, but it wasn't until about a year and a half later that I felt moved to share the experience with the late Dr. Marcus Bach, who had been the headline speaker. Dr. Bach had spoken movingly about his own spiritual journey and about his then-current interest in promoting religious understanding among peoples of various faith persuasions. One of the reasons I chose to write him was because, in some regard, I felt his generous sharing had played a part in heightening my own spiritual aspirations. He responded with a loving letter of encouragement, suggesting that I had received the experience "for a special purpose," which would be revealed "more and more as days go by." *

KUNDALINI AND THE SECOND COMING OF CHRIST

Once I was able to gain a perspective on the significance of what had happened to me, my next objective was to account for why it happened to me in particular. From my readings, I found that it was not a common occurrence, even among lifelong practitioners of Yoga and other Eastern disciplines. Since my approach to spiritual matters was completely Christian in outlook, and because of the lack of Christian-oriented case histories to draw upon, I concluded that *East* and *West* might not be that far apart after all. And after further reading, it became apparent that the differences between these two approaches revolved around emphasis and conceptualization, but that, indeed, they led to the same goal.

It seemed to me that what the Easterners called the arousal of Kundalini (or enlightenment) was referred to in the Christian tradition as the Second Coming of Christ. As will become evident throughout the book, I view the Second Coming not as a literal event, but as a psychophysical

---

*I had completely forgotten about this letter from Dr. Bach until the year 2010, when I chanced upon it while sorting through files of reader responses to MOC.

manifestation. As controversial as this statement may appear to someone whose religious views are based on a literal reading of scripture, my suggestion is to set aside judgment for the time being until the views and arguments laid out in the rest of this book to support a reinterpretation of the core message of the New Testament have been presented.

The evidence upon which I drew to propose this connection between the Second Coming of Christ and Kundalini was based primarily upon an assessment of the psychological aspects of my own experience. I was able to see that, perhaps, the primary factor that had triggered my Kundalini experience was the very strong expectation that had been building up within me concerning the Second Coming.

Let me explain. It was not that I had been literally expecting the sky to burst open to reveal a physical Christ and throngs of winged angels—my religious conceptualizations had by now already developed well beyond that. But I had been working at cultivating an attitude of reconciliation within myself, to create room in my life for the principles that Christ represented to take hold and grow. After the Kundalini experience, I felt that this had been accomplished. The peace and self-acceptance I felt were so pervasive that were Christ to have manifested in the flesh and taken up physical abode with me, I would have felt no need to change anything in my life. In every psychological way, then, Christ had indeed come for me; I had experienced my Second Coming.

While it was all well and good that I was convinced of the underlying unity of Christian doctrine as outlined in the New Testament—particularly the Gospels—and Eastern thought, how could I demonstrate this connection to others? This task was not easy at the outset, as there were no overt references to Kundalini in the Bible, and even the Saul of Tarsus account was a loose reference at best. From the Eastern side, it was also difficult to obtain any "conversion formula." Discussions of Kundalini in Yoga literature were shrouded in symbolism.

However, after several years of intensive research, success came in my endeavor to place Eastern and Western approaches to spirituality into the same general context. The key was in recognizing the main difference between them: in the East, the experience is made the objective of religious discipline, even solicited directly; while in the West, the attention is purposely directed away from the phenomenon of the experience itself. Stated another way, we have in Christianity many observances that will awaken this Kundalini energy, but these observances are all *implicit* in the core system of Christian belief and practices itself.* Also, in Christianity, many manifestations of Kundalini awakening are treated as religious rather than psychological processes. They are, for example, understood as "gifts of the Holy Ghost" or "fruits of the Spirit."

In my estimation, then, the Second Coming of Christ was to be the final chapter of unfolding in the spiritual work of the Christian believer, and this occurrence was to unite him fully with the purpose he was striving for in his Christian living.

The psychological flavor of the Second Coming is quite transparent in the writings of Paul and John. Paul says, " … unto them that look for him shall he appear the second time without sin unto salvation." It should be noted that expectation is to play a part here. Furthermore, the Second Coming is seen as assisting one "unto salvation," not granting it.

John, the purported writer of the Epistles and the Book of Revelation also indicates that the Second Coming was not an event to be looked for at any specific period of world history. In his teaching on the antichrist, whom Christians expect to *immediately* precede Christ in his coming, John said, " … and every spirit that does not confess Jesus is not from God. This is the spirit of the antichrist, which you heard was coming *and now is in the world already*" (I John 4:3, emphasis added). This unmistakably shows that the antichrist was a reality at the time of John, indicating that Christ's "return" was a reality at that time also.

---

*This is, however, true only of Christianity in its theoretical design and not as it exists today. Indeed, I believe that the further the practice of Christianity drifts from its esoteric roots, the less capable it becomes as a discipline to engender the type of transformations that can facilitate the awakening of Kundalini.

The book of Revelation also says that " ... he is coming with the clouds, and every eye will see him" (Revelation 1:7), further indicating that Christians were to interpret this symbolically. In the first place, it would be impossible for any physical event taking place on our planet to be visible everywhere at once. Secondly, we know that clouds, as meteorological phenomena, are very much of our physical world and not part of a heavenly one.

Finally, in the Gospel of Matthew, Jesus is quoted as saying, "Truly, I say to you, there are some standing here who will not taste death until they see the Son of Man coming in his kingdom" (Matthew 16:28). Does that mean there were people living at the time of Jesus who are still alive today, awaiting his coming?

THE PLACE OF KUNDALINI IN THE TEACHINGS OF JESUS

Once convinced of the premise that biblical Christianity was geared toward a solicitation of the Kundalini experience, I began searching the Gospels for an underlying structure that would substantiate this. The pattern eluded me at first, but, as in so many instances in life, it finally revealed itself when I was not looking for it.

I was conducting an impromptu Bible study session with three women from the yoga studio where I took classes. One of them had approached me and asked if I would be willing to teach her about the Bible. We had taken the same class in Yoga philosophy, and she had become intrigued by my numerous interjections, showing parallels between the teachings of Jesus and key concepts in Yoga philosophy. I had agreed to her request, on condition that she recruited enough students to constitute a small class. I opened the class of four, which subsequently convened at my apartment, by having each person read a passage of scripture, starting with Matthew. Periodically, we'd stop for discussions, which consisted mostly of their questions and my responses. But it was through these responses and off-the-cuff comments that the broad outlines of a system of teaching oriented around Kundalini became clear to me. After each meeting, when the women had left, I made notes of the ideas that had come to me during our session. These notes became seeds for further contemplation, study, and research.* These combined efforts revealed an exact parallel between the schedules of observances required to progressively awaken Kundalini and many of the instructions given in the discourses of Jesus, particularly those in Matthew. Stated another way, many of Jesus's teachings were actually instructions on how to awaken this energy within us.

It became apparent then that this was a case of something being hidden in plain sight; something that, unless you are looking specifically for it, will remain undetected. But why? Why would Kundalini not be spelled out directly in the New Testament? Because the New Testament employs a psychology of transformation that relies not on theoretical models, but on practical application. Jesus himself was to be a living symbol of active Kundalini and, furthermore, of the dynamic process of achieving it. Thus, his exhortations to "follow me," once heeded, should be all the Kundalini practice the Christian requires.

The overall objective is to engage a transformation of consciousness by following the teachings of Jesus Christ. This devotion and application realign our energies, thus facilitating an awakening Kundalini and "the return of Christ."

FROM EDEN TO GETHSEMANE

After the correspondences I was seeking between Eastern systems and those of biblical Christianity took more definite form, it became evident that the struggle to come to terms with the Kundalini process is at the foundation of biblical thought. In this regard, the story of the fall of man from

---

* It is the cumulative result of these inner and outer explorations that provided the initial ideas for this book.

the paradise enjoyed in the Garden of Eden to the plan of God for his redemption—as portrayed in the consecration by Jesus Christ of himself in the Garden of Gethsemane—can be appreciated as a highly symbolic rendition of the psychological protocol that one must observe to attain the state called enlightenment.

The first part of this story, that of the fall, deals with mankind's unsuccessful attempt to master the Kundalini factor and the principle behind it. The second part, namely Jesus's consecration of himself to the cause of the unification of God and man, represents the way in which Kundalini is eventually mastered.

The relationship between the Eden story and the process of Kundalini is explored in greater detail in chapter 4, but in anticipation of that discussion, we can consider the main symbols in the Eden story—the Tree of Life, the Tree of the Knowledge of Good and Evil, Adam and Eve, and the infamous serpent—as principles inherent in activating and mastering Kundalini.

Let's first look at the serpent. In Eastern traditions, Kundalini is referred to as "serpent power." This is probably because the psychophysical sensations experienced when this energy is activated compare to the writhing movements of the serpent. Such writhing movements also provide a fit symbol for the way in which Kundalini restructures an individual's life.

The Tree of the Knowledge of Good and Evil symbolizes the free will* that is achieved when the pent-up psychic force of Kundalini is released. This free will becomes the gateway through which mankind can affect the world for good. However, when an individual uses his energies to impose his own designs upon the world, the result is a degeneration of free will into

---

* In common usage, we use the term "will" to represent our capacity to execute our intentions, and the term "free will" to represent the absence of external interference to our capacity to make and exercise personal choices. However, in a spiritual context, free will can only be truly experienced when we have access to our will. Our access is usually impeded when we are under the influence of destructive habits and compulsions, as well as ego-directed drives, such as ambition, pride, envy, and the like.

self-will. Free will is our capacity to engage in actions that facilitate our psychological and spiritual growth. Self-will, on the other hand, is based on the drive to satisfy our personal desires. It is the cultivation of self-will that is described as eating from the Tree of the Knowledge of Good and Evil.

As for the Tree of Life, this represents the Christ Principle. This is the principle of living not unto oneself but for the common good—for collective human well-being. In the second and third chapters of Genesis, Adam and Eve are driven from the garden after they ate the fruit from the Tree of the Knowledge of Good and Evil. Their banishment occurred because God (the Elohim) feared that they will also eat of the Tree of Life and become as the Elohim. (This term, Elohim, is plural and refers to exalted Celestial Beings.) At the root of the Elohim's concerns was the spiritual protocol necessary for achieving enlightenment; in other words, it was not that the fruits of the Tree of Life were forbidden, but only that they should have been partaken of first. The Principle of Unity symbolized by the Tree of Life had to be observed before free will could be constructively used, because possessing free will without first acknowledging such unity would result in the degeneration of free will into self-will. And it is impossible to share in the unitive state of consciousness suggested by enlightenment while self-will is present. (These ideas will be explored more fully in chapter 4.)

Adam and Eve represent the two aspects of the human mind: the intellect and the emotions, or the masculine and feminine poles of consciousness. The drama of Eden tells us that the coalition of the emotional aspect of man with the pent-up psychic reserve of energy that is Kundalini (serpent power), subverts free will into self-will—and *this is the true fall of man,* whose redemption lies in the restoration of psychic energy to its proper usage, as the life of Jesus Christ as portrayed in the Gospels is intended to demonstrate.

ONE

UPDATING OUR UNDERSTANDING OF JESUS'S ROLE IN OUR SALVATION

In the forthcoming chapters of this book I will work to substantiate the claim that the Gospels contain a well-developed psychology of transformation, designed to take one to a higher level of consciousness. But before that point, I'd like to deal with just three of the number of questions you might develop in response to those chapters. Indeed, I pondered these questions for a number of years.

The first question is: Is this psychology a deliberate construction, or is it an artifact—a coincidence or an accident? Because of my training as an economist, I was accustomed to treating every result of a statistical correlation between two sets of data with skepticism until more thorough analyses could be performed. Such a practice was standard in my line of work to eliminate what is called a *spurious correlation,* which is when an apparent statistical relationship between phenomena turns out to be a fluke. In this instance, although I was not dealing with quantifiable data, I figured the same cautious approach was called for.

The second question follows on the heels of the first: If it turns out the psychology is a deliberate construction, what does that imply for our understanding of Jesus?

Finally, the third question: What are the implications for Christianity, if the main message of the Gospels turns out to be not about Jesus, but about transformation?

Before delving into these questions, however, I'd like to give you an idea of where I'm coming from personally.

MY RELIGIOUS BACKGROUND

I haven't been a member of a Christian church for several decades, yet I feel more of a Christian today than when I dutifully attended services. For some, this might seem a contradiction to how things ought to be, but it's true for me because I've always associated Christianity with a set of principles to live by, and as such, the outer trappings of religion just never had a pull on me. I've also always felt free to engage in my own inquiry into the big questions—such as those regarding the nature and existence of God, what happens after we die, and so on. Needless to say, I've never opted for prepackaged answers to these questions.

I was fortunate to have been born into a religious family. My father, though he earned his income as a farmer, was by vocation the pastor and leader of an independent Baptist Church. He never went to a seminary and was self-taught, not an unusual practice in those times* and in that part of the world. Apart from the Methodist hymnal the members used in worship, the church had no formal relationship with any church organization. Worshippers had no other creed book besides the Bible, which, of course, they interpreted literally.

During my childhood, my mother attended the Methodist Church and took us children along, my father's position notwithstanding. We were all christened as Methodists. Eventually, she joined my father in his church, while we children continued to regard ourselves as Methodists, occasionally attending services in the Methodist Church.

At the age of eighteen, I became a member of the Church of Christ. I was baptized by an American minister who had come to my native St. Vincent as a "missionary" to set up congregations there. Several months

* My father was born in 1917.

earlier, I had signed up for a Bible correspondence course offered by that minister while still living in the United States. I didn't know it at the time, but the correspondence course had been his way of making advance contact with prospective candidates for the new church congregation he was planning to start in St. Vincent. The Church of Christ perceived itself not as a denomination of Christianity, but as "the one true church" itself. It saw its role as the restoration of New Testament Christianity. Even though I was a member, I never bought into these pretentious claims, as my common sense and observations told me otherwise.

Two years after I was baptized, I left St. Vincent for Canada, where I continued to be a member of a Church of Christ congregation almost to the end of my second year of university. I eventually drifted away. Since then, I have had no affiliation, formal or informal, with any religious group or organization.

However, two church practices left an indelible imprint on me. The first was the requirement for male lay members (yes, males only) to take turns at delivering the Sunday morning and Sunday evening sermons. (This practice was only carried out in smaller congregations that couldn't afford to hire full-time ministers.) I used the opportunity to thoroughly research my sermon topics and, in the process, explored my own feelings about the Bible's stories.

The second church practice that stuck with me is that it never had the heavy emphasis on an emotional attachment to Jesus. Yes, it believed and taught that Jesus died for our sins, but it parted company with other evangelical-type churches by stressing the need for "obedience to the Word," rather than emphasizing an emotional attachment to Jesus.

THE PSYCHOLOGY OF TRANSFORMATION IN THE GOSPELS—INTENTIONAL OR ACCIDENTAL?

Now let's go back to the three main questions that will likely arise as you continue through this book. As for the first question, I can categorically state that the psychology of transformation in the Gospels is a deliberate construction—it is no accident.

For one, it's obvious that such a message couldn't have been embedded in the Gospels unless that had been the intent from the outset. Two, the psychology of transformation has an internal consistency that gives it coherence and plausibility. Further, the design of the psychology corresponds with that which underpins the Eastern disciplines of Yoga,* which predated Christianity by thousands of years. These Yoga disciplines are geared toward helping the individual organize and focus all of his energies—intellectual, emotional, volitional, and physical—on the goal of spiritual realization. The central idea within the various disciplines of Yoga is that the human being is a "God-seed," awaiting the conscious cooperation of the individual in order to awaken and progress into full flowering. That's not to say such insights into our human potential are lost to Christianity. The thirteenth-to-fourteenth-century Christian mystic Meister Eckhart expressed similar sentiments quite forcefully in his writings. He wrote, for example, "The seed of God is in us. Now the seed of a pear tree grows into a pear tree; and a hazel seed grows into a hazel tree; a seed of God grows into God."[1] Such realizations have been lost only on the mainstream expressions of Christianity.

A key component that the psychology of the Gospels shares with the various Yoga disciplines is a structural framework of human consciousness which shows us humans as having the potential to experience life at seven different levels of consciousness, with each successive level representing a higher level of relationship to Reality. In the Gospels, this framework serves as the key to a fuller understanding of the teachings and miracles of Jesus.

It's unfortunate that this structural framework lies hidden from the casual observer. If one does not have an understanding beforehand of the design that is being utilized, it goes undetected.** In my own case, had it

---

*The term yoga means union, and is the equivalent of the Christian concept of yoke. There are three main classical Yoga disciplines, widely accepted as different paths to God: Gyani Yoga (the Yoga of contemplation), Karma Yoga (the Yoga of good works), and Bhakti Yoga (the Yoga of devotion). Hatha Yoga, the most familiar form of yoga in the West, consists of physical exercises designed to strengthen and integrate the mind and the body, and is not classified as a yogic path per se.

**An exposition of this framework will be discussed more fully in Chapter 5.

not been for the personal experience with Kundalini, described in the introduction, and the search it inspired, this reality of the underlying framework to the Gospels would have remained hidden from me.

The Kundalini experience and the revelations that were to follow also awakened me to the realization that we can derive entirely new levels of meaning from religious concepts that we've been previously content to interpret literally and superficially.

During intense sessions of Bible reading and contemplation, prayers, and meditation, I was flooded with intuitive insights on the spiritual life. I realized that the most important concepts and doctrines of Christianity were more meaningful when viewed within a frame of reference that is allegorical and psychological—in other words, when viewed in ways that relate to our present, lived experience—as opposed to one that is historical and literal. My deepest intuitive insight during those early months was the realization that there is one God, meaning that all the aspirations of all peoples of all ages resulted from different levels and qualities of insight into one Ultimate Reality. This did not come to me as an intellectualization, but as a felt, embodied realization. It is this intuition that led me to familiarize myself with various world religions and mythologies. And it is because of this familiarization that I was able to see some of the common themes that permeate both Christianity and other world religious traditions.

WHAT IS THE ROLE OF JESUS IN THE PSYCHOLOGY OF TRANSFORMATION?

We can now address how best to understand the role of Jesus in light of the deliberate embedding of the psychology of transformation in the Gospels. In short, we must reassess our own views about salvation and Jesus's role in it.

In traditional Christian theology, Jesus is seen as a unique phenomenon on the screen of history. He is championed as God's answer to man's need for redemption from sin. Indeed, one of the most quoted Bible verses is John 3:16, which states, "For God so loved the world, that he gave his only Son, that whoever believes in him should not perish but have eternal life."

Unaware of the transformation that the teachings of Jesus are designed to engage in us, Christian doctrine has become primarily focused on Jesus's role in our salvation. And since there is no shared understanding of what constitutes salvation, it's up to each Christian group to settle on its own definition, which, in turn, is based on its own surface reading and interpretation of scripture. As a result, Christian teachings on salvation are as varied and diverse from one another as the preferences, prejudices, fears, and desires of the various groups within the faith. Positions in the debate range from those that regard salvation as a matter of Christian heritage to those that advocate it is achieved only by accepting Jesus Christ as savior (meaning that one must make a verbal and emotional acceptance of the salvation that Jesus is understood to have provided through his suffering and crucifixion). For those who see salvation in a more cultural context, it is entirely sufficient to be born of Christian parents, baptized in infancy, and perhaps attend church once in awhile. And on the fundamentalist end of the spectrum, we find even more polarization on issues such as whether a person who is once saved is always saved, whether faith alone is sufficient for salvation, or whether faith plus works is the key.

Yet, as diverse as these positions are, all Christian groups find common ground in the Gospel story that Jesus paid the price for our salvation through a sacrificial death by crucifixion. This knowledge is so pervasive that it's part of our cultural endowment in the West. I was a small child when, one Good Friday, I learned from an older cousin the story of Jesus dying for our sins. Though that disclosure made me feel sad that someone had to die, it made as much sense to me then as it does now. Of course, my intellect was not developed enough to frame the questions I was to pose later.

Even accepting the surface account of how Jesus came to save us, those of us who probe further could never find an intellectually satisfying Christian answer as to the mechanism by which Jesus's death actually translates into our salvation. Most times, one is told that it's something one must accept by faith. However, the typical Christian answer is aptly demonstrated in the Mel Gibson–directed movie *The Passion of the Christ.*[2] The psychological mechanism by which the death of Jesus confers salvation is through the feelings of guilt that are stirred in us when we contemplate his suffering.

It is reasonable to surmise that the architects of the Gospels relied on the appeal of the story of Jesus's birth, life, and crucifixion to engage converts at an emotional level. They likely intended this historical drama to serve as a "hook," to use a marketing expression. Most of the teachings intended to engage people were never meant to become a permanent fixture in the believer's world view. They were simply to serve as easily digestible spiritual food, meant for "infants in Christ."[*] Said another way, these teachings were meant for a sort-of spiritual kindergarten, delivered in hopes that a believer would progress to following the prescription Jesus lays out in his teachings for the saving of the soul. Provided that these teachings of love for God and one's neighbor were put into practice, believers would experience a transition to a higher level of consciousness. In turn, this higher level of consciousness would enable them to discover the true purpose of the Gospel message, thereby releasing them from the need to cling to a literal interpretation of the Gospel story. Getting people to believe the narrative was an initial first step to applying the psychology. It was not to be an end unto itself.

Two related factors suggest themselves as to the reasons why we've missed out so terribly on achieving a deeper understanding of what our salvation consists of and Jesus's role in it, as played out in the Gospel story. The first is that we do not have a clear understanding of what life requires of us as human beings; or, to put it differently, we do not know what we

---

*For example, Paul's first letter to the church at Corinth states: "I, brothers, could not address you as spiritual people, but as people of the flesh, as infants in Christ. I fed you with milk, not solid food, for you were not ready for it. And even now you are not yet ready" (I Cor. 3: 1-2).

should be making the goal of our striving. The second reason is a lack of understanding of the roles of religion and spiritual disciplines in helping us meet this requirement. In both cases, our poor understanding is directly related to our inability to distinguish mythic themes and images in scripture from actual historical events.

OUR HUMAN POTENTIAL AND THE ROLE OF RELIGION IN HELPING US ACHIEVE IT

In my early twenties, wanting to learn how to do my own car tune-ups, I took an auto mechanic course at a community college. The instructor provided a definition of a tune-up that still resonates with me; he said it was the task of returning a vehicle, as closely as possible, to the manufacturer's specifications. I've often thought of that definition when reflecting upon the role of religion in human affairs. The function of religion is to imbue each of us with a sense of our potential as a human being, a potential that includes a state of wholeness. Our religious practice should then become our human equivalent of a tune-up, restoring us to psychic wholeness. As for what life requires of us, it is nothing less than our desire for and pursuit of wholeness, together with a willingness to realize the complete truth of *what* we are—both goals that the psychology embedded in the New Testament is designed to help us achieve.

In the view of the Indian philosopher and mystic Sri Aurobindo* (1872-1950), the proper role and practice of religion is to help man in searching for, and finding, God, and to help him use the experience of the encounter with the Divine to energize a life of devotion and service. Our wholehearted turning to the Divine would, in turn, prepare the way for God to "descend" into and live through us. Says Sri Aurobindo:

---

*Sri Aurobindo is identified here as a philosopher and mystic only for the sake of convenience. Many recognized him as an Avatar of the "supramental manifestation" that defined his personal Yoga discipline.

> The deepest heart, the inmost essence of religion … is the search for God and the finding of God. Its aspiration is to discover the Infinite, the Absolute, the One, the Divine, who is all these things and yet no abstraction but a Being. Its work is a sincere living out of the true and intimate relations between man and God, relations of unity, relations of difference, relations of an illuminated knowledge, an ecstatic love and delight, an absolute surrender and service, a casting of every part of our existence out of its normal status into an uprush of man towards the Divine and a descent of the Divine into man.[3]

When viewed against such a lofty view of religion, it is easy to see why a more modest understanding of our spiritual duty and the related role of religion would lead to correspondingly less effort in our day-to-day spiritual practice. But, if the truth lies more in line with Aurobindo's vision rather than in the issue of finding personal salvation, then our failure to understand the higher standards we're being called to achieve would mean that we are shortchanging ourselves. And such shortchanging can start a cycle of self-reinforcing errors that can lead to our spiritual disenfranchisement. This cycle begins with a failure to penetrate the outer layers of our religious symbols in order to acquaint ourselves with the deeper meanings of our religious texts. This misunderstanding of scripture then leads us to misinterpret what we should be striving for in our religious practice. Finally, when we're busily engaged in expending our energy in misdirected pursuits, we miss out on opportunities to become acquainted with the knowledge and practices we need in order to make genuine spiritual progress.

Real spiritual progress consists foremost of the upliftment and eventual transformation of our natural impulses toward a life that progressively embodies the ideals attributed to Jesus—to name a few, love, charity, kindness, compassion, and obedience to the will of God.

DISCERNING MYTHIC THEMES
AND IMAGES IN SCRIPTURE

As we look at the state of Christendom today, it's hard not to conclude that a serious miscalculation was made in interpreting the message of the Gospels. Jesus was not to be the final resting place for the attention of Christians; he was to be the mobilizer, the shepherd herding the flock to greener pasture. Instead, what we have is emphasis on an emotional attachment to Jesus that cannot go beyond the literal, surface level. Believers were expected to grow out of these infantile attachments to Jesus. They were to look not to the past but to the future, to a return of the Christ not without, but within themselves. There seems to be some cosmic irony at play here, in that our belief in, and adoration of, a historical Jesus has stood in the way of the Christ Principle having a greater representation in our lives and our human affairs.

The human tendency to become fixated on a symbol while failing to assimilate into our consciousness the life lesson represented by the symbol is the target of the Zen Buddhist aphorism, "The finger pointing at the moon is not the moon."* Indeed, by becoming fixated on Jesus and the historical drama presented in the Gospels, we are staring at the finger rather than at the object to which it is pointing, and which, in our case, is the psychology of transformation in which we need to become engaged.

Once we are aware of the underlying psychology, and the intent of the historical drama, we can have a deeper appreciation of Jesus's role, and discover that this role is not unique. It belongs to a special class of symbols named *archetypes* by the renowned psychoanalyst Carl Gustav Jung. The term was used reservedly by Dr. Jung to represent "those psychic contents which have not yet been submitted to conscious elaboration and are therefore an immediate datum of psychic experience."⁴ As an archetype, Jesus was modeling principles for us to live out in our own lives, and in this

*The context here is someone pointing at the moon in conjunction with a verbal exhortation to an onlooker to "Look at the moon!"

sense, his role of world savior is hardly unique. Such a designation has been assigned to various personalities across the march of history. Although different religious traditions employ different concepts and metaphors, none can legitimately lay claim to being the exclusive embodiment of truth.

The development of a religion is simply an attempt to give local relevance to an eternal truth by drawing upon the culture from which the realization of that truth occurred. Consequently, the most appropriate way of portraying the purpose of life in one time and place may not be the most appropriate way to portray it in another, considering the bigger picture of our human unfolding and development.

REVISIONING CHRISTIANITY

One cannot help but wonder what might have been if, over the past two millennia, there had been widespread recognition within Christian communities that the true purpose of Christianity was to engage in spiritual practices that lead to a transformation of consciousness. But as intriguing as it might be to speculate on this, it has no practical benefit. What is more beneficial is to look forward, to speculate instead on the potential for Christianity should the awareness of an underlying psychology in the Gospels become common knowledge. Of course, this is not something that can be known, because we know that a characteristic of human beings is that different individuals react differently to the same information, but one can hope that greater awareness would lead to greater responsibility.

There are positives that can be hoped for, namely: first, that Christians rediscover the transformative power of their sacred symbols; second, that they rediscover contemplative practices; third, that they make the acquaintance of the *spirit of truth*; and fourth, that each individual assumes primary responsibility for his or her spiritual progress. These third and fourth "positives to be hoped for" are combined in the discussion to follow, but in anticipation of that discussion, this fourth point about personal responsibility holds the greatest promise for the renovation, not only of our spiritual practice, but our experience of life in general. For once we become aware that spiritual practice, and religious life in general, are about the transformation of consciousness, every life situation and encounter become an opportunity for spiritual advancement.

Rediscovering the Transformative
Power of Religious Symbols

I believe that religions such as Christianity are repositories of ageless symbols with transformative value.

Seeing Jesus as a symbol offers us a much better chance of understanding what he represents, much more so than when we only relate to him as a historical character. Further, a historical character, to a large extent, functions as a barrier to appreciating the Divine Principle it is supposed to represent.

Our human mind tends to get stuck at the level of admiring the personality of Jesus, losing sight of the need to move on to a more meaningful relationship with the principle he symbolizes. This is the Principle of Life, which must be understood as something transcending biological life. In this sense, biological life is only one form of expression of life as a principle. Life, as a principle, expresses itself in terms of sacrifice, and this involves the action of voluntarily consecrating one's individual energy to something greater.[5] All the other attributes ascribed to Jesus are secondary to this overriding principle of sacrifice and consecration to a higher cause. To move forward, we need to withdraw our projections and assume the responsibility of developing within ourselves those qualities we attribute to him. Until we can relate to Jesus as a representative of a Divine Principle that we must embody, no level of admiration or worship can amount to much in the way of our transformation.

Our human propensity for projecting our higher nature onto Jesus is not peculiar to Jesus alone. It is characteristic for us to reduce a transcendent reality to a symbolic form that can easily fit our individual circumstances.

This tendency ensures that the transcendent reality gets representation, albeit distorted or diminished, in our everyday reality. But it also means that to avoid becoming emotionally and spiritually stunted, we must take ownership of these higher principles and develop them within ourselves.

In the case of Jesus, he is presented in the Gospels and the apostolic letters as the perfected man, but because this presentation is too transcendent for ordinary human consciousness, he has been reduced to the symbol of the cross over millennia of institutional practices. The cross as a true religious symbol can be regarded as the epitome of sacrifice, the principle of a higher consciousness reaching down into the lower consciousness to revitalize it. To many people, however, there is an emotional barrier to this realization; the mind does not go beyond the cross as an institutional object that identifies someone or something as belonging to the Christian faith. Its potential for revitalizing the personal consciousness has become stunted, rendering it a "dead symbol."

A dead symbol is one that has lost its potential for reminding us of something higher and then propelling us toward it. To keep a symbol from going dead, we must continually take stock of whether we are drawing all possible inferences from it. The relationship between us and our symbols is therefore an interactive one.

Living symbols keep growing as we grow. As we mature in understanding and become more conscious, we are able to see more levels of meaning in the symbol, which, in turn, helps us to grow in consciousness even further. This is why we can say that certain symbols have transformative power. However, before we can access this transformative power, we must take our attention beyond the outer form of religious symbols to the kernel of higher reality that each represents.

The Promise of Contemplation

Contemplation is the exercise of going beyond the surface of things—words, ideas, concepts, and even events—to their more profound depths. When we contemplate a religious symbol, we are rewarded with the opportunity to experience that which often lies hidden behind religious formalism. This is the experience of the "Numinous," which is defined in *Webster's Dictionary* as

(1) supernatural, mysterious;

(2) filled with a sense of the presence of divinity, holy;

(3) appealing to the higher emotions or to the aesthetic sense: spiritual.

In reality, the Numinous is something that eludes precise definition. Ultimately it is that which cannot be circumscribed by words, but must be experienced to be understood. Therefore, short of having a direct personal encounter with it, the best we can do to understand the Numinous is to look at the lives of individuals who have experienced it.

Usually, those so touched talk about feeling awe, reverence, joy, enhanced mental understanding, or a sense of all-encompassing love, unity, oneness, or sense of harmony. Some even confess to receiving insight into the meaning of life. Irrespective of the form in which it is encountered, the Numinous leaves its mark. The individual may even feel that his entire life up to the point of the encounter was one long preparation for just that moment, and he may resolve as a result to give more of his life over to spiritual and humanitarian pursuits.

An immediate effect of an encounter with the Numinous at its more intense levels is an appreciation of the underlying unity of all the major world religions, with the experience of the Numinous as the common goal. That's because with the personal, direct experience of Truth that accompanies an encounter with the Numinous, one is able to move beyond the significance previously given to outer form. An encounter with the Numinous does not end our pursuit of Truth, but reenergizes and refocuses it. For in encountering the Numinous, we receive a glimpse into the larger reality of which we are part, but of which we are unaware in our ordinary states of consciousness. It is this foretaste and inner assurance that it offers which serves as our new motivation to transform our consciousness from one that is ego-driven to one that is spiritual and holistic.

It's worth emphasizing that no one religion has a monopoly on the Numinous. This is why contemplatives from different religious traditions can easily bridge institutional divides and share in one another's contemplative practices and spiritual insights. The relationship between the Numinous and various religious forms is similar to that between a mountain's peak and its sides. Just as you can reach a mountain peak by scaling its various sides, so too can the Numinous be attained from different religious perspectives. In fact, a personal encounter with the Numinous can be hastened by a familiarity with more than one major religious tradition, since such an eclectic worldview will enhance one's chances of seeing what lies beyond the formal structure into that which, by its very nature, is formless.

Generally speaking, the failure in our Christian practice to move beyond the symbolic to "the depths" in matters of the Spirit can lead to practices that are equivalent in their spiritual effects to a soccer player scoring against his own team. Chief among these practices is the delivery of the "prosperity gospel" message, popular with some brands of television-based ministries. In recent decades, with the rise of televangelism, we've seen a rising tide of believers who see and present Jesus Christ as a magic potion for all of life's problems. Not only is Jesus seen as the solution to personal problems such as of loneliness, sickness, and financial hardship, but he is presented as the secret ingredient that can make one "a winner" in "the game of life." Daily, we see individuals who claim to have proven this success formula march across the television screen, attesting to the belief that Jesus is the critical factor to their success, and each time, I am reminded of Jesus's response to those who wanted to become his followers immediately after witnessing the miracle in which he fed the five thousand: " ... you are seeking me, not because you saw signs, but because you ate your fill of the loaves" (John 6:26).

Our Individual Responsibility for
Making Acquaintance with the Spirit of Truth

The idea that the Gospels contain hidden teachings should not come as a surprise to the ardent biblical student. Indeed, in his discourses, Jesus gave several indications that there is an esoteric aspect to his teachings. On one such occasion, he referred to a time when this esoteric side would reveal itself. In this exhortation to his disciples he said:

> I still have many things to say to you, but you cannot bear them now. When the Spirit of truth comes, he will guide you into all truth, for he will not speak on his own authority, but whatever he hears he will speak, and he will declare to you the things that are to come. (John 16:12–13)

I interpret this "Spirit of Truth" as being the spirit, or the principle of eclecticism or synthesis. From personal experience, I have learned that when guided by this principle, we do not confine our search for spiritual knowledge to any one religious tradition, but extend it to several. Once we allow ourselves to be guided by the Spirit of Truth or synthesis, we see that Truth, or Reality, is undifferentiated; it does not parcel itself out into different traditions, such as Eastern or Western, Catholic or Protestant. All such traditions through which we often insist on approaching Truth are our human creations, developed in an attempt to gain understanding—from our various cultural perspectives—on something that is universal and timeless. Consequently, to gain access to Truth in its own, universal domain, we need to free ourselves from the limitations imposed by our various traditions. When one embodies the Spirit of Truth, or synthesis, one does not have to belong to an esoteric school or tradition to obtain esoteric knowledge, since such hidden knowledge can make itself available to anyone, even in the most public of domains.

Also, let me clarify that the spirit of eclecticism and synthesis is not the same thing as ecumenism, which is institutional. Curiosity and an open heart are required for the Spirit of Truth to manifest and work its alchemy in our understanding, and this can only happen at the individual, personal level.

Several years ago, I was engaged in discussion with a Catholic priest and a friend who has authored books on the transformation of consciousness. The question my friend and I had for the priest was why the type of knowledge we were so freely discussing—namely, the esoteric and mystical aspects of Christianity—was not shared more openly with the laity. To our surprise, the priest told us that he and others like him were usually kept in line by the parishioners, who would complain to the bishop if exposed to anything that deviated from the familiar doctrines. After some reflection, I realized that this made perfect sense. Until we're shaken out of our comfort zones by some form of discontinuity—job loss, illness, divorce, bereavement—we generally want things to remain as they are. There's nothing more comforting than the familiar, whether these be routines or stories. This is the same reason our children do not like us to skip portions of their favorite bedtime stories.

The simplest way to exercise individual responsibility in matters of the Spirit, then, is to be curious. Curiosity is our birthright and, as such, must be encouraged—not repressed. It is the responsibility of each of us to keep this light burning, for only those who are curious can advance in knowledge and understanding.

Two

WHY TRANSFORMATION OF CONSCIOUSNESS IS THE ONLY TRUE SALVATION

HOW ARE WE TO UNDERSTAND THE TRUE ROLE OF JESUS IN SALVATION?

Once we begin to view the Gospels as presenting a program on the transformation of consciousness, we begin also to see Jesus's role in the Gospel story as more than someone simply starring in his own life story. As will become clear as we progress in our exploration of the transformation theme of the Gospels, Jesus's role in the Gospels is that of embodying and demonstrating the Universal Life Principle. This portrayal must be understood as something transcending biological life. As a principle, Life expresses itself in terms of sacrifice—voluntarily consecrating one's energy to something greater.[1] All the other attributes ascribed to Jesus are secondary to this overriding principle of sacrifice and consecration to a higher cause.

Since Life as a principle is difficult for our human mind to grasp, it was presented in the Gospels in terms of love and service, based on the premise of the unity and brotherhood of mankind. Because of this practical emphasis, it is generally accepted that Jesus was the embodiment of the Love Principle. This misunderstanding has resulted in an overemphasis on sentimental devotion to the person of Jesus to the detriment of action to put his teachings into practice by those who claim to be his followers. Jesus portrayed the Life Principle by demonstrating Love as action. This expression of Love is impersonal, and superior to Love as emotion. It attests to the unity of all Life, of which each individual is only a unit, a cell.

However, there is a world of difference between the cells in a living body and individual human beings in a community. What cells do naturally, human beings have to learn to do. This learning requires us to fight against our natural tendencies toward separateness and self-centeredness. As we overcome these separative tendencies, we experience a greater sense of being and belonging. At the same time, we begin to play host within ourselves to the same principle of Life that Jesus demonstrated.

Once we discern this principle of Life underlining Jesus's teachings, we are better able to understand the psychological importance of doctrines that have taken shape from those teachings. For example, doctrines of sin and repentance, of forgiveness and remission of sins, of salvation and resurrection from the dead, are elements of a psychology that has as its goal the expansion of individual human consciousness. These doctrines were designed to widen the aperture of Being* in ourselves, so that more of the Universal Life Principle can flow in and find expression in our thoughts, emotions, and activities. This widening or enlargement of the aperture of Being is accomplished by the awakening, in our psyche**—processes that dissolve blockages, mobilize and recirculate energy, and integrate one into a cooperative arrangement with the external Universe. At all levels, Life as a principle operates by promoting integration and flow in place of division and blockages.

---

*The idea of "aperture" in relation to "Being," or our "Higher Self," is similar to the aperture of a camera's lens, which regulates how much light is admitted to the camera's sensors (or film in the days of film cameras). Thus, our "aperture of Being" defines our capacity to be open to the inflow of higher spiritual virtues into our consciousness. The wider our "aperture of Being," the more we will base our motivations and actions on the reality of our connectedness.

**I am using the term "psyche" in a manner consistent with its use in Jungian psychology, namely "the totality of all psychic processes, conscious as well as unconscious"; Jung, *Psychological Types*, Vol. 6 of The Collected Works, p. 563.

When we view Jesus's portrayal in the Gospels as an expression of the Universal Life Principle, some of the characteristics he claimed for himself take on new meaning. One example is the statement in the Gospel of John: "I came that they may have life and have it abundantly" (John 10:10). Another is found in the twenty-fifth chapter of Matthew, where he gave an exposition of the rewards and punishments the Son of Man would mete out at his coming. That passage is reproduced here in its entirety:

> 31 When the Son of Man comes in his glory, and all the angels with him, then he will sit on his glorious throne. 32 Before him will be gathered all the nations, and he will separate people one from another as a shepherd separates the sheep from the goats. 33 And he will place the sheep on his right, but the goats on the left. 34 Then the King will say to those on his right, 'Come, you who are blessed by my Father, inherit the kingdom prepared for you from the foundation of the world. 35 For I was hungry and you gave me food, I was thirsty and you gave me drink, I was a stranger and you welcomed me, 36 I was naked and you clothed me, I was sick and you visited me, I was in prison and you came to me.' 37 Then the righteous will answer him, saying, 'Lord, when did we see you hungry and feed you, or thirsty and give you drink? 38 And when did we see you a stranger and welcome you, or naked and clothe you? 39 And when did we see you sick or in prison and visit you?' 40 And the King will answer them, 'Truly, I say to you, as you did it to one of the least of these my brothers, you did it to me.'
> 41 Then he will say to those on his left, 'Depart from me, you cursed, into the eternal fire prepared for the devil and his angels. 42 For I was hungry and you gave me no food, I was thirsty and you gave me no drink, 43 I was a stranger

and you did not welcome me, naked and you did not clothe me, sick and in prison and you did not visit me.'[44] Then they also will answer, saying, 'Lord, when did we see you hungry or thirsty or a stranger or naked or sick or in prison, and did not minister to you?'[45] Then he will answer them, saying, 'Truly, I say to you, as you did not do it to one of the least of these, you did not do it to me.'[46] And these will go away into eternal punishment, but the righteous into eternal life. (Matthew 25:31–46)

In this discourse, Jesus equates an act of consideration done by one person for another with an act done toward him directly. This would only make sense if, when doing an act of consideration, we are putting into practice the principle that Jesus represented. In the acts of consideration listed—feeding the hungry, giving drink to the thirsty, providing shelter to the stranger, visiting the sick and imprisoned—the one who is helping is really increasing the flow of life in those who are helped. That is because in every instance where there is need, even if it is just for food, drink, shelter, or encouragement, it is *life* itself that is under threat.

By listing these acts of charity in this particular order, i.e., giving food, providing shelter, offering clothing, making visitations, Jesus is describing a process that becomes progressively more subtle in terms of the needs addressed. Offerings of food can be interpreted as helping people with the physical necessities of life; of drink to emotional sustenance; of shelter to social acceptance; of clothing to ideological tolerance; visits to the sick and imprisoned to giving encouragement. Each of these categories of assistance helps a recipient become unstuck in a particular area of personal consciousness. And there is yet a larger significance to naming these acts; they represent the facilitation of life energy through the first four chakras. These chakras are discussed in chapter 4.

THE PROGRESSIVE ASPECT TO SALVATION

An obvious characteristic of the New Testament's design for salvation is its progressive aspect. Unfortunately, most followers of the Christian faith miss this progressive aspect. Instead of appreciating salvation as an undertaking of progressive unfoldment, denominations distinguish themselves one from the other by expressing individual preferences regarding the requirements for achieving it. Even more remarkable, despite the wide spectrum of beliefs and practices that distinguish one denomination from another, all find common ground in the claim that such salvation is the prerogative solely of Christians.

The objective here is not to berate Christians, but to show how easily we can become locked into patterns of circular logic concerning the subject of salvation. A moment of insight showed me how this self-serving pattern of reasoning operated in my own life. As a consequence, I was able to achieve a de-blocking in my thinking, which allowed me to incorporate and process more information than was permissible under the set of religious beliefs to which I subscribed at the time.

This moment happened several decades ago, when I first permitted myself to overhaul the grounds of my religious convictions. At that period, I was an active member of the Church of Christ, a denomination that publicly claimed the restoration of New Testament Christianity as its primary mission. Its motto on doctrinal matters was, "We speak where the Bible speaks and are silent where the Bible is silent." This meant that any issue that did not exist two thousand years ago could not win the attention of this church. As such, most of its preoccupation was with doctrinal issues: how often communion should be held, whether instrumental music should be permitted in the service, whether water baptism was necessary for salvation, etc. Social issues were irrelevant.

Regarding salvation, the teaching was that one had to make a personal confession of faith in the divinity of Jesus Christ and then subscribe to certain beliefs. Salvation was achieved by first "believing in the truth" and then "obeying the truth." And since "the truth" was defined in terms of doctrinal beliefs, it followed that if you did not have the right doctrine, you could not obey the truth, and therefore could not be saved. Further, since this church was the only one that practiced the right doctrines, anyone outside of it could not obey the truth and thus could not be saved.

For those who subscribed to this way of thinking, the logic was airtight. What no one thought about was the most fundamental and primordial of religious questions: *How can we reconcile the idea of a just God with a scheme in which there are only two outcomes—salvation or eternal damnation—to a human situation that is infinite in variability?*

This question chose the most inauspicious of occasions to penetrate my thinking. This occurred during my attendance at a first-year university lecture in economics. It is difficult to recall precisely what triggered the initial moment of reflection. Perhaps it was the monotonous delivery by the lecturer that drove my mind into reverie, into passively scanning the lecture hall and its three hundred or so faces instead of paying attention. Whatever the trigger, once I became unfocused and took notice of my fellow students, to see that each one could have been me, or I any one of them, but for the accident of parentage, geography, and personal history, the break with my smug self-righteousness, my religious beliefs, and my church came.

The beginning of this rupture with my old beliefs was uneventful. As I surveyed those many faces, a certain thought formed in my mind, namely, *"If I believe what my church teaches, I may be the only one here entitled to salvation. But, what right do I have to claim salvation for myself and not for these others?"* This thought became a preoccupation and eventually grew into the philosophical problem of divine justice mentioned above.

I share this experience here to illustrate the point that, like myself and the church group to which I belonged, many lay claim to that thing called salvation, which is little understood and even less thought out. In their understanding of salvation, the central focus is the historical Jesus, who is presented as having come to Earth to save us from our sins. It is usually explained that this act of redemption was accomplished on the cross at the time of Jesus's crucifixion. However, for an individual to benefit from this act of redemption and become freed from his sins, he must believe in the exclusive divine heritage of Jesus (i.e., believe that he is the only son of God) and "accept him as savior."*

This acceptance is marked by the individual submitting to ceremonial acts such as baptism, a public declaration of faith, and acceptance of membership in a church, though the model has undergone various degrees of modification among the many denominations (e.g., in some groups, the concept of salvation is considered in broader terms, such as admission into the church.) So confident are many Christians of these salvation precepts that an expression of faith might be satisfied as early as infancy, in which the requirement of baptism is fulfilled by the sprinkling of water on the baby, and the confession of faith that Jesus is the only son of God met by someone acting on behalf of the unknowing infant.

VIEWING SALVATION IN THE CONTEXT OF PROCESS

As with many ideas in the Bible, there is a symbolism behind the concept of salvation that institutional Christianity appears to have missed. Perhaps many believers, not having the good fortune, as it were, of seeing their lives pivot upon a single thought, enabling them to leave behind their smug self-righteousness as a result, continue to take for granted this thing called salvation. And because the underlying symbolism is missed, salvation is presented in static, rather than dynamic, terms. It is understood as *a state of existence*, rather than *a process* or *way of life*.

---

*This requirement of "accepting Jesus as savior" has been modified by evangelical Christians in the U.S. to that of "accepting Jesus as personal savior." However, this requirement is not universal across all of the evangelical-type churches. The very conservative Church of Christ, to which I belonged, taught that this requirement of "accepting Jesus as personal savior" has no doctrinal precedent in the entire New Testament.

In some denominations, salvation is understood as an afterlife reward for present-life righteousness, fulfilled by the individual going to heaven. In others, it is presented as an entitlement in the present life to rewards that continue into the afterlife. This latter view is most propagated by the television evangelists who present Jesus as the answer to all of life's problems, both spiritual and material.

Despite apparently explicit biblical references to going to heaven, the writers of the New Testament had something more in mind than an afterlife state of bliss in their use of the term *salvation*. This is even suggested by an examination of the original meaning to the Greek word that has been translated in English versions of the New Testament as "save." According to Young's *Analytical Concordance to the Holy Bible*, this word is *sozo*, the literal meaning of which is "to make or keep sound" or "to heal, make whole, preserve." This suggests that what the architects of the Christian faith had in mind was something dynamic, namely, a way of life, or a process of unfoldment and growth. There is incontrovertible evidence that they were more concerned with the presentation of a psychology of transformation rather than establishing tenets of dogma for a religious institution.

Actually, it is possible to interpret the entire array of doctrines that form recurring themes in Christianity in psychological terms. It is also possible to correlate many of the terms that form religious and theological doctrines to psychological states. For example, for sin, which traditional Christianity views as mankind's natural state, we can substitute ideas such as psychological stagnation, encrustation, crystallization, or blockage. And for the concept of salvation—the antidote to the state of sin—we can think in terms of breaking down such psychological barriers (e.g., dissolving blockages in the psyche, and reactivating and mobilizing life energy in order to progress toward a state of wholeness). The Kingdom of Heaven, as mentioned before, may be understood as the transformation of our human consciousness. Our consciousness undergoes transformation when the process of mobilization and reactivation of life energy reaches a certain intensity or tempo. (See more on this topic in chapters 10 and 11, where we examine the parables used by Jesus to allow us to get a better understanding of what the Kingdom really represents.)

The most important distinction in viewing these familiar concepts of sin and salvation in psychological, rather than theological, terms, is that we can now relate to them as processes that can exist in our individual consciousness.

When we understand sin in psychological terms (e.g., stagnation, encrustation, crystallization, blockage), we're in a better position to understand how the factors that condition us to act in a predetermined way—our beliefs, ideas, habits, phobias, attractions, and repulsions—can become barriers to change. This shift of perspective then enables us to take responsibility for the state of our consciousness and to undertake actions that will facilitate its advancement.

Further, once sin is understood in terms of a certain functioning of our individual consciousness, so too can salvation. In this light, when Christians talk about the "name of Jesus" or the "blood of Christ" being necessary for salvation, we can see lurking beneath those words the idea of an agency of activation—something that works internally to promote or reactivate the process of growth toward a larger consciousness.*

Just because the psychology found in the New Testament is not explicit, however, does not make it any less effective. If we examine various apostolic teachings in some depth, it becomes clear that if we comply with the requirements laid down for salvation, we derive the full benefit of the respective psychology. So, looking closer at the concept of salvation as it was presented, we detect the underlying orientation toward process rather than some defined state. For example, on the surface, salvation was shown as something for which Jesus Christ already paid, with nothing more required of

---

*The idea of growth, or enlargement, as it applies to consciousness, refers to a change from ego-centeredness to other-centeredness, accompanied by a growing openness and inclusiveness to one's outlook on life.

the individual than acknowledging this already-acquired salvation. Then, in addition to this inner acceptance, or as evidence of it, the individual was to make a public declaration that Jesus was the Son of God. These two steps, together, would fulfill the declaration of Jesus in Matthew:

> So everyone who acknowledges me before men, I also will acknowledge before my Father who is in heaven, but who-ever denies me before men, I also will deny before my Father who is in heaven. (Matthew 10:32–33)

Conversely, in the teachings of the early Christian church as presented in Acts, belief in the "name" of Jesus is presented as the only means of obtaining salvation. On this score, the apostle Peter used the healing of a paralytic to make the following declaration:

> Rulers of the people and elders, [9] if we are being examined today concerning a good deed done to a crippled man, by what means this man has been healed, let it be known to all of you and to all the people of Israel that by the name of Jesus Christ of Nazareth, whom you crucified, whom God raised from the dead—by him this man is standing before you well. [11] This Jesus is the stone that was rejected by you, the builders, which has become the cornerstone. [12] And there is salvation in no one else, for there is no other name under heaven given among men by which we must be saved. (Acts 4:9–12)

Paul, too, was moved to attest to the supremacy of the name Jesus in the overall plan of God:

> Therefore God has highly exalted him and bestowed on him the name that is above every name, [10] so that at the

name of Jesus every knee should bow, in heaven and on
earth and under the earth,[11] and every tongue confess that
Jesus Christ is Lord, to the glory of God the Father. (Philippians 2:9–11)

To take advantage of the salvation found in Jesus's name, one had to
make a demonstration of faith by submitting to baptism in water. This
was done by immersion. In fact, baptism was such a central part in the
"plan of salvation" that its fulfillment and the expression of faith in the
name of Jesus became inextricably linked. We see this requirement being
enforced in the historic sermon of Peter on the day of Pentecost, when he
said of Jesus:

> [36] Let all the house of Israel therefore know for certain that
> God has made him both Lord and Christ, this Jesus whom
> you crucified. (Acts 2:36)

When those who heard him became convinced of what he said and
inquired as to what they should do in response, he said to them:

> Repent and be baptized every one of you in the name of
> Jesus Christ for the forgiveness of your sins, and you will
> receive the gift of the Holy Spirit. (Acts 2:37–38)

We find these requirements of belief in the name of Jesus and submission to water baptism being imposed again in the conversion of the eunuch
from Ethiopia, recorded in the eighth chapter of Acts. In this account, the
evangelizing apostle was Philip:

> [35] Then Philip opened his mouth, and beginning with this
> Scripture he told him the good news about Jesus. [36] And as
> they were going along the road they came to some water,

and the eunuch said, "See, here is water! What prevents me from being baptized?" [38] And he commanded the chariot to stop, and they both went down into the water, Philip and the eunuch, and he baptized him. (Acts 8:35–38)

The psychological benefits of these acts of faith, (i.e., confessing the name of Jesus and submitting to baptism), can only be fully received if the individual looks upon his salvation as "a going concern" (to borrow from the accounting definition of a viable business) and not just a once-and-for-all transaction. In other words, having been told initially that his salvation has been secured by Jesus Christ and offered to him as a matter of God's grace, the individual is nevertheless faced with an increasing tempo of responsibility for his own salvation.

Finally, from the teachings of Paul on salvation, we find the strongest evidence that the messages of Jesus and the apostles pointed to the activation of a process, rather than the achievement of a fixed state. For example, writing to the church at Ephesus, Paul said:

And you were dead in the trespasses and sins [2] in which you once walked, following the course of this world, following the prince of the power of the air, the spirit that is now at work in the sons of disobedience—[3]among whom we all once lived in the passions of our flesh, carrying out the desires of the body and the mind, and were by nature children of wrath, like the rest of mankind. [4] But God, being rich in mercy, because of the great love with which he loved us, [5] even when we were dead in our trespasses, made us alive together with Christ—by grace you have been saved—[6] and raised us up with him and seated us with him in the heavenly places in Christ Jesus, [7] so that in the coming ages he might show the immeasurable riches of his grace in kindness toward us in Christ Jesus. [8] For by grace you have been

saved through faith. And this is not your own doing; it is
the gift of God, [9] not a result of works, so that no one may
boast. [10] For we are his workmanship, created in Christ Jesus
for good works, which God prepared beforehand, that we
should walk in them. (Ephesians 2:1–10)

Within this discourse, we see three progressive conditions of salvation.
First, Paul tells the recipients of his letter that it is by the grace of God that
one is saved: "by grace you have been saved." Next, they are told that they
must avail themselves of this salvation through their own faith: "by grace
you have been saved through faith." Finally, despite the fact that they are
told that salvation is "not a result of works, so that no one may boast," they
are further instructed that by virtue of this salvation, they owe it to their savior to live for him. They are told that they have been "created in Christ Jesus
for good works, which God prepared beforehand, that we should walk in
them." In other words, by virtue of being saved, the individual is expected
to pursue a certain life path of good works that God has prescribed.

Paul elaborated on this theme in other discourses. For example, in his
first letter to the church at Corinth, he wrote, "… for you were bought
with a price. So glorify God in your body" (1 Corinthians 6:20).

These conditions of salvation can be compared to a contemporary life
situation in which a financial institution grants someone a debt-consoli-
dation loan to enable him to pay off several creditors, leaving him with
only one regularly scheduled payment to make instead of many.

In the next section, we shall examine two of the premier acts of faith
identified as necessary to enable one to take advantage of salvation—a salvation to which one is already entitled as a matter of God's grace. We will
see, from a psychological perspective, how these two requirements respectively form the *keystone** and *touchstone* conditions essential for someone

---

*A keystone is defined by Webster's online dictionary as: 1: the wedge-shaped piece at the
crown of an arch that locks the other pieces in place. 2: something on which associated
things depend for support. Touchstone is defined as: "a test or criterion for determining
the quality or genuineness of a thing."

to start taking an active role in the expansion of his own personal consciousness. These acts of faith are:

- Confession of belief in the name of Jesus Christ, and
- Submission to water baptism.

We shall also look at the immediate benefit of these expressions of faith, namely the acquisition of "the gift of the holy spirit" as taught by the apostles.

The Deeper Significance of the Name of Jesus

In the requirement of belief in the divinity of Jesus as a condition for salvation, one encounters, at its widest point, the gulf that can exist between the underlying meaning of a religious symbol and its literal, surface interpretation. When a Christian accepts, at a literal level, that the name of the historical personage, Jesus, is the "only name under heaven" by which salvation can be attained, he may actually hinder the cause of Christ, rather than promote it. This is by virtue of the limit that this position imposes on the applicability of Christianity across different time periods and cultures.

In the first place, it is impossible for anyone with no model, or lived experience, of what characterizes a human being as divine, to express a meaningful statement of belief in the divinity of anyone; and this task is made even more difficult when separated from the person in question by some two thousand years. Second, by doggedly adhering to the literal interpretation that the name of Jesus is the only one by which a person can achieve salvation, one is automatically denying the possibility of salvation to the billions who lived before the time of Jesus, not to mention those who have lived since and not heard of him. So unless there is some other explanation for, or meaning behind, the "name of Jesus," salvation becomes something reserved for those lucky few who were born in an area of the world where Christianity is the common religion, and in an era postdating the time ascribed to Jesus.

To better understand what it means to believe in the name of Jesus and to confess that he is divine, then, let us examine the incident in the Gospels of the first public expression that Jesus was the Son of God. In this incident, we see Jesus responding with an enthusiasm that appears, at first glance, unwarranted, especially in view of the fact that Peter was carrying out a confession of faith that every Sunday School child now makes with ease. Considering also that Peter was with Jesus and had firsthand knowledge of his mode of being, Jesus's enthusiastic response seems even more peculiar. He tells Peter that "flesh and blood" had not revealed the knowledge of his divinity to Peter, meaning that this insight had come from Peter's intuition. It is this fact that makes Peter's confession a meaningful one and distinguishes it from that of someone who can only arrive at it through hearsay.

Peter's confession was also revolutionary because he was crediting a human being with divinity. This was a situation that he had not previously experienced. By saying that Jesus was *the Christ*, he was doing much more than venerating Jesus; he was ascribing to the man Jesus the consciousness of the Christ, or the "Anointed One." In ordinary language, Peter was saying, "Here, in tangible, physical representation, is the reality of God and man, superimposed, one upon the other, without conflict."

In similar fashion, when the apostles made an expression of faith in the divinity of Jesus the focal point of their conversion program, they were really planting the suggestion in an individual's consciousness that it is possible for humans to achieve union with the Divine, and that such union ought to be the culmination point of our life's strivings. If the apostles had meant anything else by the requirement of believing in the "name" of Jesus other than giving us a point of focus for our aspirations and will, they would, in effect, have been expecting us make perjurers of ourselves.

By making belief in the divinity of Jesus the key to salvation, the apostles were also establishing the foundation for a psychology of personal integration. They were asking the individual to accept Jesus as the Principle of Life, and, as such, to use his teachings as a blueprint for a reorganization of his or her personal life. In complying with such a program, the individual would be opening himself up emotionally to the principle that Jesus represented, as well as accepting the challenge of striving for a better reflection of it in his own life. And since this is the Life Principle, such an acceptance of Jesus means that the individual would be striving to let Life express itself more fully through him. The result of such an effort would be a personal life lived in pursuit of our human unity and the expansion of human consciousness, both individually and collectively.

There was also another sense—apart from the context of personal salvation—in which the name of Jesus Christ was used and presented in the New Testament. This was in terms of a "password" to divine favors. In the Gospel of John, for example, Jesus tells his disciples that if they asked the Father anything in his (i.e., Jesus's) name that it would be granted (John I 5:23). We see this promise put to the test in subsequent miracles of healing, as well as in exorcisms recorded in Acts.

However, this practical orientation aside, the underlying sense in which the name of Jesus is meant is the same as that pertaining to the issue of personal salvation. In both cases, we are not dealing with the word-name of Jesus, but the *consciousness-name.*

WORD-NAME VERSUS CONSCIOUSNESS-NAME

When we make a request in the word-name of another person, we are doing so *in the authority* of that person. As such, the request is usually made with the authority and power of the person whose name is being invoked, and the individual to whom the request is being made is ultimately answerable to the person whose name is being used.

On the other hand, when we make a request in the consciousness-name of someone, we are asking *on behalf of* that person. The distinction is more than a matter of semantics. The word-name of someone is really a label or symbol for his material reality. The consciousness-name, on the other hand, reflects the reality of his true nature. Recognition of this distinction is shown in the secular advertising slogan, "The quality went in before the name went on," to aptly demonstrate the meaning of the consciousness-name of Jesus Christ; it has to do with the spirit, or consciousness, that Jesus Christ represents.

It therefore makes sense that if one asks in the name of Jesus Christ, in the sense that one asks on behalf of Jesus Christ, the request would be granted. This is because when one asks "on behalf of Jesus Christ," one is asking in the spirit that characterizes the principle that Jesus Christ represented—the principle of advancing the cause of Life, of facilitating flow where there is blockage, and of arresting entropy. When one asks in this spirit, one asks so as to channel that which is received to a perceived need. Viewed in this light, then, the idea of asking in the name of Jesus becomes an exercise of offering oneself to become the means, or a conduit, through which a perceived need finds redress or fulfillment.

Failure to see this underlying principle of channeling behind the idea of asking in the name of Jesus explains why some Christians express discouragement and loss of faith when their prayers are not answered in the manner they expect. It is in anticipation of such misunderstanding that the apostle James wrote concerning prayer, "You ask and do not receive, because you ask wrongly, to spend it on your passions" (James 4:3). This emphasizes the point that asking in Jesus's name is not asking in his authority, but rather on his behalf.

Finally, as if to demonstrate that the name of Jesus had a deeper significance than the simple recitation of words, a story is recorded in Acts in which certain individuals tried to exploit what they perceived as magic in the word-name of Jesus Christ. To their humiliation, they found out that the only true magic was to be found in the consciousness of the user:

> [11] And God was doing extraordinary miracles by the hands of Paul, [12] so that even handkerchiefs or aprons that had touched his skin were carried away to the sick, and their diseases left them and the evil spirits came out of them. [13] Then some of the itinerant Jewish exorcists undertook to invoke

the name of the Lord Jesus over those who had evil spirits, saying, "I adjure you by the Jesus whom Paul proclaims." [14] Seven sons of a Jewish high priest named Sceva were doing this. [15] But the evil spirit answered them, "Jesus I know, and Paul I recognize, but who are you?" [16] And the man in whom was the evil spirit leaped on them, mastered all of them and overpowered them, so that they fled out of that house naked and wounded. [17] And this became known to all the residents of Ephesus, both Jews and Greeks. And fear fell upon them all, and the name of the Lord Jesus was extolled. (Acts 19:11–17)

THE PSYCHOLOGY BEHIND THE REQUIREMENT OF BAPTISM

If we regard belief in the name of Jesus Christ as the keystone condition for salvation, then submitting oneself to baptism is the first test of that belief. Baptism is, therefore, the touchstone condition, meaning the condition that seals the deal, in a manner of speaking.

It must be noted, however, that the practice of baptism was not restricted to the teachings of Jesus and his disciples (later to become apostles). According to the Gospels, it was instituted by John the Baptist, whose name really means "John the Baptizer." Jesus also submitted to baptism under John, marking the occasion as that point at which he took up his ministry. This act by Jesus is additional evidence that baptism was not something mystical and unknowable, but a tangible event in the here and now. It symbolized a punctuation mark, a point of turning. Just as Jesus used it to separate his life into the years before and after he assumed his spiritual mission, we were to regard it as the point of change between the old life and the new. After all, baptism is to symbolize the triune process of death, burial, and rebirth, as emphasized by Paul in his Epistle to the Romans:

³ Do you not know that all of us who have been baptized into Christ Jesus were baptized into his death? ⁴ We were buried therefore with him by baptism into death, in order that, just as Christ was raised from the dead by the glory of the Father, we too might walk in newness of life. ⁵ For if we have been united with him in a death like his, we shall certainly be united with him in a resurrection like his. ⁶ We know that our old self was crucified with him in order that the body of sin might be brought to nothing, so that we would no longer be enslaved to sin. ⁷ For one who has died has been set free from sin. ⁸ Now if we have died with Christ, we believe that we will also live with him. ⁹ We know that Christ, being raised from the dead, will never die again; death no longer has dominion over him. ¹⁰ For the death he died he died to sin, once for all, but the life he lives he lives to God ¹¹ So you also must consider yourselves dead to sin and alive to God in Christ Jesus. (Romans 6:3–1)

The idea expressed here is that the individual ceremoniously accepts the penalty for sin, which is death. But in the case of baptism, it is a ceremonial death, a form of initiation that takes one through the doorway of death and into a new way of life. Paul refers to the old lifestyle as the "old self" and, in another context (Galatians 3:27), refers to the act of baptism as "putting on Christ." The implication is that, through baptism, a metamorphosis is enacted—the old self, complete with old habits, compulsions, and outlooks, enters into the watery grave and gives way to the new man, the consciousness of Christ operating in him.

Psychologically speaking, baptism is a ritual that impresses itself on the mind at both a conscious and unconscious level. At the conscious level, it impregnates the mind with the sense of a point of departure, thus meeting the requirement that every undertaking, before it can succeed, must have a birth in a moment of time. This is because it is harder for someone to turn his back on his commitment to expand his own consciousness if that commitment exists as a historical fact in time and space, rather than as an idea only.

At the unconscious level, which includes the level of the emotions, baptism acted to erode feelings of guilt and to help clear the "hearth of the conscience" so that the fire of genuine aspirations could be lit. This idea was expressed by the apostles, and particularly Peter, who wrote, "Baptism, which corresponds to this, now saves you, not as a removal of dirt from the body but as an appeal to God for a good conscience, through the resurrection of Jesus Christ" (1 Peter 3:21). The idea is that the value of baptism is not derived from the function or utility of water, but rather that its value is psychological. Just as two individuals concluding a business arrangement may seal their agreement with a handshake as a demonstration of good conscience toward each other, baptism puts a seal on the new relationship between the individual and God. By submitting to this act, the individual is indicating that he is ready to begin, in earnest, the process of the transformation of his personal consciousness.

As for eroding guilt, baptism accomplishes this by helping one acquire a positive self-image. Guilt results from feeling badly about oneself on account of something that was done in the past. In this state of negative self-reflection, transformation is impeded, since the individual, by virtue of these negative feelings, remains stuck in old patterns of thinking and behaving. The stagnation is sustained by its own dynamic: the one who's feeling guilty about something strives to balance the ledger of his conscience by generating negative feelings about himself for his past misdeeds. Next, these negative feelings are unconsciously accepted by him as the price for his misdeeds. He therefore feels no need to change his ways; since he accepts the negative feelings he bears towards himself as fair exchange.

The other psychological value of baptism lies in its ability to insert a wedge into and break the vicious cycle that is generated from having a guilty conscience. Someone might feel guilt for a past indiscretion, but instead of changing for the better, feels resentful for having these guilty feelings. This resentment can then lead to further indiscretions.

When one entitles oneself to the forgiveness of sins that is supposed to accompany baptism, the slate of conscience is wiped clean, psychologically speaking. With a clear conscience, one is able to start afresh, as one's actions are no longer tied to the legacy of one's past. However, this freedom from one's past comes with the price of added responsibility. Since one's actions are no longer reactions to causes set in motion in the past, one comes under pressure to find justifications for one's current actions. Through this process, foresight is learned, since one must now ascertain the inherent value, or consequence, of an activity before participating in it. This is how personal consciousness is made to grow—by the individual assuming more responsibility for his actions.

THE GUIDANCE OF THE HOLY SPIRIT

The Holy Spirit enters the design for salvation as a reciprocation by God to the convert who believed in the name of Jesus, repented of his sins, and submitted to water baptism. If we return to the sermon of Peter on the day of Pentecost, we would recall that Peter told the crowd that if they repented and were baptized, they would receive the gift of the Holy Spirit.

The role of the Holy Spirit in salvation must be understood in terms of process, just as the role of Jesus Christ can be best understood as the Principle of Life, and salvation seen as the process of the renewal and growth of personal consciousness towards the Universal. In the scheme of salvation, the Holy Spirit represents the Reconciling Principle of God as it manifests at an individual and personal level, in contrast to the Christ Principle, which represents the transpersonal and mental manifestation.* This can be detected from the teachings of Jesus as recorded in the Gospel of John.

---

*These two principles operate cooperatively; the role of the Holy Spirit in the process of salvation can be compared to the action of charging a battery, while the Christ Principle relates to putting the charged battery to use.

In John's Gospel, as we find Jesus preparing his disciples for his eventual departure, he tells them that unless he went away, the "Helper," meaning the Holy Spirit, could not come to them.

> ^{16} And I will ask the Father, and he will give you another Helper, to be with you forever, ^{17} even the Spirit of truth, whom the world cannot receive, because it neither sees him nor knows him. You know him, for he dwells with you and will be in you.
> ^{18} "I will not leave you as orphans; I will come to you. ^{19} Yet a little while and the world will see me no more, but you will see me. Because I live, you also will live. (John 14:16–19)

The point Jesus is making in this discourse is that his physical presence would block the arrival of the Helper (or "Comforter" in the King James Version). Moreover, Jesus assured the disciples that the Helper would more than compensate for the loss they would experience from his departure. The Helper, he said, would teach them, reminding them of all that he himself had taught:

> But the Helper, the Holy Spirit, whom the Father will send in my name, he will teach you all things and bring to your remembrance all that I have said to you. (John 14:26)

From additional discourses by Jesus, we get the impression that the Helper, or the Holy Spirit in the form of a distinct personality, was a special creation designed to get the disciples (and individuals in general) to shift their focus from outward to inward. It is this inward look that enables one to make the acquaintance of the Divine spark found in each soul and nurture it to its fullest expression. As a representative of the Life Principle, Jesus's role was that of a light-bearer to the world, in order to impress upon it the necessity of reorganizing and giving expression to this principle in its fullness. However, in order to get people in general—who are only used to relating to the Divine as something outside of themselves—to turn their gaze inward, their attention was directed to the new, divine personality of the Holy Spirit.

In fact, the entire life drama of Jesus, as found in the Gospels, could be regarded as an attempt by those responsible for creating this literature, to focus our attention on the Divine Light, in the person of Jesus, then take it away—as an external phenomenon—so that we would seek and find it again, but within ourselves. Since the idea of salvation is to encourage us to lend our conscious cooperation to the process of transforming our personal consciousness, the scheme of bringing our collective attention to the phenomenon of the Divine-human, who then leaves the scene, might actually be considered foolproof. When one has been acquainted with the Light, which in this case is embodied in the Divine-human, life is not the same thereafter. Therefore, one would need to seek another Light source after the first one was taken away.

The life drama of Jesus, therefore, was to serve as means to an end—namely, an event to get us to recognize our own divine potential. The next step was for us to marshal our energies to realize this potential. This was why Jesus emphasized that, as long as he remained in the flesh, or more accurately, as something "other," the Holy Spirit could not come to the disciples:

> Nevertheless, I tell you the truth: it is to your advantage that
> I go away, for if I do not go away, the Helper will not come
> to you. But if I go, I will send him to you. (John 16:7)

This method of introducing the redeeming process of the Holy Spirit into our awareness was especially chosen to effect a smooth transition in the human mind to a new way of looking at the Divine: no longer was it sufficient to look for God outside of oneself; one must look within. The operation is similar to a radar operator watching an airplane take off with the naked eye, and then shifting his gaze to watch the action from his radar screen. A blip on a screen, for all practical purposes, now becomes the aircraft. The purpose behind this change in observation is to extend the operator's normal powers of observation; he can now see the craft long after it has gone outside the range of his naked eye.

Likewise, as our capacity to relate to the Divine through Jesus exhausts itself, we must learn to turn our eyes inward.

The psychological workings of the Holy Spirit are explained in the following exhortation of Jesus that the Holy Spirit would convict the world of sin, righteousness, and judgment:

> And when he comes, he will convict the world concerning sin and righteousness and judgment: concerning sin, because they do not believe in me; concerning righteousness, because I go to the Father, and you will see me no longer; concerning judgment, because the ruler of this world is judged. (John 16:8–11)

The different workings of the Holy Spirit (i.e., the various convictions) mentioned above represent levels of deepening in our relationship with the Divine. One of the first effects of being imbued with the Holy Spirit is the stimulation of the faculty of conscience. Conscience is part of our legacy as human beings and is our innate sense of "doing the right thing." However, like any of our other faculties, it can become dulled through neglect and disuse. It is through our conscience that we become convicted of sin and realize that we are living at a level of existence below that which our intelligence and experience tell us is right for us.* Conscience also acts like a mirror, reflecting our outer self and its interactions with the world back to our innermost self. In this sense, it is our counselor-judge.

---

*This is why someone with a highly developed conscience would do good as a matter of course and not expect special recognition or reward for behaving with kindness, compassion, and fairness. To do less would be to live below his own expectation of himself.

Next, there's an awakening of the intuition. Intuition convicts the world of judgment by revealing to us the inadequacy of accepted legal and moral frameworks by which the world functions. By comparison, the faculty of intuition allows us to have a deeper understanding of the moral principles on which the Universe functions. With this understanding comes the ability to act responsibly, to make correct decisions, and to act in a manner consistent with a sense of purpose.

Thirdly, there's a strengthening of the will, and it is in this sense that the Holy Spirit convicts the world of righteousness. Will, in the spiritual sense, is more than focused intention; it is our capacity to apply ourselves to accomplishing what we know in our hearts to be in our best interest. This is really what constitutes true righteousness—it is our capacity to be true to our ideals.

Finally, the Holy Spirit was to give the disciples the gift of prophecy: "[H]e will show you things to come," said Jesus. The association of the Holy Spirit with prophecy and other miracles was made to enable one to relate consciously to the transformative work taking place within. As one's sense of connection with others increases as a result of giving expression to the Christ Principle through acts of service, certain manifestations may occur to reassure us that the inner work is progressing on schedule. These results inwardly impress upon us in an objective way the validity of the path we are pursuing in our outer life.

These "special effects" were not meant to cause alarm, or yet, make one feel special. Furthermore, one was not meant to solicit them, for to do so would result in one's being distracted from doing the essential work, which is the expression of the Christ Principle in one's daily life. By attributing these experiences to the work of the Holy Spirit, the architects of this psychology intended for the individual to take whatever assurances he could from them, and go about the task of making as accurate an expression as possible of the Life Principle in his daily existence.

THREE

AN ESOTERIC APPROACH
TO THE GOSPELS

ESOTERIC TEACHINGS IN THE NEW TESTAMENT

Before we get to the task of uncovering the transformational psychology in the Gospels, let's reflect on a certain design feature built into the movement of Christianity that has accounted for this knowledge remaining hidden. This feature relates to the intentional dissemination of spiritual information at multiple levels. The outermost, or exoteric, level is the one generally available to the multitudes, or the masses. The innermost level is the esoteric, and this is hidden from all but the most serious, committed, and sincere practitioners.

The idea of Christian knowledge being made available at different levels should not come as a surprise to anyone familiar with the practice of Jesus speaking to the multitudes in parables, but plainly to the disciples. When the disciples asked the reason for this approach, his reply was:

> "To you it has been given to know the secrets of the Kingdom of Heaven, but to them it has not been given. [12] For to the one who has, more will be given, and he will have an abundance, but from the one who has not, even what he has will be taken away. [13] This is why I speak to them in parables, because seeing they do not see, and hearing they do not

hear, nor do they understand. [14] Indeed, in their case, the prophecy of Isaiah is fulfilled that says:

> 'You will indeed hear but never understand, and you will indeed see but never perceive. [15] For this people's heart has grown dull, and with their ears they can barely hear, and their eyes they have closed, lest they should see with their eyes and hear with their ears and understand with their heart and turn, and I would heal them.'

[16] But blessed are your eyes, for they see, and your ears, for they hear." (Matthew 13:11–16)

In no uncertain terms, Jesus is upholding the parable as a device for metering out "the secrets" of the Kingdom of Heaven. The reason for such metering is our varying capacities of understanding and readiness to act on whatever knowledge we receive. The secrets of the Kingdom of Heaven really relate to the expansion of consciousness, both collectively and individually. Since the disciples had already indicated by their commitment that they were ready to receive these secrets, Jesus spoke in plain language to them.

The reason for restricting knowledge of this nature is given in the quotation from Isaiah cited by Jesus: The multitudes had closed ears, eyes, and hearts, because they did not want to hear, see, and understand, and be healed. This assessment describes the mind-set of everyone who is afraid of the challenges that change can bring, and more so if the needed change is the type of life-course correction that's required for a transformation of consciousness. Because, in reality, this is the healing that Jesus and Isaiah are referring to; it is healing for our entire life, for our existence. Since such healing, and the change of consciousness it requires, is always perceived as a venture into the unknown, when we are introduced to knowledge we are not prepared to act upon, our natural response is to recoil, which then expresses itself as disbelief.

The device of the parable represents neutral ground. It does not back one into a corner. If one is willing and ready to undertake necessary work to improve oneself, the way leading to understanding the deeper meaning of the parable becomes clear. This explains the puzzling statement of Jesus that says, "For to the one who has, more will be given, and he will have an abundance, but from the one who has not, even what he has will be taken away." (Matthew 13:12).

This statement sets out one of the principles of spiritual growth. It seems to be a universal law that if we have the aspiration to change, to actively participate in the process of growing our consciousness, then we will find the knowledge and the experiences necessary to make this aspiration a reality. If, however, we lack the required level of aspiration and are exposed prematurely to this knowledge, the result will be disbelief and a consequent blunting of our will. This occurs because, when we take the position of disbelieving something, or an idea, we establish a position of opposition in our consciousness to the reality underlying the premise that we're rejecting. This stance of opposition is reinforced by intellectual arguments that we construct to justify our position. Eventually, when we later acquire the life experiences that would enable us to receive the knowledge that we previously rejected, we typically find it difficult to change our position because the mind, having invested itself with arguments favoring rejection, now has a vested interest in maintaining its opposition.

Accessing Esoteric Teachings in the New Testament

The religion that has sprung up around Jesus's teachings is based mostly on its exoteric aspects. It is what we get from a literal reading of the Gospels. The consequence is that many of the instructions concerning inner psychological processes that accompany the transformation of consciousness are missed; they are misinterpreted as incidents occurring in the world, outside oneself. As said previously, this misinterpretation has given rise to disparate doctrines and denominations within the Christian faith.

The esoteric aspect, on the other hand, comes from having direct insight into the psychological principles behind the Gospels' reporting of events and instructions. Esoteric knowledge is not book knowledge; it is insight into a deeper Reality. It is knowledge that we acquire with our total being. The question, therefore, is: How do we get from the exoteric to the esoteric?

Perhaps in earlier times, individuals who were initiated into the deeper wisdom of the scriptures served as a guide for others who were ready to deepen their understanding. Since spirituality is really about what's going on within us, those individuals ready to advance would have announced their readiness through their inner experiences and questions. However, given the fragmentation of the Christian faith, there is no standard access point to esoteric knowledge within the church as an institution. This means that most individuals who want access to esoteric knowledge have to become self-initiated.

Normally, self-initiation should be a natural process of spiritual maturation, the result of living by the spiritual knowledge that we already have. The lived experiences that would emerge from practicing our spirituality would then give us the perspective and courage to pose questions about life for which we do not already have answers. I acknowledge that this process, though natural, may not be easy due to the various interferences that could develop, such as factors that repress our curiosity, or lull us into thinking that we are already in possession of that which we should be striving for.

Asking, Seeking, and Knocking

The main requirements for gaining access to esoteric knowledge are contained in Matthew 7:7-8:

Ask, and it will be given to you; seek, and you will find; knock, and it will be opened to you. For everyone who asks receives, and the one who seeks finds, and to the one who knocks it will be opened.

Thus, *asking, seeking,* and *knocking* represent ways that we can progressively express our desire for meaning—which in this context is a sense of connectedness to the Cosmos. As such, the utilization of these modes, or avenues of access—asking, seeking, and knocking—represents a threefold strategy for obtaining esoteric knowledge. In a practical sense, the activity of asking is related to our acquisition of objective values, of seeking to our level of sincerity, and of knocking to our degree of perseverance, or strength of will. From an inner perspective, i.e., the perspective of Spirit, in our daily life, we will be presented with opportunities, or tests, to demonstrate our values, sincerity, and perseverance as a way of evaluating our readiness to receive esoteric insight into the deeper mysteries of life.

The Test of Our Values: *"Ask, and it will be given to you"*
In our search to find meaning, *asking* can be understood as our ongoing evaluation of our life experiences in relation to the ideals that we hold. This evaluation creates a juxtaposition in consciousness, of our ideal world, on one hand, and our everyday experiences of the world, on the other. The foundation of this ideal world that we create internally is built on the values that we hold; and the more objective our value system, the more the events in the outer world would seem to clash with the inner one. It is thus from the inner tension, or discomfort, that is manifested from the conflicting presentations from our inner and outer worlds, that we formulate the questions that can motivate us at an intellectual level to find answers; questions about the meaning of life, about divine justice, about how we can make a more meaningful contribution to the world.

When our questions arise, they set up a dialogue with our Higher Self. It is this dialogue that eventually guides us to a deeper insight, such that we may see the need to refine our understanding of the spiritual values we hold, or learn to see the world differently, perhaps more compassionately. Understandably, since it is our values that enable us to construct an internal model of how we would like the world to be, without a system of objective values, there is no ideal counterpoint to the world of our everyday experiences. And without this dynamic of contrast functioning in our consciousness, meaningful questions cannot arise, since we would feel that everything is as it should be. Usually, it is when we are not satisfied with the status quo that we allow questions to form. So in a sense, asking questions is not so much about pursuing specific information as it is about finding deeper insights into existence as a result of our pursuit of a more meaningful relationship with life.

When we have a well-developed, objective value system, we will become aware of alerts in the Gospels that indicate when we must seek more than a literal interpretation of an event or discourse that we read about. Sometimes these alerts are quite direct, such as the words, "He who has ears, let him hear" (Matthew 13:9). On this occasion, Jesus had just related the parable of the sower. At other times, the alerts function through our values by presenting situations that offend our sense of divine justice. A clear example of such a values-related alert is the fig tree incident in Mark. Another type of alert occurs in terms of paradoxes, or outright absurdities, which we will only be able to acknowledge if we are sufficiently comfortable within ourselves. An example of a paradox-type alert is contained in a parable in Matthew about a wedding celebration. And it is only when we've developed an objective value system that we will allow ourselves to feel this level of comfort with the Gospels to find a literal interpretation unacceptable.

Let's look at the fig tree incident. In Mark's telling of this story, Jesus, being hungry, approached a fig tree hoping to find figs. He found only leaves on the tree, because "it was not the season for figs," states Mark. Jesus then curses the fig tree, causing it to wither:

¹² On the following day, when they came from Bethany, he was hungry. ¹³ And seeing in the distance a fig tree in leaf, he went to see if he could find anything on it. When he came to it, he found nothing but leaves, for it was not the season for figs. ¹⁴ And he said to it, "May no one ever eat fruit from you again." And his disciples heard it (Mark 11: 12-14).

By telling us that it was not the season for figs, Mark is alerting us that there's something else going on. He wants us to pay particular attention. For those of us who are familiar with the Gospels, this is the same Jesus who knew that the Samaritan woman at the well had five husbands (John 5:19), who was privy to the secrets of the Kingdom of God, which he shared with his close disciples, yet he went up to a fig tree in the off-season expecting to find figs!

It is obvious that this incident does not make any sense at a literal level. In the first instance, wouldn't Jesus have known that there weren't figs on the out-of-season fig tree before going up to the tree to take issue with it for doing exactly what Nature intended for it? Secondly, what sort of moral lesson would Jesus intend for us to take from his treatment of the fig tree? Indeed, if we insist on taking this story as an actual event, it does not support our characterization of Jesus as someone who is perfect and faultless. To summarily condemn a fig tree simply because one is disappointed at not finding it in fruit, even when it is acknowledged that it was not the season for fruit, would characterize the one passing judgment as petulant and prone to misusing power. Such conduct, coming from someone like Jesus, would make his behavior all too human, and flawed at that.

Apart from the aspersions that this incident would cast on Jesus's own character, it would raise a significant issue surrounding our notion of divine justice. Unless we see something awry in the fig tree incident, we should be prepared to say goodbye to whatever notion we have of the justice of God, as divine justice gives place to unpredictability and capriciousness.

Interpreting this incident esoterically means that we should see it as a parable for us to apply to ourselves in our quest for spiritual understanding. As with parables in general, the subject of the action is not an external agent, but an internal dynamic in our own consciousness.

In interpreting this story, as a parable, I would suggest that Jesus, being hungry and approaching an out-of-season fig tree for food, really stands for our emergent Christ Consciousness, which requires nurturance. In this scheme, the fig tree represents the natural order. The fact that figs are out of season suggests that the natural order may regard the appearance of Christ Consciousness as a temporal inconvenience, and may not be in a state of readiness to play a supporting role.

Christ Consciousness requires extraordinary measures to develop, obliging us to go the extra mile. It does not emerge out of the natural order, as it is not the product of natural evolution. Nature can only perform within the scope that has been defined for it. And in order to support the development of Christ Consciousness, Nature—including our own natures—must make a special accommodation, which may exceed the capacity of Nature's resources and our own natural inclinations or gifts. In other words, the pursuit of spiritual development may very well dictate that we do things that do not come to us naturally, or extend ourselves in ways that are difficult for us. As such, for Christ Consciousness to emerge in our individual psyche, the rest of our life must make an accommodation, must find ways to rise to the occasion to support the nurturance and growth of this emergent reality. The gist of this principle is this: If the world of the Spirit needs support, we cannot hide behind our natural limits; otherwise, the opportunity may be forever lost. This is what it means for the fig tree to fall under a curse. If we cannot rise to the occasion to lend support to our Christ Self when it appears, we might as well not have been born, as we would be missing out on the whole point of human existence.

The Test of Our Sincerity: "Seek, and you will find"

Spiritually speaking, *seeking* is represented by three related conditions appearing in our consciousness. First, there is a recognition and acknowledgement of a need for something other than what we have. Second, there is awareness that we should prepare ourselves internally to receive the missing element when we encounter it. Third, we arrive at a subjective understanding of what we are prepared to give in exchange for the missing element that is sought. Seeking and finding are inseparable and, to state the obvious, there's no finding without seeking, because when we come upon something of value, we might not recognize it for what it is unless we're looking for it.

Seeking implies a certain kind of integrity of comportment, which I refer to as *sincerity*. This kind of sincerity defines our posture before Life. The three conditions, which constitute seeking, must hold simultaneously for us to demonstrate sincerity; otherwise our seeking cannot be true seeking. Said another way, our spiritual search will lack sincerity if we have not demonstrated a willingness to take on the higher level of responsibility that corresponds with the spiritual knowledge we're seeking.

The challenge of acquiring sincerity is increased because it's easy for us to deceive ourselves that we're sincere when, in reality, we're not. The person who is sincere would be prepared to accept the advice of Job's friend Elihu to "Let not the greatness of the ransom turn you aside" (Job 36:18). The easiest way for us to tell if we're sincere is to do some introspection and ask, "What have I done with the knowledge that I already have?"

Of course, there are practical reasons for anyone who professes to seek spiritual knowledge to demonstrate that he or she is capable of using the knowledge when received, and the only way to assure this is to have already tested and applied the knowledge we've previously gained. If we try to discover esoteric knowledge before we are ready, gaps might appear in our understanding that will later prove harmful. Jesus conveys a warning to those of us who ignore his instructions. From an esoteric perspective, Jesus's reference to "these words of mine" is to be interpreted as referring to the promptings of our own Higher, or Christ Self:

[24] Everyone then who hears these words of mine and does them will be like a wise man who built his house on the rock. [25] And the rain fell, and the floods came, and the winds blew and beat on that house, but it did not fall, because it had been founded on the rock. [26] And everyone who hears these words of mine and does not do them will be like a foolish man who built his house on the sand. [27] And the rain fell, and the floods came, and the winds blew and beat against that house, and it fell, and great was the fall of it. (Matthew 7:24–27)

The symbols that Jesus used in this warning are significant in and of themselves. By likening someone who is exposed to his teachings to one who is building a house, Jesus is suggesting that everyone exposed to spiritual knowledge is making a decision about his or her own future. A house symbolizes personal consciousness, and just as being in our own house gives us a feeling of personal security, our consciousness gives us a sense of psychic security. It is from this secure core that we find the strength to establish relationships with people and things in our environment. And in order to create such feelings of security, we must draw from ideas and concepts proven by our own experiences. These experiences constitute the foundation of rock.

The consciousness that is constructed from experiences that we have acquired from *doing* provides us with a sense of certainty. It is this certainty, this groundedness, that will enable us to withstand doubts (rain), assaults of the desires emanating from our feelings of neediness (floods), and ridicule from others (winds). If, however, we have gone through life being dependent on fantasy and speculation, not proving things for ourselves by our own doing, we are building our consciousness—our allegorical house—on sand.

Of the different aspects of seeking spiritual knowledge, the most crucial relates to our readiness to receive what we are seeking. Of course, if we are

truly seeking—meaning if we're motivated from a place of inner hunger—
then chances are that we'd be ready to seize the opportunity when we
encounter the object of our search. However, there is always a chance that
our search may not be very well defined, and that preparations for undertaking it may have been inadequate. It is just such a situation that is
addressed in the parable of the wedding garment in Matthew 22. In this
instance, however, the esoteric information with which we need to acquaint
ourselves is contained in a paradoxical situation within the parable.

> [1] And again Jesus spoke to them in parables, saying, [2] "The
> kingdom of heaven may be compared to a king who gave a
> wedding feast for his son, [3] and sent his servants to call those
> who were invited to the wedding feast, but they would not
> come. [4] Again he sent other servants, saying, 'Tell those who
> are invited, See, I have prepared my dinner, my oxen and
> my fat calves have been slaughtered, and everything is ready.
> Come to the wedding feast.' [5] But they paid no attention
> and went off, one to his farm, another to his business, [6] while
> the rest seized his servants, treated them shamefully, and
> killed them. [7] The king was angry, and he sent his troops
> and destroyed those murderers and burned their city. [8] Then
> he said to his servants, 'The wedding feast is ready, but those
> invited were not worthy. [9] Go therefore to the main roads
> and invite to the wedding feast as many as you find.' [10] And
> those servants went out into the roads and gathered all
> whom they found, both bad and good. So the wedding hall
> was filled with guests.
> [11] But when the king came in to look at the guests, he
> saw there a man who had no wedding garment. [12] And he
> said to him, 'Friend, how did you get in here without a wed-
> ding garment?' And he was speechless. [13] Then the king said
> to the attendants, 'Bind him hand and foot and cast him

into the outer darkness. In that place there will be weeping
and gnashing of teeth.' [14] For many are called, but few are
chosen" (Matthew 22: 1-13).

The king's son, whose wedding is being celebrated, is Christ Consciousness, which is emerging in us all, possibly as an evolutionary advance
of our species. An invitation to the wedding feast means that we all have
an opportunity to have various forms of mystical experiences, even
"enlightenment."

We can see in this parable more than one of the aspects of sincerity.
First, those invitees who refuse the invitation symbolize those of us who
take on the outer trappings of religion but, when presented with an opportunity to realize the very thing we claim to be seeking, do not recognize it.
We are so committed to our own approaches for achieving spiritual knowledge that our approaches become ends in themselves. We become so doc-
trinaire that when opportunities arise for us to broaden our knowledge
and deepen our understanding, we assess them by the canons of our various traditions and find them wanting. In short, the unresponsive invitees
in the parable more than likely represent formal religion in its various
expressions. These religions, by their own admission, are supposed to be
means of taking us closer to the Divine, but instead, they become lost in
their own individual agendas.

However, as with the wedding celebration, it is inevitable that the celebration of our species' coming of age takes place, and it is for that reason
that God extends his grace to all and sundry. The show must go on, even
if that means bestowing the honor of an invitation on those who, out-
wardly, may appear not to have paid their dues. But, although all are
invited, no one is absolved of the responsibility of being prepared.

The parable contains a paradoxical situation, which alerts us that an
esoteric principle lurks: while the celebration was in progress, the king
confronted one of the guests for not being suitably dressed, even though
it was he himself who gave the command to have everyone rounded up

without warning and ushered helter-skelter into the wedding celebration. No wonder the guest was speechless. From an ordinary perspective, this situation defies logic, since the chances of having everyone conform to a strict dress code would be slim to nonexistent if we roamed the streets and forced everyone we meet into a highly prestigious event, such as a wedding reception.

The paradoxical situation in the parable is resolved if we understand that the wedding celebration is a symbol for spiritual realization at the collective level. To be hauled into the wedding feast is to have a spiritual experience that lifts one out of ordinary reality into a higher state of being. However, the only way we'll be allowed to remain in the exalted state is if we have the right "presentation"—the equivalent of what the parable calls a wedding garment. The only presentation that would be suitable for an ongoing participation in our collective spiritual realization is an open mind and a pure heart.

An open mind means that we're curious and free of intellectual bias, and a pure heart means that we're humble and free of pride. These two qualities—openness of mind and purity of heart—are the ultimate tests of our sincerity, for together, they define a mode of being that will enable us to be always ready to receive God's grace whenever and wherever it should manifest in our life

The Test of Our Commitment: "Knock, and it will be opened to you"

In the context of a search for spiritual understanding, *how*, and *with what*, do we knock? Usually, when we knock on a door or a gate, we are requesting admittance into a building or to a property. Also, knocking at a door or gate generally implies that we've arrived at the end of a journey and reached a destination of sorts. Similarly, with a spiritual search, the idea of *knocking* presupposes that we've been on a journey and have arrived at a point where we're signaling our readiness to make a change to our life, to take the next step, and to gain admittance to the next level. How do we present ourselves in such a way that we announce our desire to take a step in a new direction?

Let's return to the first part of the question posed above: *How* do we knock? Since we're dealing with the subtle dimension of existence, we need to understand that there is no equivalency of action in a spiritual search that would correspond to the physical act of knocking in the physical world. What we do have, however, is an equivalency of function, meaning that there are actions we can take in our search that will serve as the functional equivalent of knocking in the physical world.

Spiritually, we knock by signaling that we're finished with the old life. We know within ourselves, in no uncertain terms, that the old life, old customs, old habits, no longer have a hold on us. Just as our presence at a door or a gate can imply that we've arrived at our destination after a journey, so too does our readiness to leave our old life behind suggest that such a mode of living no longer serves what we've discovered ourselves to be. For indeed, this is the journey we've been on, a journey of self-discovery.

And now for the second part of the question: *With what* do we knock? Expressed in terms of spiritual seeking, we knock by utilizing our faculty of will. But here, we must understand that we're not referring to the familiar idea of will as the force of our intent. This type of will is ineffective for gaining us entrance to the next level of being. If we insist on using this kind of will to impose order on our impulses and urges, we will only meet with limited success, since they could come back stronger when we least expect them, as in our moments of weakened resolve when our impulses masquerading as needs assert themselves. If we've learned anything of value from our journey of self-discovery, it is that our "needs" do not share in our sense of morality, and we cannot teach it to them. We can only find agreement in our various parts when we understand that all needs emanate from some sense of lack that we experience in ourselves. It is this sense of lack that we must target if we are to overcome our fragmentation, announce our presence at "the door" and signal our readiness to advance to the next stage of our spiritual journey. And it is only when we get a sense of ourselves liberated from any feelings of lack that we can override our perceived needs and the desires and impulses to which they give rise.

Our strength comes from another kind of will, the kind that functions like the force of attraction between a planetary body and its sun. In our case, the vision of a fuller, more authentic life that we hold functions like our sun, which exerts a pull of attraction on our various parts, domiciled in the body, mind, and spirit. In this sense, as our various parts share in our vision and yield to this attraction, we develop *will*.

It must be borne in mind that in terms of spiritual seeking, we may have to knock on many doors, and may have to signal over and over again our readiness to take yet another step to heretofore unknown vistas. This is why spiritual seeking is such an adventure and why we must be able to give an open-ended commitment to the Spirit. It is this need for our open-ended commitment that is referred to in the story of the rich man in Matthew 19: 16-24.

> [16] And behold, a man came up to him, saying, "Teacher, what good deed must I do to have eternal life?" [17] And he said to him, "Why do you ask me about what is good? There is only one who is good. If you would enter life, keep the commandments." [18] He said to him, "Which ones?" And Jesus said, "You shall not murder, You shall not commit adultery, You shall not steal, You shall not bear false witness, [19] Honor your father and mother, and, You shall love your neighbor as yourself." [20] The young man said to him, "All these I have kept. What do I still lack?" [21] Jesus said to him, "If you would be perfect, go, sell what you possess and give to the poor, and you will have treasure in heaven; and come, follow me." [22] When the young man heard this he went away sorrowful, for he had great possessions.
>
> [23] And Jesus said to his disciples, "Truly, I say to you, only with difficulty will a rich person enter the kingdom of

heaven. [24] Again I tell you, it is easier for a camel to go through the eye of a needle than for a rich person to enter the kingdom of God."

In his exchange, the rich man confessed to a desire for eternal life and wanted Jesus's advice on the next step he should take to achieve this aim. When told that he ought to keep the commandments, he proudly declared that he'd been keeping them already and wanted to know what else he should be doing. He was told that if he really wanted to take the next step—which Jesus defined as the pursuit of perfection—he ought to sell all his possessions, give the proceeds to the poor, and follow Jesus. We are told that, upon hearing these instructions, the young man went away sorrowful as he found the requirement too onerous.

From an esoteric perspective, there's a great deal going on in this exchange between Jesus and the rich young man, and between Jesus and the disciples. In a sense, the rich man's initial enquiry represents a desire for being in control of his spiritual destiny, as can be intuited from his focus on doing. His second question, "What do I still lack?" implies that he anticipated more challenges that he felt confident he could accomplish. After all, it's no small achievement to have kept all the commandments from his youth. However, Jesus turned the tables on him by upping the ante; he asked him to leave his entire life and identity behind, for this is what is entailed by the requirement to sell all his possessions, give away the proceeds, and follow Jesus. In other words, he was shown that the Kingdom of God is ultimately not about doing, but about *being*. But to make this adjustment from doing to being, he had to perform the final act that would pave the way for him to transition to a different mode of seeking, based on being.

On an esoteric level, this story of the rich young man is told to demonstrate the difficulty that we can experience when it comes to making the transition from doing to being. This change represents a discontinuity, but must be made because the journey is one of transformation, requiring us to change into something else along the way. Because of this ongoing process of change, we eventually find that the identity with which we started off on our spiritual quest must eventually give way to another. As the door of new possibilities opens to our knock, we must part company with our past at the threshold. As for the young man of wealth, he has knocked at the door, figuratively speaking, but when it opens, he turns away. His turning away is suggestive of our inability to surrender owing to the large investment we may have in our present identity.

Jesus's remarks, upon the rich man's leaving, that it's easier for a camel to go through the eye of a needle than for a rich man to enter the kingdom of God, is thrown in by the Gospel writers to deliver a jolt to the minds of the readers of this teaching story. When we contemplate the physical impossibility of a camel passing through a needle's eye, and are confronted with the prospect that this impossibility has a greater change of being accomplished than a rich man gaining entry to God's kingdom, the mind is boggled. Upon hearing this comparison, the disciples also needed reassurance, which Jesus provided by telling them that what may seem impossible from mankind's perspective is quite within the realm of possibility for God.

But why give us a comparison that we can't even get our minds around? Again, owing to the absurdity of this comparison, we know that we must be on the alert for esoteric insight.

The rich man is used in the story as an example of our human need to be in control, to set the terms for our life and our spiritual search. The instructions to the young man to "Sell all your possessions...and follow me" are like saying, "Bring an end to your life as you've known it and start anew with me in control," understanding, of course, that the one giving the command is the Higher, or Christ Self. The young man's wealth is a proxy for his identity, and telling us that he had a lot of possessions conveys to us that he had a lot vested in his present identity. As mentioned before, we signal our readiness for a new, transformed consciousness, or the Kingdom of God—by showing that we're finished with our old life and our old identity.

The story is structured to show how the things that give us an advantage in this world inhibit our ability to transition to the next. It's like planning for entry to another country where the laws are different, where the currency is different and nonconvertible with ours. In other words, there are no terms, or rates of exchange, by which we can convert the advantages we've enjoyed in one world into credits usable in the other one. That is what "sell all that you have" is meant to conjure up—the impossibility of setting our own terms for entering God's kingdom. There must be a radical discontinuity with our known self. It means that we have to surrender absolutely—to give an open option to the Spirit, to God.

After Jesus made his remark about the camel having an easier time going through the eye of a needle than it would be for a rich person to enter the kingdom of God, the disciples asked: "Who then can be saved?" (Matthew 19:25-26). Jesus replied: "With man this is impossible, but with God all things are possible." The effect of this verbal exchange is to impress upon us that it is not possible to know with precision what it will take to enter God's kingdom. This is because it will never be on our terms, but on God's. That's why Jesus assured the disciples that what is impossible with man is possible with God. This reassurance is to confirm the need to surrender all our accumulated power and advantages and submit to God's terms.

Finally, before we move on, let's take another look, from a different perspective, at the camel-through-the-eye-of-the-needle analogy to illustrate the predicament of anyone who thinks they can set their own terms to achieve the transformation of consciousness symbolized by the idea of God's kingdom. Looking at the analogy scientifically, we may have to acknowledge that the chances of a camel going through the eye of a needle might not even be the complete physical impossibility that we initially imagined it to be. If we think in terms of evolutionary time, it's quite possible for Nature to craft a miniaturized camel to the point where it's small enough to go through a needle's eye. With evolution, there's little Nature cannot accomplish, given the time. But our relationship to our accumulated identity—symbolized by the rich man and his wealth—is not something on which Nature can work its magic. And it is this relationship that will always prevent "the rich man"—meaning anyone with a large vested interest in his current identity—from accessing God's kingdom. The only solution must come from within, by a detachment from that identity, through surrender to discontinuity, so that God can complete us as he sees fit.

THE BIRTH OF EXOTERIC CHRISTIANITY

We can attribute the multiplicity of denominations in Christianity to the simple fact that Christians at large remain unaware of the esoteric current in the New Testament. Such unawareness has resulted in a confusion of tongues within the faith, since once the esoteric aspect is missed, the symbols that form the exoteric aspects lend themselves to all sorts of diverse interpretations. This has nothing to do with the sincerity of one's faith. What seems to be more important in determining the quality of interpretation are the inner needs and purity of heart of the believers.

The obscuration of the esoteric element by the exoteric that has so characterized popular Christianity over the past two millennia was already evident when the concept of "church" first surfaced in one of Jesus's verbal exchanges with the disciples. In this exchange, found in Matthew, the ambiguity at the root of the idea of "church" is quite evident, if not altogether deliberate. Nonetheless, this incident came to have one of the strongest influences on institutional Christianity, becoming the basis for a keystone doctrine. This verbal interaction, which holds the first mention of "church," also addresses the issue of the divinity of Jesus.

> [13] Now when Jesus came into the district of Caesarea Philippi, he asked his disciples, "Who do people say that the Son of Man is?" [14] And they said, "Some say John the Baptist, others say Elijah, and others Jeremiah or one of the prophets." [15] He said to them, "But who do you say that I

am?" [16] Simon Peter replied, "You are the Christ, the Son of the living God." [17] And Jesus answered him, "Blessed are you, Simon Bar-Jonah! For flesh and blood has not revealed this to you, but my Father who is in heaven. [18] And I tell you, you are Peter, and on this rock I will build my church, and the gates of hell shall not prevail against it. [19] I will give you the keys of the Kingdom of Heaven, and whatever you bind on earth shall be bound in heaven, and whatever you loose on earth shall be loosed in heaven." [20] Then he strictly charged the disciples to tell no one that he was the Christ. (Matthew16:12–20)

Viewing this exchange exoterically, one would see, as traditional theology has, two separate issues: (1) Peter's confession of the divinity of Jesus, and (2) the establishment of the foundation of the church. Viewed esoterically, however, one sees these two issues as parts of one whole event. This becomes evident by examining all of the possible meanings for the ambiguous expressions used in the exchange. The first evidence is found in the nature of Jesus's response to Peter's confession that Jesus was the Christ:

> Blessed are you, Simon Bar-Jonah! For flesh and blood has not revealed this to you, but my Father who is in heaven. [18] And I tell you, you are Peter, and on this rock I will build my church, and the gates of hell shall not prevail against it. (Matthew 16:18)

Jesus went on to tell Peter:

> I will give you the keys of the Kingdom of Heaven, and whatever you bind on earth shall be bound in heaven, and whatever you loose on earth shall be loosed in heaven. (Matthew 16:19)

Interpreting this last passage on the surface level, one might assume Jesus is paying a personal tribute to Peter and veritably giving him the keys to the Kingdom of Heaven (whatever those might be). If that were the case, the whole exchange would take on an illogical shading indeed. In the first place, Jesus attributed Peter's declaration to the Father and not to Peter. What Jesus is really telling Peter is that his knowledge did not come from the realm of the conscious mind, but from the realm of the collective unconscious.[1] Jesus is crediting Peter with a burst of intuitive insight.*

We can see further consequences of the failure to spot the built-in ambiguity in this exchange. What was Jesus making the foundation of "his" church—a man, or intuition? In the traditional interpretation, it is assumed that Jesus was making Peter the foundation of the church when he said to him, "You are Peter, and upon this rock I will build my church." The authority for this assumption is derived from the fact that the name Peter also means *rock*, giving the impression that Jesus was indulging in word games by punning on the word "rock."

It is unlikely that Jesus expressed any such intention. If he'd intended Peter to be the foundation of the church, couldn't he have chosen terms less ambiguous to express this? Further, it is unlikely that he would have engaged in word games on an occasion as solemn as this. What is more likely is a deliberate attempt to obscure esoteric truth. The traditional interpretation of this exchange—that Jesus is making Peter the foundation of "his" church—seems more the consequence of chance than design. This assessment is supported when Jesus's statement is considered from the point of view of the language he likely would have used, i.e., Palestinian Aramaic. According to the annotated *New Oxford Bible*, Jesus's remarks to Peter give less indication that a play on the word *rock* was intended. In Palestinian Aramaic, the same word would have been used to indicate the proper noun *Peter* and the common noun *rock* (*cephas*, in the Greek). Had

---

*This quality of intuition is distinguishable from a hunch, which usually also goes by the name intuition. The kind of intuition accredited to Peter is an act of recognizing a universal principle in action. It is cognizance of a structure beneath the outward activities of life.

Jesus intended a pun, he would therefore have addressed Peter in the following manner: "You are *Kepha* and upon this *kepha* I will build my church." This would have changed the cryptic nature of the statement into something more straightforward, though no less ambiguous.

The key to determining to what Jesus was alluding in the exchange, then, is found by trying to better understand what he meant by the term *church*. This term is usually assumed to refer to something institutional. But in this context, that is not the case. Actually, its true meaning here is the very antithesis of something institutional. The word *church* means "the called out," suggesting those who have awakened from the slumber of a matter-bound existence to more conscious living. The foundation of this type of church is to be the faculty of intuition, since this faculty is what enables us to awaken to possibilities to expand our consciousness. (Remember that Jesus identified the source of Peter's insight as intuition by attributing Peter's revelation to the Father, as opposed to flesh and blood [the conscious mind]). So in short, *intuition*, the rock of the true Self, is also the rock upon which Jesus's Church was to be constructed.

It also makes sense that it is to intuition that the "keys to the kingdom of heaven" are given, so that what it binds on earth would be bound in heaven, and what it looses on earth would be loosed in heaven. This is because, without intuition, we cannot consciously participate in the process of Consciousness expanding into our awareness and daily life—and that process *is* the Kingdom of Heaven. This interpretation is reinforced by Jesus's teaching on the "unforgivable sin," or the sin of "blasphemy against the Holy Spirit" (Matthew 12:22–33). Recall that this is the single sin that Jesus said cannot be forgiven in this world or in the world to come. That is because this "sin" is not a single act, per se, but a certain dynamic in personal consciousness that leads to the repression of intuition.

Refer to "Appendix I: A Meditation on the Unforgivable Sin" for a standalone exposition on this psychological dynamic and its role in inhibiting the growth of consciousness, thereby interfering in the process of "salvation."

FOUR

THE TRANSFORMATIONAL PSYCHOLOGY EMBEDDED IN THE NEW TESTAMENT

ITS SCOPE AND OUTLINE

To appreciate the scope of the psychology of transformation inherent in the Gospels, we must first establish some commonsense criteria by which to evaluate it.

To be effective, a spiritual psychology must be multifaceted. First, it must offer us a framework for understanding ourselves, generally speaking. This framework must be capable of providing us with insight into our full capacities and potentials as human beings. Second, it must indicate where we are, mentally and emotionally, relative to that potential; something akin to a map a traveler would consult during a journey. Third, it must provide a prescribed set of observances that we can engage in to lead us closer to our goal of fulfilling our potential.

The psychology of the New Testament contains these three elements, but they are overshadowed by a fourth—a "working model" in the form of the life drama and teachings of Jesus. It is this life drama and teachings that Christians regard as "the Gospel of Jesus Christ." It can be shown, however, that the complete Gospel includes the above four components, with the life drama of Jesus serving the function of modeling otherwise abstract principles, presenting them in a form to which ordinary individuals can relate. Stated another way, in the life of Jesus, we find a dramatization of higher principles of being, which helps us to better understand them. His life story serves the dual roles of being a catalyst and what we might call "a distant light."

As a catalyst, the life events recounted plant suggestions in our minds as to what is possible for us as human beings. In short, we are motivated as individuals to strive to raise the expressions of our ordinary human characteristics into their higher counterparts. In the role of "a distant light," the principles portrayed by Jesus become focused in our minds, providing us with ideals to aim for, but which we may only feel capable of achieving in some distant future rather than in the present. In many respects, then, the catalyst aspect of Jesus's life story acts on our emotions, while the distant light aspect mostly affects our intellect.

THE STRUCTURAL FRAMEWORK LINKING THE COMPONENTS OF NEW TESTAMENT PSYCHOLOGY

As mentioned, the structural framework that integrates the psychological components of the New Testament is hidden from the casual observer. In this framework, a human being is seen as capable of giving expression to a spectrum of life characteristics ranging from those we share with the animal kingdom, i.e., those concerned with basic survival needs, to those that express higher attributes such as love, compassion, wisdom, and equanimity.[*]

Without awareness of this framework, however, we cannot take full advantage of the teachings of Jesus or understand his extraordinary deeds, the miracles. And as a result of such unawareness, Christian doctrine has become focused on how we can achieve salvation. Further, since there is no one definition that constitutes "salvation," various Christian doctrines have emerged that outline how salvation is to be achieved.

Equanimity is used here in the sense of "joyous acceptance."

It just so happens, however, that the framework underlying the Gospel message is the same as that which underpins the Eastern disciplines of Yoga. The common goal of these various Yoga disciplines is the same as that of Christianity at its core, which is to transform our consciousness to a higher level.

The central idea within the various disciplines of Yoga is that the human being is a God-seed, awaiting the necessary conditions to awaken and progress into full flowering. As different from accepted Christian teachings as this might seem, the idea has a counterpart in the New Testament. The main difference is that, in biblical teachings, this framework of "man's divine possibilities" remains in the background, while in Eastern approaches, it lies up front. Despite this difference, we can find corroborative evidence in the New Testament that this particular vision of human possibility is what structured most of the teachings of Jesus, as well as Paul's.

Take, for example, the following sermon in Acts, into which Paul weaves the theme of the dormant God-nature of man, along with his ability to achieve a better expression of this God-nature:

> [22] So Paul, standing in the midst of the Areopagus, said: "Men of Athens, I perceive that in every way you are very religious. [23] For as I passed along and observed the objects of your worship, I found also an altar with this inscription, 'To the unknown god.' What therefore you worship as unknown, this I proclaim to you. [24] The God who made the world and everything in it, being Lord of heaven and earth, does not live in temples made by man, [25] nor is he served by human hands, as though he needed anything, since he himself gives to all mankind life and breath and everything. [26] And he made from one man every nation of mankind to live on all the face of the earth, having determined allotted periods and the boundaries of their dwelling place, [27] that

they should seek God, in the hope that they might feel their way toward him and find him. Yet he is actually not far from each one of us, [28] for

"'In him we live and move and have our being';

as even some of your own poets have said,

"'For we are indeed his offspring.'

[29] Being then God's offspring, we ought not to think that the divine being is like gold or silver or stone, an image formed by the art and imagination of man. [30] The times of ignorance God overlooked, but now he commands all people everywhere to repent, [31] because he has fixed a day on which he will judge the world in righteousness by a man whom he has appointed; and of this he has given assurance to all by raising him from the dead." (Acts. 17: 22–31)

The thesis that Paul expounds here is that we humans, as God's offspring, must seek out and express our divine heritage ("that they should seek God, in the hope that they might feel their way toward him and find him"). But this idea is not one preached from the pulpits of Christian churches. As far as Paul is concerned, God is a part of every individual's reality, a fact of which we are not generally conscious.

Paul further develops this view of God in his letters. He talks about the individual being a temple in which God dwells: "Do you not know that you are God's temple and that God's Spirit dwells in you? If anyone destroys God's temple, God will destroy him. For God's temple is holy, and you are that temple." (1 Cor. 3:16–17)

One can also go to the Old Testament, in the very first of the Ten Commandments (Exodus 20:3), to find the idea that divinity was to be the goal of humankind. Hidden behind the words of the commandment "You shall have no other gods before me" is the idea that we should not let anything separate us from the *true* God.* Therefore, anything that poses or creates a barrier to the true God becomes a god of sorts, circumscribing the limits of one's striving. By systematically eliminating these little gods that mankind is prone to worshipping, then, one is progressively taken closer to the true God, to Ultimate Reality. Perhaps it was this thought that moved Paul to give the following exhortation to the church at Corinth:

> [18] And we all, with unveiled face, beholding the glory of the Lord, are being transformed into the same image from one degree of glory to another. For this comes from the Lord who is the Spirit. (2 Corinthians 3:18)

The poetic beauty of the language aside, the only value in such a vision lies in the use one makes of it.

THE BLUEPRINT OF OUR HUMAN POSSIBILITIES UNDERPINNING JESUS'S TEACHINGS

In the Gospel of Matthew, in particular, the teachings of Jesus can be shown to be structured around a model of our human potential to express life at seven different hierarchical levels of consciousness. These teachings are specifically directed at encouraging us to move up the hierarchy, which can be called the Ladder of Being.** Whenever we learn to express life at a higher level of consciousness, we progress up the "Ladder."

Each of the seven rungs represents a level of consciousness that is

---

*The idea of a "true" God implies a Reality that exists beyond our capacity to define or circumscribe it. Whatever the human mind can define cannot be the True God, in the sense that our power to define and circumscribe will make us equal to or greater than it; and whatever we can define or circumscribe cannot be God. This implies that our God, to be True—in the sense of being Ultimate Reality—must forever remain a Mystery.

**This term occurs rather frequently in esoteric, spiritual literature.

significantly higher than the previous. At the lowest level, most of our energy would be spent on issues relating to ensuring our physical survival. Thus, we would be preoccupied with competing with one another to secure our personal survival needs. As such, if our consciousness is arrested at this level, our behavior would have more in common with the animal kingdom than what we've come to expect of humans. As we conceptually move up the ladder, we experience progressive refinements such that, at the seventh level, we would be expressing more of our Divine nature—or being more Christlike—than the lower aspects of our human nature.

Although this hierarchical model in its fully developed form is borrowed from the Eastern religions, it is sufficiently flexible to accommodate the ideas of other world religions—their common goal being to help an adherent elevate the quality of expression of Life in himself. In terms of this model of sevenfoldedness, progress involves moving one's consciousness from one rung of the Ladder of Being to the next. The different terms of reference of various world religions result from the architects of those religions giving their respective peoples a meaningful and workable understanding of this underlying principle that is suited to their respective cultural conditions. To achieve this, then, they resorted to symbols and metaphors. For example, instead of discussing levels of consciousness and processes of transformation, popular Christianity speaks of salvation and attaining "the Kingdom of Heaven."

In the seven-tiered model of consciousness, the body plays an integrating role between all of the levels of reality represented by the rungs on the Ladder of Being. The physical body, then, despite its material density, performs an anchoring function to higher-level, subtler "bodies," which correspond to the respective states of consciousness belonging to the other six rungs on the Ladder.

According to the literature of the East and West, the seven levels of consciousness have their correspondences with seven specific locations in the physical body. In the Sanskrit language in which these ideas were originally articulated, the seven related sites, or areas of interphase, are called *chakras.*

With the spinal column as the vertical reference point, the seven chakras are distributed along its length.¹ The first is found at the base of the spine, the second in the sacral region, the third in the lumbar region, the fourth in the dorsal, the fifth in the cervical, the sixth in an area horizontally aligned with the spot between the eyebrows, and the seventh in the crown of the head. Table 1, below, shows the Sanskrit names given to these chakras:

Table 1
THE SEVEN MAJOR CHAKRAS

The First	Muladhara
The Second	Svadvishthana
The Third	Manipura
The Fourth	Anahata
The Fifth	Vishuddha
The Sixth	Ajna
The Seventh	Sahasrara

Since each chakra represents an area of interphase with higher levels of existence, the process of expanding our consciousness is expressed in terms of "opening up" these chakras. Opening up a chakra does not mean exercising control over the corresponding level of existence. Actually, it is the individual who opens up to a chakra, since it is the ordinary consciousness that must be elevated to synchronize its functioning with a higher level of existence. When such synchronization occurs, the area of interphase (and therefore exchange) between the physical body and the higher level becomes operational.

Figure 1, on page 86, shows the physical location of the seven major chakras.

Figure 1: The Seven Major Chakras

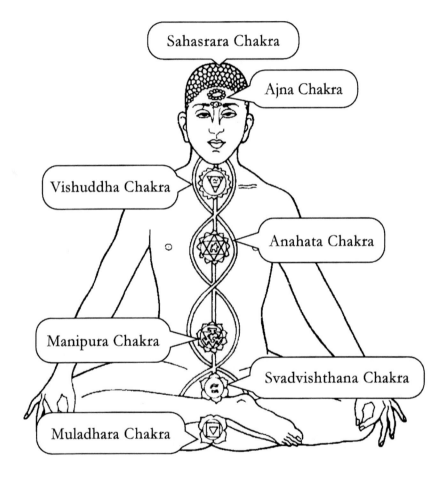

THE CHAKRAS AS QUALITIES OF ENGAGEMENT IN LIFE

Seen in the light of our efforts to elevate our consciousness to higher levels, each chakra becomes associated with a certain quality of striving in the spiritual sense. By "striving," we mean the intensity with which we engage our physical, mental, and spiritual abilities to pursue goals we feel to be worthwhile. In terms of the seven-tiered model of Being, we would therefore have seven levels of striving (or qualities of engagement with life) to coincide with the seven chakras.

According to classical literature on the subject, the first chakra, Muladhara, corresponds to a level of striving in which we see physical survival as our objective. If our consciousness is arrested at this chakra, the bulk of our energies will be expended trying to satisfy our physical needs and appetites. As this preoccupation will bring us into direct competition with others, the principle of existence that rules at this level is "survival of the fittest."

At the second chakra, Svadvishthana, the goal of striving becomes emotional gratification. The principle expressed here is polarization. When our consciousness is arrested here, we have difficulty achieving emotional stability, as our feelings fluctuate between pairs of opposites—liking and disliking, loving and hating, pain and pleasure, etc.—without end. Because life in the physical finds its most complete polarization in the division of the sexes, most of the manifestations of second-chakra consciousness are oriented toward the subject of sex. It is for this reason that the Svadvishthana Chakra has been called the sex center.

At the third chakra, Manipura, the main objective of striving is social position, or status. When our consciousness is arrested here, we enjoy displaying power and dominating others. Our primary concern is with advancing and protecting our sense of self-importance. We are generally obsessed with gamesmanship or any type of interpersonal interaction that offers the possibility of a payoff. The principle at play here is that of "vanity" or "feeding the ego." This center is commonly called the solar plexus, or the center of self-will.

The objective of striving at the fourth chakra, Anahata, is to achieve a state of acceptance and belonging. At this level, our consciousness has achieved some liberation from the "lower forces," meaning the forces that promote individual strife and inhibit collective human advancement. When our consciousness reaches this level of development, our actions are more likely to flow from a sense of higher purpose than as a response to external stimuli. The principle of life expressed here is that of "inclusion" or "empathy." There is, however, a danger that someone who has reached this level could spend too much time seeking approval from others. Because the affairs of life are conducted on a higher emotional level when the consciousness is elevated to this level, the Anahata Chakra is called the heart center.

When the goal of striving becomes the need to see an objective purpose to human life, the consciousness becomes centered at the fifth chakra, Vishuddha. At this level, we are driven to discover the laws of nature and other hidden principles of life. Since the faculty of speech plays an important part in giving structure to our thoughts as we strive to impose a mental order on nature, the fifth chakra is also called the speech center. It is also credited with being the center of objectification of the personal consciousness.

When we succeed in elevating goals for the betterment of the general human condition over those that benefit ourselves, our consciousness would become centered at the sixth chakra, Ajna. The principle that governs this expression of life is "impersonal love," or "love as a mode of being." For this reason, this chakra has been called the Christ Consciousness center in Western esoteric literature.

Overall, when the sixth chakra is "open" and functioning, the goal of achieving personal satisfaction gives place to efforts to bring higher principles of existence into manifestation. At this level, we are also able to function in the intuitive mode of the mind, which implies the capability to directly perceive the hidden principles that govern life in the material world and to apply this higher understanding to daily life.

Finally, as the consciousness becomes anchored in the seventh chakra, Sahasrara, we come to the highest level of being according to this model. When life is expressed from this level, the individual becomes a point of expression between the temporal and the Eternal. Since the personal energy of expressing life at this level is not being co-opted by personal preoccupations, such an individual becomes a vehicle of the Divine Will. Such a person therefore embodies the characteristics of the divine emissary, since his or her existence is no longer a matter of a human being trying to improve him or herself, but rather a Divine Principle seeking to establish a presence in an earthly body.

The foregoing information on the seven chakras and their main attributes are summarized in Table 2 below.

Table 2
CHAKRAS: AN OVERVIEW OF THEIR ATTRIBUTES

LEVEL	CHAKRA	GOAL OF STRIVING	PRINCIPLE EXPRESSED
I	Muladhara	Physical Needs and Appetites	Physical Survival
II	Svadvishthana	Emotional Gratification	Polarization
III	Manipura	Social Position and Status	Vanity
IV	Anahata	To be Accepted and to Belong	Empathy
V	Vishuddha	Exploring Nature's Secrets	Finding Purpose of Life
VI	Ajna	Human Advancement	Impersonal Love
VII	Sahasrara	To Express Divine Will	Striving Itself

THE CHAKRAS AND THE ENDOCRINE SYSTEM

Although expositors of the chakra network are quick to point out that these belong to the "subtle body" and cannot be anatomically proven, two pieces of scientific observation have helped to establish the validity of the concept. For one, although the chakra concept predates Western science by thousands of years, the positions ascribed to the chakras correlate with seven nerve plexuses that service seven of the major systems of the body. Second, the general characteristics of the chakras correlate with the broad functions of seven major glands of the endocrine system.

We shall now examine the relationship between the broad functions of the endocrine glands and the characteristics of the chakras to which they are related. The seven endocrine glands, and the ways in which they complement their chakra counterparts, are as follows:

(1) The gonads, incorporating the ovaries in the female and the testes in the male, correspond with the Muladhara Chakra, which is concerned with the survival of an individual on the physical plane. The gonads are also concerned with survival, though in this case, of the species through reproduction.

(2) The leydig cells in the testes of the male, and the hilar cells in the female; the related glands are responsible for the secretion of hormones that promote secondary sex differentiation—voice, distribution of body hair and body fat, body contours, etc. The leydig and hilar cells provide the endocrine counterpart to the Svadvishthana Chakra, which deals with emotional gratification as it relates to sexual desire. This "need" is perpetuated through the polarization of the sexes and the attraction between them.

(3) The adrenal glands correspond to the Manipura Chakra, which relates to the power complex in the individual and the desire to advance socially. In a sense, this chakra is concerned with the "need" to maintain individual sovereignty. The function of the adrenals

can also be said to promote and defend individual sovereignty through two of the hormones they produce: adrenaline and noradrenaline (or epinephrine and norepinephrine, as they are also known). Since these hormones prepare us physically for perceived threats, the adrenals have thus been called the "fight or flight" glands. Emotions such as anger, envy, jealousy, fear, etc., as well as acts of courage, result from the impact of adrenaline and noradrenaline on the system.

(4) The thymus gland relates to the Anahata Chakra. This chakra triggers the need for security, which is then fulfilled through acts that promote empathy and inclusiveness. The function of the thymus is tied up with the immune system of the body. In the sense that immunity to diseases allows one to survive in an otherwise hostile environment, it can also be said to foster a spirit of inclusiveness and belonging.

(5) The thyroid gland is located at the site of the Vishuddha Chakra. This chakra is concerned with the individual's need to give order to the perpetual flux of existence, achieved through the urge to discover what the principles are that make things work. The thyroid gland, through its wide-ranging effects on body metabolism, regulates an individual's adaptability to the external environment. This is accomplished chiefly through the regulation of the individual's perception of external stimuli.

(6) The Ajna Chakra is related to the individual's need to embody universal principles and to thereby foster the growth of the collective consciousness. The pineal gland, to which this chakra is related, has been shown to be sensitive to light and to secrete certain hormones (endorphins) that regulate an individual's ability to tolerate pain. The pineal also has a repressive effect on sexual development, in a way reversing the sexual differentiation that is promoted at the second chakra. These and other characteristics of this gland support the categorization of the Ajna Chakra as the Christ Consciousness center.

(7) The Sahasrara Chakra is associated with the desire in the individual to became a point of expression between the Eternal and the temporal. The related pituitary gland, situated deep in the limbic brain, is recognized as the master gland of the body. Its main task is to coordinate the functioning of all other glands in the body. One of its functions is to regulate physical growth, and malfunctioning in this regard can cause dwarfism (underactivity) or gigantism (overactivity). Because of its relationship to growth, the pituitary is said be related to the expansion of the whole being. This implies getting rid of restrictions on the being, which inversely can be regarded as the exercise of will. The pituitary, then, can quite justifiably be called the seat of will and aspiration. It adjusts the organism to accommodate new aspirations and new objectives of striving in life.

THE CHAKRA MODEL IN ITS DYNAMIC ASPECTS

The seven-tiered model can be thought of as the static representation of consciousness as it is expressed in us—a map, so to speak. The dynamic aspect of the model has to do with how we can activate these latent centers, thereby accessing higher-level realities, and, in the process, enhance and transform our ordinary consciousness. As an elaboration of the chakra system, then, another level of detail deals with how the chakras are awakened.

At this level of detail, we learn that the chakras are not isolated centers, but are part of a network that includes three "channels" that function to conduct "nerve currents." These channels, or *nadis*, as they are called, are the *Ida*, the *Sushumna*, and the *Pingala*. The nadis are differentiated according to electrical conductivity; the Pingala is positive, the Ida negative, and the Sushumna neutral. The Sushumna channel runs through the center of the spinal cord, with the Pingala and Ida channels meandering and crisscrossing it (see Figure 1 on page 86). All three nadis begin at the first chakra and meet again at the sites of the other chakras.

The basic idea behind the dynamic aspect of this model is that Consciousness exists in a polarized state in each individual, with each person having the potential for uniting the two poles of Consciousness within himself. These two poles consist of an active principle, called *Prana*, which is associated with the life impulse, and a latent energy, called *Kundalini Shakti*. This latent energy is metaphorically described as a sleeping serpent, coiled three-and-a-half times around the lower pole of the spinal axis in the region of the Muladhara Chakra.

One of the implications for our human existence of the separation of Consciousness into its two poles (Kundalini at the unmanifest pole, and Prana at the manifest) is that we are able to relate to Reality only partially, on the basis of surface appearances. (It is this recognition that has led many expositors of Eastern philosophy to say that reality as we know and experience it is an illusion.) In order for us to have an undistorted relationship with Reality, the two poles of Consciousness must once again become unified. This is accomplished when the Kundalini Shakti awakens and liberates itself from its home in the Muladhara Chakra and journeys to the other, positive pole of Consciousness at the Sahasrara, or seventh chakra. This process is described in Lama Anagarika Govinda's book *Foundations of Tibetan Mysticism* as follows:

> The *susumna* is closed at its lower end, as long as the latent creative forces of Kundalini (or "libido," as modem psychologists would say) are not awakened. In this state the Kundalini, which is likened to a coiled serpent (the symbol of latent energy) blocks the entrance to the *susumna*. By awakening the Kundalini's dormant forces, which otherwise are absorbed in subconscious and purely bodily functions, and by directing them to the higher centers, the energies thus released are transformed and sublimated until their perfect unfoldment and conscious realization is achieved in the highest center. This is the aim and purpose

of the Kundalini Yoga, or *pranayama*, and of all other exercises through which the chakras are activated and made into centers of conscious realization.[2]

THE CHAKRAS AND MEDITATION

Readers who are interested in gaining more practical insight about the chakras are encouraged to pursue the work of the late Dr. Brugh Joy (1939–2009), who made an independent discovery of the chakras in the 1970s. During the course of his work as a physician, Dr. Joy learned to become sensitive to the energy field around the human body. Over the course of exploring his newfound ability, he mapped out particular areas of the body where energy was strongest. He subsequently discovered that these points of high energy corresponded with the locations of the chakras.

Amazingly, Dr. Joy had no knowledge of the concept of chakras before he began mapping out the high-energy centers on the body. He became aware of the significance of what he had discovered only after he found a corresponding distribution pattern as he browsed a text on Yoga at a bookstore. His discovery is presented in his book *Joy's Way*. In addition to the traditional seven major chakras, Dr. Joy was able to map out several others. He stated in his book:

> The chakra system is a real physical aspect of the body but very subtle in comparison to ordinary physical aspects. Many of the traditional drawings are in error as to placement of different chakras, especially the heart chakra. Some omit the spleen chakra or the lower-abdominal chakra, and none I have seen show the chakras of the knees, hands, feet, elbows and shoulders. After almost five years of exploring these energy fields, I have found more than forty such fields

radiating from the body surface in the normal individual. The major chakras, however, are the ones I have described and are the ones with which I work. [3]

Dr. Joy was able to use his discovery to develop an energy-sharing technique that he called the Spiral Meditation. In its simplest form,* the practice of this technique requires two participants: one lying on a table as the recipient, and the other taking an active role. The active participant uses his hands to sense the location of the chakras (in this case, twelve points) in an alternating fashion, such that a spiral pattern is created. The object is to induce a meditative state in the recipient.

I have had the opportunity to experience the profound effects of this exercise performed by Dr. Richard Moss, who practices a version of it in the transformational workshops he conducts worldwide. Dr. Moss, who duly credits Brugh Joy for introducing him to the technique, provides readers with a concise description of the Spiral Meditation in one of his books, *The Black Butterfly—An Invitation to Radical Aliveness*:

> The Spiral was a way to make consecutive contact with each of the chakras, starting from the heart at the center of the chest and progressing to the solar plexus, the high chest, the spleen, the lower abdomen, the throat, the base of the spine, the forehead, the knees, the top of the head (crown), the feet, and, finally, a space above the head representing transpersonal energies. [4]

The chakras can also be incorporated into our private contemplative practice to facilitate spiritual attunement, as outlined in the exercise with the Lord's Prayer in Appendix IV.

---

*The technique can also involve several individuals sharing energy with a single recipient. This can have the effect of intensifying the experience.

TECHNIQUE-DRIVEN VERSUS PROCESS-DRIVEN
APPROACHES TO WAKENING KUNDALINI

Various practices have been prescribed by the various traditions for the awakening of Kundalini. These approaches fall between what I would call a purely *process-driven* approach at one end of the spectrum, and a purely *technique-driven* approach at the other end. Approaches closest to the process-driven end of the spectrum are more concerned with the development of character through moral and spiritual observances, while the technique-driven ones are more reliant on various disciplines, which may combine meditation and bodily purification regimes such as yoga postures and breathing exercises.

Usually, a technique-driven approach for awakening Kundalini relies heavily on the personal guidance of a teacher who has undergone the experience and has the ability to activate it in others. This approach, which is more concerned with techniques aimed specifically at achieving Kundalini and less with philosophical matters, is called "opening from below."

Conversely, the process-driven approach emphasizes philosophical and spiritual practices. Within this school, teachers may be totally unconcerned with Kundalini, focusing instead on the acquisition of spiritual virtues. It is thought that in giving expression to these virtues, Kundalini awakening will occur as a matter of course. This approach, which emphasizes the need to live toward high ideals, has been regarded as "opening from above," an expression suggesting that when focused on embodying spiritual principles, we gradually awaken to higher levels of inspiration and intuition. Once these faculties are aroused, we can receive both conscious and unconscious guidance from a higher intelligence into awakening Kundalini. (This awakening may take place spontaneously without interference from the conscious mind.) More important, on account of the spiritual training that a person has undergone with the process-driven approach, he or she will be able to achieve the necessary inner equilibrium and peace required to withstand the emotional turbulence experienced as the mental structures formerly relied upon disintegrate* and are replaced by new ones. There is ample indication that this is the route taken by the New Testament.

These concepts, "opening from above" and "opening from below," are further explained by Satprem in his book *Sri Aurobindo or the Adventure of Consciousness*, in which he provides an overview of the teachings of the mystic, yogi, and philosopher Sri Aurobindo. Of the psychic centers or chakras, he says:

> Generally, in "normal" man, these centres are asleep or closed, or they only let through the very small current necessary to his shallow existence; he is really walled inside himself and communicates only indirectly with the outside world, within a very limited circle—in fact, he does not see other people or things, but himself in others, himself in things and everywhere, without getting out of it. With yoga, the centres open. They can do so in two ways, from bottom to top or from top to bottom, depending on whether we practice traditional yogic and spiritual methods, or Sri Aurobindo's yoga. As mentioned earlier, through repeated concentration and exercises, we can one day feel a Force awakening at the bottom of the spine and ascending from

---

* In my personal experience with this process (as recounted in the Introduction), I lost the ability to focus on mundane tasks, as my mind was continually drawn into a meditative state. For several years after the Kundalini experience, I found also that I could not listen to popular radio or watch TV, as my mind would dwell too much on things I'd seen and heard from those media. In the case of popular music, lyrics would keep repeating in my mind so much that I had to limit myself to classical music. I had to make my apartment a TV-free zone.

level to level up to the top of the head with an undulating movement, quite like a serpent; at each level this Force pierces (rather violently) through the corresponding centre, which opens, and at the same time opens us to all the universal vibrations or energies that correspond to the frequency of that particular centre. With Sri Aurobindo's yoga, the descending Force opens the same centres, slowly and gently, from top to bottom. Often, the lower centres do not even open fully until much later. This process has its advantage, if we understand that each centre corresponds to a universal mode of consciousness or energy: to open the lower centres of the vital and subconscient right at the start is to run the risk of being submerged, not by our personal little problems any more, but by universal torrents of mud: we have automatically tuned in to the world's Confusion and Mud. Besides, that is why traditional yogas absolutely insist on the protective presence of a Master. With the descending Force this pitfall is avoided, for we confront the lower centres only after our being is firmly established in the higher, superconscient light. [5]

To expound on the dangers of "opening from below," the physiological phenomena that characterize Kundalini are really outer manifestations of an inner psychological process, in which barriers in consciousness are destroyed. Efforts at achieving an awakening could therefore lead to an unbalancing of the personality, with resulting psychological problems.

Another danger to focusing solely on the physiological aspects of Kundalini is misplaced effort. Looking for a single lever of enlightenment is a waste of time, since enlightenment cannot be coaxed into being by techniques. It happens on its own, when we've demonstrated that we no longer need to maintain our ordinary perception of the world. As long as this need remains, however, enlightenment cannot manifest, irrespective of the techniques used.

A proper understanding of how Kundalini figures in the transformation quest is so important that this process has formed a key element in biblical thought. The way in which this problem is dealt with is presented in the following chapter.

FIVE

KUNDALINI AND THE PSYCHOLOGY OF SELF-TRANSFORMATION

THE PROMISE AND CHALLENGE OF SELF-TRANSFORMATION

The role Kundalini assumes in the psychology of self-transformation is complex. This is by reason of self-transformation itself being a very complex psychological process. What we call self-transformation involves both objective and subjective developments, comprised of biological and psychic changes on the one hand, and spiritual changes on the other. In the absence of much training, anyone involved in the process generally has difficulty identifying which experiences are subjective and which are objective—that is, which experiences result from peculiarities in the individual having the experience and which result from a genuine change of consciousness.

The individual working toward a change in consciousness is really playing host to two conflicting forces in his being. The first force originates from the historical self with all its habits, likes and dislikes, prejudices and preferences, and generally narrow outlook on life. The second force emanates from the promise of a life more enduring and worthwhile. It is the drawing force of the Higher Self,* and its objective of striving is more

---

*The Higher Self can be thought of as our truest, deepest reality. It has been referred to by other terms, namely, the Self (spelt with a capital "S") in Eastern philosophy and Jungian Psychology, or Soul (also with a capital "S") in Western esoteric thought.

distant than the day-to-day concerns of the historical self. Put simply, then, the task of self-transformation is to lessen the hold of the historical self on our being while allowing the Higher Self to increase its influence.

This can be a challenging undertaking, since any insight we encounter that has the potential to advance the transformational process in us must first be channeled through mental faculties dominated by the lower self. And to expect the lower self—that part of us that's oriented to the finite and the personal—to accurately process information intended to help us transition to a more spiritual existence is not quite realistic. It would amount to getting the lower self to release the mind and faculties from its control, thereby presiding over its own demise. However, we can only expect the mind, under the control of the lower self, to endeavor to sabotage any progress toward transformation by distorting or misinterpreting the insight it receives. Thus it is this subjective aspect of transformation that creates the biggest challenge. It is also this aspect that is represented in the drama of the Garden of Eden, recorded in the second and third chapters of Genesis.

The message of the Eden story, which is lost in traditional interpretations of its symbology, is a statement about the purpose of human beings in the world. This purpose is the pursuit of a sense of "Self" in which, ultimately, nothing is excluded. In other words, our purpose is to work at universalizing our beings. On top of that, we have to learn how to do this the right way, as opposed to the more automatic and expedient way, which leads us to a dead end.

THE INDUCTIVE APPROACH TO INTERPRETING THE SYMBOLS IN THE EDEN MYTH

Traditional interpretations of the Eden myth seek one-to-one correspondences between its symbols and elements of reality, thus arriving at a composite meaning. Such an approach can be called deductive, or additive.

The approach I propose for untangling the Eden story, however, is inductive. In this approach, the meaning of each symbol comes from the overall meaning derived from the interactions of all the symbols in the story. In other words, the overall message of the story gives meaning to individual symbols, rather than the other way around.

I readily acknowledge that there are no set rules for interpreting symbols, as we are not dealing with mathematical equations, but with feeling states, or impressions. However, I believe that we can understand the message carried by a set of symbols better by determining their dynamic interrelationships than by interpreting each of the symbols separately. In my experience, the more fruitful approach to interpreting religious symbolism in general is to achieve an integrative understanding at a feeling level of the overall interactions of the symbols; then, and only then, should we affix specific interpretations to them. I elaborated on this approach in the introduction to my book *Meditations on the Apocalypse,* but have reproduced my reflections here for the reader's convenience:

> I would like to explain how I approached the task of interpreting the symbols in Revelation. First, I approached it with an open mind—a mind free of all preconceived ideas as to what its many symbols mean. My approach to these symbols was to not attempt an interpretation as they were encountered. Indeed, it was not my objective to find a one-to-one correspondence between each symbol and something in the outer world, but to find meaning in the sense of personal relevance.
>
> Second, as my understanding about Revelation was emerging at a feeling level, I "measured" this against all my beliefs and against all that I held as truth. As a consequence, I had to modify some of my previously held beliefs. At the same time, my own sense of truth (i.e., what I had already proven by experience to be truth) helped to guide my enquiry by providing me with parallels, similarities, and cor-

respondences between the symbols in Revelation and systems of knowledge besides Christianity.

Third, as my understanding of Revelation's message increased at an integral level, I was able to place an interpretation on individual symbols. For me, this ensured that the individual symbols take their meaning from the overall message of Revelation rather than vice versa.[1]

The lesson of the Eden story is that the mission to transform ourselves is a double quest, or a quest within a quest, as some aspects of one quest overlap with the other. This is our first major clue in determining the meaning of this myth. The first quest of transformation deals with the pursuit of identity, or individuality, while the second deals with defining that identity in terms that are harmonious to the entire Universe.

The problem is that the first and second quests appear to be at cross-purposes. In the first, the pursuit of identity is achieved through the exercise of the powers of our individual ego, which differentiates itself by separation. The second quest requires finding a context larger than the ego around which to forge a new identity.

We can sharpen our understanding of this double quest by examining the main symbols in the Eden drama, as well as the interactions among them. The prominent symbols here are the Garden of Eden itself, Adam and Eve, the Tree of Knowledge of Good and Evil, the Tree of Life, and the Serpent. Each of these symbols represents an entire subprocess in the transformation quest. As such, each one also represents a universal principle, and each affects the transformation process in a specific way.

We begin our task of interpretation by regarding these symbols as representations of principles in a state of potentiality. In a sense, it is as if the elements of a highly structured game, such as chess, are present. Only when interaction begins can the course to follow be determined, but not before. Just as the idea behind chess is to conduct a series of movements with the pieces that are favorable to one party, the idea behind transforming consciousness is to have a set of principles interact in the life of the individual to bring about the most beneficial outcome.

However, before we delve into the double-quested nature of the transformation process represented by the interaction of symbols in the Garden of Eden, let's examine these symbols individually.

The Garden of Eden

When the Eden myth is seen as a model of the transformation process, the Garden of Eden itself represents potentiality as viewed from a virginal state of Consciousness; that is, a state in which Consciousness, the divine principle, has not yet become condensed to form the human mind. It should be noted that the etymological meaning of the word "Eden" is "delight." It represents primordiality—unspoiled and undifferentiated nature. It is futile for us to aspire to an "Eden Consciousness," however, because as innocence or primordiality goes, it can be had only once. So the real question for mankind is this: What should we pursue in exchange for the innocence that is no longer ours?

Adam and Eve

Adam and Eve do not represent man and woman, but the universal principles that men and women characteristically express. Adam represents the principle of intellect. The etymological meaning of the name Adam is "firm, ground." He represents the logical mind, the function located on the left side of the brain. Eve, on the other hand, represents the emotional side of our human nature. The name means "life giving." It is the emotional aspect that gives human life its characteristic flavor. When an individual has lost the capacity to feel, that person has lost his capacity for sane, caring behavior. A common symptom of criminally insane individuals is that they have lost the capacity to feel. Such individuals are usually called sociopaths. The qualities represented by Eve can be relegated to the right side of the brain.

It is significant that it was Eve whom the serpent approached. What this scene is really saying is that the impulse to subjectivity, or to "self-assertion" (which the serpent represents), stems from the emotional side of our nature. When Adam and Eve ate the fruit from the Tree of Knowledge of Good and Evil, they experienced a separation from the natural order of things. The Genesis account says that "the eyes of both were opened, and they knew that they were naked" (Genesis 3:7).

Psychologically speaking, then, discovering themselves to be naked and desiring to cover themselves suggest a differentiation from the natural order, from Nature. The flip side of this splitting off from the natural order is a sense of being separate (mentally) and alienated (emotionally). This really is the source of the legendary fall of man. It must also be remembered that Adam was never deceived. He ate willingly to support his mate, and the result was the "fall" of the intellect in addition to that of the emotional nature. It is out of this coalition that the human mind was born.

The Serpent

As stated in the Introduction, the Eden Serpent represents the biopsychic process of Kundalini. In the East, Kundalini is referred to as "serpent power," and the imagery used to represent the process is a snake uncoiling from its home at the base of the spine and climbing up toward the brain. The Serpent of Eden and the Kundalini Serpent are not equated just because the same physical imagery is used, however. Their affiliation comes from the fact that, in both cases, the serpent symbolizes a certain stage in the process of self-transformation. This stage is the first of the "double quest" mentioned earlier. Specifically, the serpent represents the initial impulse to experience and express identity and individuality. It is the impulse toward subjectivity, toward "I-ness," that is stimulated during the quest for transformation.

Initially, our quest for self-transformation is born out of our feelings of spiritual alienation from not having any direct experience of our place in the Cosmos. This gives rise to our need to find personal relevance—a need that can only be satisfied by a quest to discover and realize our true identity, the Self.[2] However, because we have no template as to what constitutes the Self, we may settle for something to "realize" that is other than the true Self. Thus, when we give in to the impulse to assert what we might think to be the Self, we may be really acting out of the familiar, historical, or "lower" self.

In reality, it's not always easy to determine which of our impulses emanate from the Higher Self and which from the lower. This is because it's all too easy to attribute noble motivations to the impulses and acts whose ultimate aim is to serve the lower self. In practical terms, we might justify our acts with the rationalizations that we are acting for the good of the other, or that we are being true to ourselves, or that we are committed to a greater good, or that we're doing God's will. However, in the final analysis, the only true test of whether our actions emanate from the Higher Self is whether we can act without the anticipation of a reward, no matter how subtle its nature. If we can think of any reward for our actions, no matter how subtle such rewards might be (for example, social status or praise) then the true motivations for these acts emerge from the lower self. More typically, acts that truly emerge from the Higher Self emerge from a place of choicelessness, in that the situation is such that it leaves us with no alternative but to act.

The affinity of the Eden Serpent with Kundalini is evident in that Kundalini can cause various biopsychic adjustments, which can be mistaken for signs of spiritual advancement or even completion of the transformational quest to realize the Self. These adjustments may open up different extrasensory faculties such as clairvoyance (i.e., receiving premonitions), sensing the thoughts and moods of others, sending thoughts to others, and a host of other "gifts." It is quite possible for someone to mistake these "gifts" as the rightful result of the work of transformation and become distracted from carrying on the work. This is why in every tradition, spiritual teachers instruct the student not to be sidetracked by psychic powers, but rather to acknowledge them with a certain amount of detachment and move on. The danger they pose is that one may succumb to the temptation to "realize" the proceeds of the transformational work by regarding these "gifts" as signs of spiritual mastery. Were this to occur, the second leg of the quest would suffer. In this sense then, Kundalini, like the Serpent of Eden, presents a continuous temptation, since one might be tricked into feeling that the work of transformation is completed at various stages along the way.

The Tree of Knowledge of Good and Evil

The Tree of Knowledge of Good and Evil speaks to the process of achieving "selfhood," or individuation, which is facilitated by eating its fruit. The fruit—namely, knowledge of good and evil—then represents free will. With the selfhood that is achieved through free will, mankind would have the power to affect the destiny of the universe, positively or negatively. However, there is no assurance that the achievement of selfhood would result in harmonious interactions, because, according to the Eden story, God had to take a defensive position, forcing Adam and Eve to leave the garden. They had to leave because the Elohim[3] (God) realized that they had become like one of them: "Behold, the man has become as one of us"(Genesis 3:22).

Adam and Eve having to leave the garden after eating of the tree had little to do with disobeying God. Rather, it had to do with a breach of cosmic protocol—a protocol by which God adds to his family, or his own being. Various properties comprise the nature of divinity, and free will is one of them. However, for this free will to operate in harmony with the will of God, it must be obtained only after other faculties have been mastered. These other faculties ensure that one's free will does not pose a threat to the "harmony of heaven." Thus, when free will is achieved in a manner consistent with proper cosmic protocol, then the individual has already brought self-will—which pertains to the will of the lower self—under the direction of the Divine Will. Of course, this sounds rather abstract, but it means that the lower self and all its contrary impulses must be subsumed to the will of the Higher Self before one can be truly free. Thus, for the one who aspires to selfhood and freedom, the realization must come that there is ultimately one Self and one Will. One must realize that the Divine is All in all.

Any sense of selfhood that is claimed that does not internalize this Principle of Unity is therefore incomplete—and the will that one may wield from such an incomplete state is not free will, but self-will. Self-will is rooted in the impulse to wield power for the sake or self-gratification and self-indulgence.

In summary, what is it in the transformation process that corresponds with Eve being tempted by the Serpent to eat the Fruit from the Tree of Knowledge of Good and Evil? It is the false notion we can get from the biopsychic process of Kundalini that we are complete, or have achieved union with Ultimate Reality, even as we may still be under the influence of our ego drives and needs.

The Tree of Life

The Tree of Life in the garden represents the Principle of the Unity of all Life. It also represents the second leg of the double quest of transformation. This is the endeavor to return to unity, to empty oneself into the Ocean of Being, metaphorically speaking.

The Tree of Life in the Garden of Eden is therefore representative of the Christ Principle. This is the principle of redemption, of absorption into the embrace of the One Life. In this context, we are reminded of Paul's teaching that in Christ, God was reconciling the world unto himself (2 Corinthians 5:19).

In terms of the transformation process, Adam and Eve being turned out of the Garden of Eden relates to mankind's loss of awareness of its divine heritage. This loss of contact persists until we are able to come to a realization of Self based on the Oneness of Creation. When we feel that we have achieved selfhood, we will be challenged to prove that it is authentic Selfhood and not something that exists only in our imagination. This challenge can be met only by demonstrating our capability of acting on behalf of Life as a principle, rather than only for ourselves and our own individual interests. The most direct way that we can prove to ourselves that we have passed the test is if we are able to renounce personal claim to our spiritual attainments.* We have to become totally un-self-willed.

The dilemma posed by the double-quested nature of transformation may be disguised by other theological and philosophical issues. For example, the ancient debate that is still alive in Buddhism as to whether there is a soul,[4] or the issue in Hinduism as to the relationship between the *Atman* (Soul) and *Brahman* (Spirit). Both of these debates stem from the desire to establish a perspective from which to assess the transformation process.

Buddhist writings record that when Buddha was asked[5] if there was a soul, he remained silent. There has been much commentary as to what Buddha's silence meant. Perhaps there was no way to answer this question without counseling his questioner to error. Or perhaps Buddha perceived this question as a distraction that neither followed from his teachings, nor had any bearing on them. Regardless, to better understand his silence, we need to consider the cultural context in which Buddhist teachings took birth. At that time in India, there was, and still is, much concern about the realization of the Self, or Atman, as it is called in Sanskrit. Nothing is to be spared in such a quest, and everything may be shunned, including responsibilities toward one's family. For example, a man abandoning his wife and children and seeking self-realization at the feet of a guru is regarded as noble.

Many spiritual seekers engaged in the quest of the Self may not realize that, in truth, there is only one Self. That is, what we call the Atman, or Soul, is really just a surrogate or provisional self. Buddha may have been silent on this question of the Soul, then, because to have said, "Yes, there is a Soul," he would have acknowledged a self separate from the One Self,

---

*This universal principle is recognized and enshrined in Buddhism as the Bodhisattva Vow, in which the seeker on the path to enlightenment avows not to rest on the fruits of his own liberation, but consecrates himself to the liberation of all sentient beings.

or a life separate from the One Life. On the other hand, to have denied that there is a Soul or Self may have counseled others to error, giving tacit approval to the stagnation, inertia, and ignorance to which mankind is prone. Buddha knew these characteristics should be overcome, and that doing so would require establishing a target of striving that might exist for only as long as it takes to gather together the scattered elements of one's being into an effective instrument for growth.

To view the process of striving and growth from the perspective of the Tree of Life is to view it in its totality, to see the One Grand Realization as the only realization that may be perceived as individual realizations. One eye is on the microcosm and one is on the macrocosm; there is constant recognition of the miniature design within the Grand Design. The path represented by the Tree of Life is that of surrender to the Grand Design.

GOD'S GRAND DESIGN

Another pertinent lesson to the transformation quest, and one worth extracting from the Eden story, is that of the divine protocol mentioned earlier. This protocol can be said to govern the process through which God adds to his being. Otherwise, he (or they) would not have said, "Let us make man in our image, after our likeness" (Genesis 1:16). In other words, God wants to replicate himself in humanity.

The first act of this desire for expansion requires God to take a chance, to allow his essence to flow outward, sending his vibrations forth over what we call Space. As these vibrations stream forth from God, they eventually slow down and ultimately form Matter. The test is now for God to find himself outside of himself—to rediscover himself in Matter. This is accomplished by agitating Matter to recall its source, which results in the process of evolution in nature. This evolution, however, is not the mechanistic process envisioned by Darwinian evolution theorists, but a reawakening of Consciousness within Matter.

When this reawakening reaches a certain critical stage, refinements must be undertaken before reunification with God occurs. At this stage, mankind enters the scene. Through humanity, the impulse toward God must be refined; it must receive the cooperation of our will, which must be reoriented from its impulse toward separation and individualization. The responsibility of mankind is to experience a realization of the need to submit to the Will of God, and to give up self-will.

EVOLUTION, SPIRITUALITY, AND THE TRANSFORMATION OF CONSCIOUSNESS

I'm deeply and eternally indebted to the writings of Sri Aurobindo, which came to my notice over thirty years ago, for guiding my intellectual understanding of the mystery and purpose of human existence and how these integrate—up to a point—with the current scientific understanding of human evolution. While Sri Aurobindo's spiritual findings are amply articulated in the many volumes comprising his collected works, his thoughts on humanity's role in creation are succinctly summed up in the short essay "The Evolution of Consciousness," found in *Essays Divine and Human*, Volume Twelve of his Collected Works. Here, he states:

> All life here is a stage or a circumstance in an unfolding progressive evolution of a Spirit that has involved itself in Matter and is labouring to manifest itself in that reluctant substance. This is the whole secret of earthly existence.
>
> But the key of that secret is not to be found in life itself or in the body; its hieroglyph is not in embryo or organism,—for these are only a physical means or base: the one significant mystery of this universe is the appearance and growth of consciousness in the vast mute unintelligence of Matter. The escape of Consciousness out of an apparent initial Inconscience,—but it was there all the time masked

and latent, for the inconscience of Matter is itself only a hooded consciousness—its struggle to find itself, its reaching out to its own inherent completeness, perfection, joy, light, strength, mastery, harmony, freedom, this is the prolonged miracle and yet the natural and all-explaining phenomenon of which we are at once the observers and a part, instrument and vehicle.

A Consciousness, a Being, a Power, a Joy was here from the beginning darkly imprisoned in this apparent denial of itself, this original night, this obscurity and nescience of material Nature. That which is and was forever, free, perfect, eternal and infinite, That which all is, That which we call God, Brahman, Spirit, has here shut itself up in its own self-created opposite. The Omniscient has plunged itself into Nescience, the All-Conscious into Inconscience, the All-Wise into perpetual Ignorance. The Omnipotent has formulated itself in a vast cosmic self-driven Inertia that by disintegration creates; the Infinite is self-expressed here in a boundless fragmentation; the All-Blissful has put on a huge insensibility out of which it struggles by pain and hunger and desire and sorrow. Elsewhere the Divine is; here in physical life, in this obscure material world, it would seem almost as if the Divine is not but is only becoming.... This gradual becoming of the Divine out of its own phenomenal opposites is the meaning and purpose of the terrestrial evolution. [6]

Viewed in the context of the role that humanity has to play in awakening Consciousness in Matter, we can return to the Eden myth with a fuller appreciation of the dynamics that are being played out in our human consciousness. Although God foresaw the temptation that Adam and Eve were to face, the temptation had to be allowed, since the being of God grows when mankind voluntarily renounces self-seeking and self-will for God's Will. When this happens, that which God previously sent out from himself would have returned. The prodigal son would have returned home, but with a difference. The difference would lie in the fact that parts of God had been sent forth into every conceivable facet of expression anti-thetical to the principles that God represents, and they would have not only survived, but triumphed.

One can find a situation not altogether dissimilar in human families. Take, for example, parents who have the foresight to trust their children and give them room to grow in responsibility and develop self-worth. It is these parents who usually enjoy the best relationships with their grown children. The children "return" to the parents, in the form of a close relationship of love and respect. On the other hand, parents who try to hold onto their children in fear of losing them stand the greater chance of actually losing them in the end. When parents desire to see their values perpetuated, their best bet is to give their children room to evaluate those beliefs for themselves. If the values are sound, children will usually adopt them.

It also follows that it is the love that children voluntarily return to parents that delights them the most. Love that is demanded is never delightful; it places the recipient in the position of a hostage taker. In God's dealings with mankind, it is our voluntary love that causes God to take delight in his creation.

Is There a "Proper" Approach to Kundalini?

In the early 1990s, I had the occasion to visit a nuclear electricity generating plant that was under construction in Ontario, Canada. Although the visit was related to my job at the time as a public policy economist, I also had a strong personal interest. While I was curious about the mysterious and controversial world of nuclear generation itself, the area of my immediate, personal interest was somewhat more mundane. Simply stated,

I wanted to see with my own eyes what could be bought with the then gargantuan sum of $14 billion, the estimated cost of the facility at the time. During our tour of the plant, I was surprised to discover how "simple" the technology behind nuclear generation is. Basically, water is poured over rods of enriched uranium, resulting in the generation of steam. The steam is then harnessed to drive the turbines that produce the electricity. I also discovered that the lion's share of the costs of a nuclear facility was not related to harnessing nuclear power as such, but for its containment, to protect the plant workers and the public at large from the harmful effects of radiation.

When I think of transformational energies, such as those represented by Kundalini, I cannot help but reflect on my nuclear plant visit. The energies of consciousness, which are released as the ego is displaced and the transformational process is fast-tracked, require similar containment. While it is a significant achievement to displace the ego sufficiently so that the primordial energies represented by Kundalini are experienced, this is not the end-point of the transformational process. The energies themselves must be tamed, harnessed, and focused. And this is where many of the New Age techniques dedicated to the purpose of evoking these energies put their practitioners at risk if the means of containing them are not made part of the practice.

It really is paradoxical that although the transformational journey consists of freeing personal consciousness (i.e., our capacities for thinking, feeling, and willing) from the domination of the ego, the successful completion of the transformational process requires a healthy ego that functions in cooperation with the Higher Self. Because of this important requirement, transformational technologies—single-focused techniques that can provoke a radical altering of consciousness—can put one at risk if the task is done without adequate preparation, and the ego is weakened to the point where it falls under the influence of sub-egoic, or elemental forces. In this case, the application of transformational technologies would have simply exchanged one danger with another—the danger to the Self from unrelenting ego domination is replaced by danger to the ego by domination from the sub-egoic realm.

Indeed, the proper application of transformational technologies is to free our perception of reality from the limited perspective of a historically anchored ego, so that we can progressively extend our concept of what constitutes the Self, and as a result get a widened appreciation of what's in our interest. But having achieved this task, the second challenge is to be able to use our new perception and understanding to make positive contributions to life around us. This is where spiritual practices that help us to transform our values and build character become invaluable. They will constitute our containment efforts to safely handle Kundalini, the spiritual world's equivalent of nuclear energy.

So, if we return to the question, *Should one engage in techniques aimed specifically at the awakening of Kundalini?*, my personal advice is: Don't! Kundalini represents a primordial force, a phenomenon that exists outside of our capacity to control and dominate. On one hand, the arousal of Kundalini can be life-changing, but on the other, its activation can present serious health challenges if it occurs before one has developed the emotional and mental maturity and physical stamina to withstand the changes that it ushers in. Once confined to yogic ashrams and esoteric groups, the awakening of Kundalini has been occurring more frequently in our time, as evidenced by the clinical interest it has attracted from practitioners in the fields of medicine and psychology. Knowledge of Kundalini is helpful so that one can be prepared to understand the process if it does occur. Cases have been documented where individuals experiencing a spontaneous Kundalini-awakening were misdiagnosed as undergoing a psychotic episode.[7]

My view is that the safe approach to the awakening of Kundalini is to not be concerned with it as a specific target or goal. I believe that Kundalini has its own built-in maturation process, and like a fruit that falls from a tree when it has ripened, its arousal is facilitated organically when we're diligent at our spiritual practice, which essentially should be about giving expression to behaviors and practices in our daily life that attest to the unity of life. Meditation must be a regular part of this effort to ensure that all parts of our being share in our perceptions of, and commitment to, a spiritual way of life. As we continue in our practice, Kundalini may become awakened to assist us in liberating our consciousness from its imprisonment in a materialistic perception of life. This is because a key task of Kundalini is to erode the barriers in our consciousness that prevent us from perceiving and experiencing our unity. It is therefore ironic that anyone would relate to Kundalini as an object of desire, because when we lust after Kundalini, we are running the risk of creating more barriers in our consciousness than the Kundalini process, even when released, may be capable of destroying.

Ultimately, every strategy that we can devise from the perspective of the lower self to achieve liberation, or the realization of the Self, impedes it. This is why regarding Kundalini as a transformation lever to be sought after is shortsighted. By focusing all our attention on only one thing, namely pulling the Kundalini lever, we would be forgetting the path of pursuing just relationships with other people, which, incidentally, is the "path" of the Tree of Life.

One teacher who had foreseen the problems created when Kundalini is turned into an object of desire, and who devised a conceptual means of getting around it as a stumbling block, is Gurdjieff.[8] He taught that portraying liberation as the acquisition of something is dangerous. He even went as far as ridiculing the notion of the existence of Kundalini by telling his students that Kundalini is really a construct of the imagination. He advised them that instead of looking for Kundalini, they should concentrate on ridding themselves of the unpleasant properties inherent in man that are a holdover from a previous era of human development. He attributed these unpleasant properties to "the organ Kundabuffer," an organ which, he said, was implanted in man at an earlier stage of evolution. The only worthwhile task for the individual intent on achieving liberation is to rid himself of the unpleasant consequences of this organ, which are given as "egoism, self-love, vanity, pride, self-conceit, credulity, suggestibility, and many other properties quite abnormal and unbecoming."[9]

Whether or not Gurdjieff was justified in creating the "organ Kundabuffer" is difficult to judge, as it would depend on whether it assisted in his aim of advancing transformation in those he taught. However, his approach has a certain genius to it in that it creates the right kind of imagery in the minds of his students—imagery that fosters a climate favorable to genuine transformation by encouraging a mindset that is eliminative rather than acquisitive. An eliminative consciousness helps to liberate us from self-seeking and self-will, while an acquisitive consciousness strengthens our bondage to materiality. Incidentally, it is this approach of adopting eliminative strategies, as opposed to acquisitive ones, that will enable us rise above the limitations of the mind, which is under the allegiance of the lower self.

Six

LAYING THE FOUNDATION
FOR THE TRANSFORMATION
OF CONSCIOUSNESS

SPIRITUALITY AND THE TRANSFORMATION
OF CONSCIOUSNESS

Before delving further into the predominant theme of this book—namely, that the Gospel of Matthew's portrayal of the life and teachings of Jesus is an invitation for us to engage in a way of life that will progressively lead to a transformation of consciousness—perhaps we should ask: What defines a transformation of consciousness? And, more important, what is the difference between transformation of consciousness and spiritual growth?

Although we generally think of spirituality in terms of possessing and practicing various virtues, as well as having an absence of vices, the key characteristic of spiritual growth is our sense of connectedness with other people and the rest of existence. As such, spiritual growth involves personal changes that make us more considerate, loving, and giving; more capable of experiencing and expressing empathy; and more responsible toward life. Any virtue that we traditionally classify as spiritual that does not lead to these outcomes ends up being an end in itself.

Transformation of consciousness refers to the elevation of consciousness to a higher level and the resulting readjustment of our relationships with others and our environment. Each higher level of consciousness results in a greater understanding of life, existence, or Reality, and is accompanied by a higher intelligence and a deeper sense of connection with life. With a lifting of consciousness, our frame of reference for viewing and relating to life changes, becoming broader as well as deeper.

Paradoxically, spiritual growth—in the traditional sense of virtuousness—and the transformation of consciousness are not always synonymous. Some can live their entire lives in spiritually oriented endeavors without experiencing a significant transformational experience,* while others who are uninterested in conventional expressions of spirituality can undergo significant transformational experiences. The ideal situation, though, is for individuals undergoing a transformation of consciousness to use the experience of an expanded consciousness to better understand and then redefine their relationships with their environment. And, of course, it is also desirable for individuals who are committed to a spiritual way of life to undergo experiences that lead to a transformation of consciousness.

The interaction of spirituality and transformation can best be explained by the following illustration: At an ordinary level of consciousness, such as one dominated by our ego-centered view of reality, following the commandment of Jesus that we love our neighbor as ourselves would be carried out only with a great deal of effort. And since we would be acting against our natural impulses, we would not be able to carry it out without the feeling of making a sacrifice. Complying with this commandment, then, would require us to adjust our perspective from one that is narrowly focused on pursuing

---

*This occurs particularly when our attempts to live a spiritual life take place within the context of a traditionally religious setting. We run the danger of letting our doctrinal beliefs and preconceived ideas get in the way of a genuinely transformational breakthrough experience. Truth is independent of, and not subservient to, our doctrines and beliefs, and it is often a requirement that we liberate ourselves from our manmade concepts and institutional divisions in order to make its acquaintance. Our attitudes must be supple enough to recognize genuine revelation when we encounter it. We also run the risk of blocking our own moments of transformational insight when we try to force transcendental truths into the straightjacket of our religious doctrines. In this case, we succumb to the proverbial error of trying to pour new wine (new revelatory experience) into the old wineskins of our familiar concepts (Matthew 9:17).

our own needs and desires to one that gives equal or greater consideration to the needs and interests of others. In simple terms, this shift in perspective represents a change from "me-centeredness" to "we-centeredness."

As we undergo a transformation of consciousness, however, we find it progressively easier to think and act out of the premise of we-centeredness. Further, our experience and definition of "we" grows in line with our expanding consciousness. At an ordinary level of consciousness, our sense of "we" might be limited to our immediate family or some tight-knit social groups to which we belong, but as our consciousness expands, our sense of "we" expands to the point where less and less becomes excluded from the definition. Consequently, at the higher level of consciousness, we would experience loving our neighbor as less of a sacrifice and more of a natural outflowing of our being, since the welfare of our neighbor and our own are no longer perceived as being in conflict.

This is one of the benefits of a transformed consciousness—it leads to a change in our nature, where the practice of virtue becomes natural for us. In the above example, loving others would require no effort, because we would come to the understanding that what we do for others, we are ultimately doing for ourselves. Transformation, then, enables us to arrive at a place where we do good as a natural and spontaneous outflowing from within.

LAYERS OF ESOTERIC KNOWLEDGE IN THE GOSPEL OF MATTHEW

Most of the Sermon on the Mount, as recorded in the fifth, sixth, and seventh chapters of Matthew, illustrates the quality of commitment and the steadiness of effort required for us to successfully undertake the journey of transforming our consciousness. Although Matthew is laid out in terms of our following a program of spiritual teachings to attain the "Kingdom of Heaven," these teachings are coincidentally organized to achieve progressive breakthroughs in the growth of consciousness. Moreover, this progression coincides with the stages that characterize Kundalini awakening.

Table 3:
THE CONTENT AND STRUCTURE OF MATTHEW IN
RELATION TO TRANSFORMATION OF CONSCIOUSNESS

Layers of Instructions	Target	Spiritual Practice	Transformational Objective
First Layer			
The Beatitudes (Matthew 5:3–20)	Sharpening the Intellect	Reexamining our assumptions about the nature of reality and the purpose of life	Overhauling our value system from subjective to objective values
Second Layer			
Matthew 5:21–48	Refining the Emotions	Routing out blockages in the psyche by focusing on the spirit of the law rather than on the letter of the law	Reprogramming our emotions by arresting the misdirection of life energy at the various energy centers or chakras
Third Layer			
Matthew 6 and 7	Developing Will	Practicing spiritual exercises that affirm our common humanity	Facilitating the flow of life energy into higher levels of expression

Specifically, the higher-level knowledge in Matthew comprises three separate layers of instructions, with each layer providing the protocol necessary for refining and thereby enhancing the functioning of our essential human faculties of thinking, feeling, and willing. The enhancement (or upgrade) of these faculties will facilitate the movement of consciousness to a higher level. Table 3 provides a schematic of how this information can be used to facilitate the awakening of consciousness.

As you can see, the first layer of instructions is the Beatitudes, presented in Matthew 5:3–20. These instructions are directed at the intellect, with the object of getting us to change our value system by reexamining our assumptions about the nature of reality and the purpose of life.

The second layer of instructions, covering Matthew 5:21–48, is directed at recalibrating our emotions through a change in our belief system. Since certain ideas, especially those concerning our relationships with others, influence the way we feel about life in general, changing them usually has the effect of altering our emotional states. In essence, when we exchange our existing belief system for one that offers greater openness and inclusiveness, we remove blockages in our psyche that restrict the flow of life energy through us.

The third layer of instructions deals with the will, and is covered in the sixth and seventh chapters of Matthew. This layer of instructions profiles principles that we need to incorporate into our being if we are to open up to a fuller expression of life.

Amazingly, these instructions found in the fifth, sixth, and seventh chapters of Matthew are based on two systems of knowledge that predate Christianity.

The first system of knowledge is astrology, upon which the Beatitudes themselves are structured. Each of the familiar sayings in this section of Matthew is really telling us how we should strive to refocus and refine the way we express impulses that may arise in us. Rather than letting us identify with these impulses and regard them as part of our inherited nature, as we would usually do, the Beatitudes aim to help us to see these impulses as the impersonal forces that they actually are, which is the first step in distancing ourselves from them.

The second system of knowledge is derived from the model of the "seven-foldedness" of our being, which finds expression in the seven chakras.

In this chapter, we will deal briefly with the astrological orientation of the Beatitudes as a background to their thorough exposition. The other two layers of instructions using the chakra model will be the subject of upcoming chapters.

THE ASTROLOGICAL ORIENTATION OF THE BEATITUDES

Since the idea behind the Beatitudes is to provide values for us to strive toward incorporating into ourselves, it made sense to present those values in the context of how the human mind naturally functions. For example, there are nine Beatitudes of the "Blessed are …" genre and three exhortations that comprise the earlier part of Jesus's exegesis on the Mosaic Code. This makes for twelve target values to strive for, to enable our mind to transcend its linear mode of functioning.

The ordinary mind functions linearly due to its dependence on the structure of time for orientation. In simpler terms, because the mind organizes itself around the past, present, and future, its ability to apprehend reality is limited to provable "facts." This means that the mind, in its natural linear state, cannot deal with matters such as aspiration and faith, and, therefore, cannot help us deal with important issues that arise during a spiritual search, such as questions about the purpose of life, or what we ought to make the objective of our striving. The work of self-transformation is thus hindered by this linear mode of functioning, because, while transformation demands that we leave outmoded ways of being for ways that are more in line with the higher levels of reason, the linear mind is locked into habitual patterns of functioning. In its linear mode, the mind is bound in loyalty to the historical self. As such, its only interest is in continuing established patterns, by imposing habitual and repetitive tasks on the being. In this manner, it stifles whatever creative desire we might have.

The linear mode of mental functioning is best illustrated by a simple astrological view of man. One of the basic ideas behind astrology is that the nature of an individual is partially determined by his or her astrological sign of birth.* This sign is one of the twelve into which the Ancients partitioned the heavens: Aries, Taurus, Gemini, Cancer, Leo, Virgo, Libra, Scorpio, Sagittarius, Capricorn, Aquarius, and Pisces. Each of these signs is said to give a certain hue to the natural tendencies of people who are born under it. In a manner of speaking, each sign's characteristic becomes a mental filter through which an individual perceives and reacts to reality.

When viewed psychologically, these sign characteristics might be called archetypes—objective patterns expressed in the guise of individual, personal characteristics. While conventional astrologers may interpret these characteristics in various ways, they are only hinted at in the Beatitudes as factors to be overcome. In other words, each Beatitude encourages us to go beyond the limitations imposed by astrological archetypes by adopting a particular value, or mental stance, which can serve as an antidote, in a manner of speaking. More accurately, it is not the astrological archetype itself that is the problem to overcome, but the ordinary mind's distortion of the "energy" of the related astrological sign.

Table 4, following, presents the twelve astrological signs, their affiliated archetypes, and the resulting mental distortions of these archetypes. Against this backdrop, each Beatitude can be appreciated as a message of encouragement toward our efforts to reflect these archetypal psychological principles.

---

*Astrological birth signs determine one's nature only in the sense of representing tendencies and impulses. They do not determine one's character, which is formed out of the conscious choices we make on a daily basis.

Table 4:
ZODIACAL SIGNS AND THEIR KEY QUALITIES

Sign	Archetypal Energy of Sign	Sign Energy Expressed in Distorted Form
Aries	Leadership	Aggressiveness
Taurus	Stewardship	Acquisitiveness
Gemini	Mindfulness	Conceitedness
Cancer	Sensitivity	Cliquishness
Leo	Determination	Overbearance
Virgo	Circumspection	Disorientation
Libra	Jurisprudence	Vacillation
Scorpio	Perseverance	Fanaticism
Sagittarius	Inspiration	Impulsiveness
Capricorn	Purposiveness	Ambition
Aquarius	Inventiveness	Eccentricity
Pisces	Impartiality	Vagueness

LOGICAL CONSTRUCTION OF THE BEATITUDES

Indeed, the Beatitudes are more than they appear to be. On the surface, each seems to offer a promise provided we adopt a particular attitude. However, under deeper scrutiny, we will see that the Beatitudes do not fall under that category of statements called conditionals, but rather under the umbrella of statements called categoricals.

Conditional statements deal with cause-and-effect relationships, as when we offer someone a reward for a task we want them to perform. Categorical statements, on the other hand, are descriptive, as in the case of showing how two objects, sets of facts, or events are related to each other (e.g., 1 mile is equal to 1.6 kilometers).

The Beatitudes, instead of offering us promises for acts that we perform, describe states of mind and being that naturally emerge in us when we live by certain principles. This perspective will be supported in the next chapter, as we examine each Beatitude in detail.

Figure 2: The Beatitudes and the Zodiac

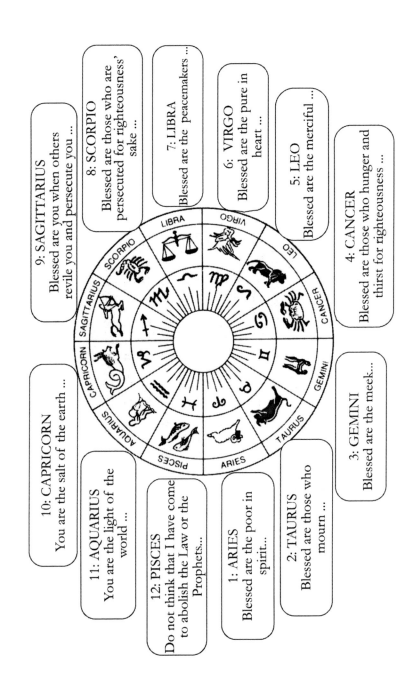

9: SAGITTARIUS
Blessed are you when others revile you and persecute you ...

8: SCORPIO
Blessed are those who are persecuted for righteousness' sake ...

7: LIBRA
Blessed are the peacemakers ...

6: VIRGO
Blessed are the pure in heart ...

5: LEO
Blessed are the merciful ...

4: CANCER
Blessed are those who hunger and thirst for righteousness ...

3: GEMINI
Blessed are the meek...

2: TAURUS
Blessed are those who mourn ...

1: ARIES
Blessed are the poor in spirit...

12: PISCES
Do not think that I have come to abolish the Law or the Prophets...

11: AQUARIUS
You are the light of the world ...

10: CAPRICORN
You are the salt of the earth ...

SEVEN

VIEWING THE BEATITUDES AS A SYSTEM OF OBJECTIVE VALUES

UNDERSTANDING OBJECTIVE VALUES

Objective values are a category of beliefs and attitudes that assist us in building our character. Because these beliefs and attitudes encourage us to look at life objectively, they strengthen our capacity for ethical discernment—that is, our ability to know right from wrong. Objective values are distinguishable from subjective values in that the former relate to unchanging principles. Subjective values, on the other hand, are relative to personal likes and dislikes, as well as to particular times and cultures. Objective values are important because they are the only means by which we can connect with higher-level realities* and achieve growth of consciousness in the process.

Without a system of objective values upon which to base decisions, our response to any given situation would depend merely on the mood we're in. And our mood is often a reflection of our desires or perceived

*I consider "higher-level realities" to be inhabitants of the spiritual world (and not of the "spirit world" as it is understood in occultism). These inhabitants can contact the individual in the form of conveying intuitions, or insights into the principles of the Universe. However, only when we are committed to an external or objective value system (i.e., not making up the rules as we go along) does it becomes possible for these higher energy forms (angels, if you will) to make contact.

needs in the moment. Without objective values to act as a referee, our needs and desires dominate our being until they are satisfied. They call the shots in our life, using us as a tunnel through time and space to seek their own fulfillment.

By adopting a system of objective values, then, we can "un-become" the means by which desires and needs find fulfillment. A value system allows us to examine the merits and consequences of committing the rest of our being to the fulfillment of each need or desire. In this manner, we can earn a degree of permanence in our being; as our feelings about situations are replaced with feelings about universally applicable principles, subjectivity gives way to objectivity.

OVERVIEW OF THE BEATITUDES

The Beatitudes are reproduced here for the reader's convenience:

> [2] And he opened his mouth and taught them, saying:
> [3] "Blessed are the poor in spirit, for theirs is the Kingdom of Heaven.
> [4] "Blessed are those who mourn, for they shall be comforted.
> [5] "Blessed are the meek, for they shall inherit the earth.
> [6] "Blessed are those who hunger and thirst for righteousness, for they shall be satisfied.
> [7] "Blessed are the merciful, for they shall receive mercy.
> [8] "Blessed are the pure in heart, for they shall see God.
> [9] "Blessed are the peacemakers, for they shall be called sons of God.
> [10] "Blessed are those who are persecuted for righteousness' sake, for theirs is the Kingdom of Heaven.
> [11] "Blessed are you when others revile you and persecute you and utter all kinds of evil against you falsely on my

account. [12] Rejoice and be glad, for your reward is great in heaven, for so they persecuted the prophets who were before you.

[13] "You are the salt of the earth, but if salt has lost its taste, how shall its saltiness be restored? It is no longer good for anything except to be thrown out and trampled under people's feet.

[14] "You are the light of the world. A city set on a hill cannot be hidden. [15] Nor do people light a lamp and put it under a basket, but on a stand, and it gives light to all in the house. [16] In the same way, let your light shine before others, so that they may see your good works and give glory to your Father who is in heaven.

[17] "Do not think that I have come to abolish the Law or the Prophets; I have not come to abolish them but to fulfill them. [18] For truly, I say to you, until heaven and earth pass away, not an iota, not a dot, will pass from the Law until all is accomplished. [19] Therefore whoever relaxes one of the least of these commandments and teaches others to do the same will be called least in the Kingdom of Heaven, but whoever does them and teaches them will be called great in the Kingdom of Heaven. [20] For I tell you, unless your righteousness exceeds that of the scribes and Pharisees, you will never enter the Kingdom of Heaven." (Matt. 5:3–20)

As mentioned in the previous chapter, the way in which the Beatitudes are presented can give the erroneous impression that they are promises. Sometimes the language, being in the future tense (e.g., "for they shall") seems to support such an interpretation. Another source of misinterpretation is the imprecise rendering of original terms in the King James and Revised Standard versions of the Bible, in particular. In these versions, for example, the expression "Blessed are" gives the impression that Jesus is promising a divine blessing to those who possess a particular state of being.

However, as said earlier, the Beatitudes really represent the exposition of spiritual principles as they naturally exist. To support this perspective, we will look at the meanings of certain key words in each Beatitude, as they existed in the original Greek language in which the New Testament was written. To accomplish this task, I have used the previously referenced *Analytical Concordance to the Holy Bible.*[1]

KEY WORDS IN THE BEATITUDES

1. Blessed are the poor in spirit, for theirs is the Kingdom of Heaven.

We will begin our analysis by examining the meaning of the term *blessed,* which is found in many places and contexts in the Bible. Several different Greek words have been translated into this single term. For example, *Webster's Dictionary* defines *to bless* as "to invoke divine care for," meaning that when a blessing is conferred by one person upon another, the one blessed receives a benefit. However, the Greek word that conveys the idea of invoking divine favor is *eulogeo,* meaning "to speak well of." It is from this word that the English *eulogy* has been obtained. But this is not the word that was translated as *blessed* in the Beatitudes. Instead, the original Greek word is *makarios,* which conveys a totally different concept; the meaning of *makarios* is "happy."

Thus, the expression "Blessed are" really means "Happy are." The difference is significant. Instead of suggesting a promised benefit in exchange for an attitude, it suggests that the attitude itself is its own reward. It is equivalent to the satisfaction a dying farmer would get from planting a seed of a fruit-bearing tree, or someone helping a stranger that he would likely never see again. Similarly, a Beatitude should not be regarded as pointing to some future state of affairs, but to something to be realized here-and-now.

As we look at the rest of the first Beatitude, the key to its interpretation lies in also understanding "poor in spirit." The meaning of this phrase has nothing to do with a lack of spirit, as we understand the term; it does not imply weakness, impoverisation, or timidity. Instead, it means "a lack of self-will." The spirit that this Beatitude addresses is the human spirit—that is, the personalized spirit of the individual— and not the divine, All-Pervading Spirit. Another way to interpret this phrase, then, would be "poor in ego."

To be poor in spirit, or in ego, is to be patient, or lacking in impulsiveness—impulsiveness being an attribute that accords with the astrological sign of Aries. In astrological analysis, the characteristics represented by Aries are those also attributed to the mythological personage of Mars, the Roman god of war, with the most salient characteristic being aggressiveness, or impetuousness. And it is this attribute that the first Beatitude is discouraging, by upholding its opposite, a gentleness of demeanor.

Further, the "Kingdom of Heaven" being given to the poor in spirit does not refer to a future place, or state, but to a present, possible reality. Note the present tense, "for theirs *is* the Kingdom of Heaven" (emphasis added). We will look at the Kingdom of Heaven in more detail in chapters 10 and 11, but suffice it to say at this point that, by putting all of these insights together, the first Beatitude becomes: Happy are those who lack the impulsiveness of self-will, for theirs is the Kingdom of Heaven.

2. Blessed are those who mourn, for they shall be comforted.

The Concordance reveals seventeen Greek words that have been rendered as *mourn* in English translations. In this Beatitude, the original word used was *pentheo*, meaning to grieve or to sorrow. In the context of grieving or having sorrow without a specific cause, the word that most accurately expresses this idea is *alienation*, as when one longs for one's home. This word is borne out by the idea of being comforted, represented by the Greek word *parakaleo*, meaning to call near, or exhort. It is apt that a sense of alienation be righted by closeness, by reconciliation.

The resulting message of this Beatitude is, "Happy is the one who feels alienated in a material setting, who is not so enamored with earthly possessions and comforts that he forgets the true objective of life." In realizing that the success of a life is not measured by how much one accumulates, this sense of alienation in the outer, material world is counterbalanced by a sense of fulfillment in the inner, spiritual one.

This Beatitude counters the characteristic energy of the astrological archetype of Taurus, with its tendencies to be too acquisitive and materialistic.

3. Blessed are the meek, for they shall inherit the earth.

The third Beatitude is somewhat of a departure from the others. Instead of heavenly or ethereal joys, it seems to offer the earth, the very reality that Christians usually think necessary to renounce. To understand this Beatitude, we must delve into the origins of the terms *meek*, *inherit*, and *earth*.

The word translated as *meek* is the Greek *praus*. A more accurate meaning of *praus* is "easy" or "mild in temperament." An individual who is mild in temperament is not given to bravado and grandiosity (i.e., products of conceit), but is reflective.

It would be logical for such a person to inherit the earth, taking into account the original concept of the word *earth*. The earth mentioned here is the earth made new, as described in Revelation 21:1, "Then I saw a new heaven and a new earth, for the first heaven and the first earth had passed away."

Finally, the Greek word that has been translated to *inherit* is *kleronomeo*. The meaning of this word is given by Dr. Young as "to obtain by lot." This does not coincide with our present-day concept of inheritance, which, as *Webster's Dictionary* tells us, means "to receive as a right or title discernable by law from an ancestor at his death." This latter definition, instead, is expressed by the Greek word *nachal. Inherit*, then, is not the best word to convey the meaning of *kleronomeo*. A more appropriate term would be *realize*.

By applying these new expressions to the third Beatitude, we get the following: "Happy are those who are mild in temperament for they shall realize the earth." The meaning is clear: The mild in temperament, the gentle, will become stewards of the new earth, because the impetuous and conceited will have disqualified themselves. The issue addressed by this Beatitude relates to our effort to express the characteristics of the astrological archetype of Gemini, which is said to deal with mental processes that, when misused, can lead to conceit. To avoid this, the individual must strive to express mildness of temperament.

4. Blessed are those who hunger and thirst for righteousness, for they shall be satisfied.

The fourth Beatitude expresses an idea that is quite universal: focusing our energy specifically on what we seek. The idea is that if we become aware of that which is missing in our life and then experience that missing quality in the utmost, it will manifest itself.

The original ideas behind the words *hunger* and *thirst* in this Beatitude are close to our present understandings of them. The term *righteousness,* however, is more accurately rendered as *justness* or *equity.* It owes its presence here to the Greek word *dikaiosune.*

Our rendition of this Beatitude when viewed as a categorical, rather than conditional, statement gives us this: "Happy are those who hunger and thirst after justness, for certain fulfillment, in time, is theirs." This is just the expression of the principle that is called *Tantra* in Eastern philosophy. This principle has been greatly misunderstood in the West. Properly interpreted, it is not restricted to a specific act or a classification of acts.[2] It relates to the process of living out one's particular existential dilemma as consciously as one can.

The words *hunger* and *thirst* are used in this context, because they are ideal metaphors for the internal void, or vacuum, the seeker experiences with respect to the virtue he is trying to embody. The exhortation that this vacuum will be filled is not a promise, however. It is the description of a process that applies to the natural world. This process ensures that no vacuums persist in nature; when one does occur, material (e.g., air) rushes in to fill the void. Similarly, when we focus on a spiritual reality and become alert to the life situations in which that reality can make a difference, something happens to bring this spiritual reality into existence.

In astrological terms, this Beatitude combats the characteristics typical of the sign of Cancer, which deals with feelings of sensitivity and closeness, or the idea of relational bonding in the general sense. Rather than using this impulse to form cliques, we should, according to this Beatitude, seek a broader bond with humanity, with justice being the binding element.

5. Blessed are the merciful, for they shall receive mercy.

The fifth Beatitude addresses the principle of reciprocity. The spiritual idea embodied by the concept of being *merciful* is not that of condescension, but of compassion. The difference is that with condescension, we act out of magnanimity, whereas with compassion, we emotionally place ourselves in the position of the person needing help. In short, we experience another's need and try to fill it. Whatever action we take to do so, then, comes from empathy—a sense of a common destiny. What is not too evident in a surface reading of this Beatitude is the thought that the compassion we show others comes back to us.

A consideration of the various situations that may place us in a position to show mercy confirms this interpretation. Certainly, it is due to differences in personal power and privilege that such situations arise. Showing compassion to one who is indebted means that we understand the fickleness of success and power, and make accommodations for it through our attitudes. Compassion is born from understanding that the situation could easily be reversed.

Another important point is that when such compassion is given, there is no question as to whether the receiver is deserving of it. The real question is whether the situation warrants it; the emphasis is not on the person, but on the principle.

According to this Beatitude, if we exercise mercy, in the sense of showing compassion or expressing continuity-of-being with others, we receive the same consideration from the Divine Powers. Actually, as we express continuity-of-being in our actions toward others, we are at the same time opening ourselves up to higher, spiritual influences. Perhaps this is what the apostle Peter had in mind when he said, "Above all, keep loving one another earnestly, since love covers a multitude of sins" (I Peter 4:8). Indeed, when we are open and receptive to others, all motivation toward, and opportunities for, sin dissipate in the same way that certain bacteria are destroyed when exposed to open air. After all, what is the impetus to sin but a lack of consideration for others, which then manifests itself in various deeds? It is therefore plausible that when we begin to express such consideration for others spontaneously, we rise beyond occasions to sin and attract the notice, and thus the mercy and compassion, of the Higher Forces.*

This Beatitude counters characteristics represented by the astrological archetype Leo. Astrology connects Leo to the need to exercise power and assume authority in situations where leadership is required. This characteristic, in its pure form, is intended to give us a sense of determination and commitment. However, in many instances in which we have access to power and authority, we may allow personal gratification to destroy our sense of compassion. By practicing mercy and compassion consciously, we can resist temptations of self-aggrandizement.

---

*See comment regarding "higher-level realities" in the previous footnote, this chapter.

6. Blessed are the pure in heart, for they shall see God.

As a promise or a conditional statement, this is confusing. On the surface, it suggests that those who have pure hearts get to see God. However, it does not define purity of heart, nor what it means to see God.

As a categorical statement, however, this Beatitude makes sense. The purity of heart talked about here is not intended to be interpreted in the ordinary sense of being chaste, which reflects the Greek *hagnos*, but rather in the sense of being clear. This latter definition is derived from the Greek *katharos*, and when used in conjunction with *heart*, means being clear in our emotions, or clearly seeing the motives for our actions. The heart is a symbol for the emotional side of our nature; a clear heart would therefore mean feelings that are unjumbled and appropriate, and motives that are known. This last point is important, for it implies taking responsibility for all our actions, even those which may not appear to be deliberate. It means no longer attributing the events of our life to mistakes, accidents, or misfortune, but looking to the hidden causes in ourselves.

The concluding part of this Beatitude suggests that the one with a clear heart would see God. To *see,* here, does not mean to perceive with the physical eye, or even to understand, but seeing as in making sure, or taking heed, of something. The word translated as "see" was derived from the Greek word *horao.* Other examples of its use are found in Matthew 8:4 "See (*horao*) that you tell no man" and Matthew 24:6 "See (*horao*) that you be not troubled." The Greek word used to represent the physical act of seeing is *theoreo,* as in John 6:19, which says "they see (*theoreo*) Jesus walking on the sea."

The resulting message of this Beatitude is that clarity in the emotional aspect of our being enables us to take heed of God. This idea conveys that "seeing" God, in the sense of taking heed of his presence, depends wholly upon the individual. The implication is that

God is always present; it's our conflicting emotions that obscure his presence. When we reword this Beatitude, we get: "Happy are those who are clear in their hearts, for they shall take heed of the presence of God."

This Beatitude speaks to the way an individual must strive to accurately express the archetypal characteristics of Virgo. Virgo represents the mental impulse to verify things for oneself, to "experience." In expressing this impulse, it's easy to lose one's bearings, to get lost in the details. To avoid losing oneself in the experiencing, which can lead to disorientation and disorganization—the impulse to verify must begin with oneself, with our desires and motives. It is only when we are clear about our own motives and desires that we can be objective, and it is only by being objective that we can benefit from our various experiences.

7. Blessed are the peacemakers, for they shall be called sons of God.

This Beatitude begins a new subcycle of six. Beatitudes 1 through 6 comprise the first subcycle, which deals with inner attunement, but beginning with the seventh, they speak to outer-world action.

The only modification to this Beatitude in terms of its intended meaning is the phrase *sons of God.* To be a son of God goes beyond gender; it refers to a stage of maturity in our relationship with the Creator.

The idea of equating peacemaking with sonship to God can be attributed to the phenomenon that by helping to bring peace to warring factions, we exercise one of the first attributes of divinity: establishing order out of chaos. It should be noted, too, that this concept of sonship is that which Jesus used to describe himself in relationship to God. So, in reality, the peacemaker is credited with having Christlike characteristics.

In its relationship to astrological archetypes, this Beatitude concerns the characteristics of the sign Libra. This is the seventh zodiacal sign and relates to the impulse to come to grips with pairs of opposites. Inner conflict is the most common psychological expression of this impulse, and to conquer it, the individual must turn his attention to the outside world in the capacity of a peacemaker.

8. Blessed are those who are persecuted for righteousness' sake, for theirs is the Kingdom of Heaven.

This Beatitude is the second one dealing with outer-world action. What is encouraged here is not an attitude that courts persecution, but one that calls forth courage in the face of opposition to a life dedicated to the cause of righteousness.

The righteousness encouraged here, and that upon which persecution acts to facilitate one's self-transformation, is not self-righteousness, but a personal commitment to justness (from the Greek *dikaiosune*). It refers to individuals who are committed to the common good, to "the Way of Life." For indeed, the pursuit of the common good is *the way of life* in the same way that the pursuit of individual glory is *the way of death*.

The part persecution plays in transformation is that it provides the individual with verification that he is following the right course of action. If our actions always meet with popular approval, it might mean that we are basing our actions not on conviction and understanding of principles, but on expediency.

This Beatitude addresses problems encountered in expressing the archetypal energies of the sign Scorpio. In the annals of astrology, the impulse attributed to Scorpio is that of perseverance and tenacity. These characteristics can become fanaticism, if not expressed as an effort of righteous living, or living for the common good.

9. Blessed are you when others revile you and persecute you and utter all kinds of evil against you falsely on my account....

The ninth Beatitude is rounded off by an additional verse that says, "Rejoice and be glad, for your reward is great in heaven, for so they persecuted the prophets who were before you." This Beatitude is directed at those who respond to the inner call to share their faith and live out the principles attributed to Christ. Jesus is saying that such individuals are in the company of the prophets who have gone before them. Consequently, they should not feel discouraged, but should rejoice, since they will receive compensation for their work.

This Beatitude is related to the astrological sign of Sagittarius. The archetypal impulses attributed to this sign deal with receiving and disseminating knowledge to foster higher learning and philosophical pursuits.

10. You are the salt of the earth, but if salt has lost its taste, how shall its saltiness be restored? It is no longer good for anything except to be thrown out and trampled under people's feet.

This particular Beatitude and the two that follow do not fit the pattern of the previous nine. Here, Jesus is giving an exhortation to those who have difficulty expressing their understanding of the purpose of life. The imagery of salt, especially when used as a metaphor for someone involved in a spiritual search, suggests that if we can sense the purpose of life, we should be able to benefit others on contact. After all, it is an understanding of life's inner meaning that makes the events of life palatable. Those who appreciate life's meaning, then, should act as a source of encouragement to those not yet so blessed; otherwise, their knowledge and understanding add to naught.

This Beatitude addresses the characteristics of the archetype of Capricorn. The impulse of this archetype is to give a practical orientation to life. Improperly interpreted, this impulse can become materialism, in which case, we become as salt that has lost its seasoning properties.

11. **You are the light of the world. A city set on a hill cannot be hidden. Nor do people light a lamp and put it under a basket, but on a stand, and it gives light to all in the house.**

This exhortation is similar to the previous one. Here, Jesus is addressing those who have obtained inner realizations of Truth. However, there are no commendations in this Beatitude as in the previous one. This suggests that being a light, or a source of illumination, is its own fulfillment.

The term *light* used here was translated from the Greek term *phos,* and was also used to describe Jesus's appearance at the transfiguration and the radiance experienced by Paul (alias Saul) at his conversion. The word connotes more a sense of radiation than of visible light. Thus, to be a light to the world in this sense is to positively influence those with whom we interact by offering them a practical demonstration of how spiritual principles play out in our lives.

The symbols that Jesus used in this and the previous Beatitude (salt and light) represent different levels of influencing the world at large. Salt works by giving of itself, and light by being true to itself. As such, these items represent two modes of facilitating the spiritual advancement of mankind—salt symbolizing practical orientation and light the embodiment of principles.

This Beatitude is directed at the impulse attributed to the astrological archetype of Aquarius. This impulse finds expression in the need to be a trendsetter, an inventor, and an innovator. Those responding to the Aquarian impulse become the visionaries and reformers in society. The negative potential to expressing this archetypal impulse is that an individual so occupied could become eccentric and cut off from the rest of mankind, instead of becoming its inspiration.

12. Do not think that I have come to abolish the Law or the Prophets; I have not come to abolish them, but to fulfill them.

Although the seventeenth through twentieth verses of Matthew 5 present a radical departure from the format of the Beatitudes proper, the address here completes the full cycle of twelve Beatitudes, to correspond with twelve astrological signs. The full text of these verses is as follows:

> Do not think that I have come to abolish the Law or the Prophets; I have not come to abolish them but to fulfill them. [18] For truly, I say to you, until heaven and earth pass away, not an iota, not a dot, will pass from the Law until all is accomplished. [19] Therefore whoever relaxes one of the least of these commandments and teaches others to do the same will be called least in the Kingdom of Heaven, but whoever does them and teaches them will be called great in the Kingdom of Heaven. [20] For I tell you, unless your righteousness exceeds that of the scribes and Pharisees, you will never enter the Kingdom of Heaven.

In the eleven preceding instructions, Jesus pinpointed the values that we should try to cultivate and express. Here, he is talking about what to expect from one who has succeeded in mastering the first eleven stages.

Up to the ninth Beatitude, we saw a progression of values being promoted. In the tenth and eleventh Beatitudes, then, we saw injunctions concerning our being a source of influence and inspiration for others. Once those stages of development are completed, questions may arise as to the status of the "old order" in relation to this "new being" that has emerged as a result of this program of transformation engineered by the prior series of instructions. Here, Jesus stands as a symbol, a representative, of this the new being. In this role, he discloses that he is not come to destroy the law (or more accurately, "loose down," from the Greek *kataluo*) but to fulfill it, (or more accurately, amplify, from the Greek *pleroo)*. This suggests that it is the responsibility of the one experiencing a transformation of being not to use the freedom he experiences from his new-found liberation from conventional wisdom to destroy systems other people need to support their spiritual development.

In the context of astrology, Jesus's statement speaks to the end of one era, or astrological Age, and the beginning of another. More specifically, his closing comments deal indirectly with the archetypal impulse of the sign of Pisces. One of the main characteristics of the Pisces archetype is the urge to validate personal experiences by erecting and associating with institutions that enshrine and protect social values (e.g., government, community establishments). By referencing himself here, Jesus identified himself with the impulse of the Pisces archetype. Astrologically, the impulse of Pisces was to be the keynote for world history for the next two thousand years.

Incidentally, it is said in astrological circles that the Age of Pisces was ushered in around the time of Jesus, meaning that the spring equinox was, at that time, oriented to the sign of Pisces.

This concept of Ages is derived from the fact that Earth regresses in space slightly each year after completing one revolution around the sun. The value of this regression amounts to only fifty seconds of arc, but over the course of seventy-two years, this would result in the start of the astronomical year (i.e., at the spring equinox or the first degree of Aries) being "precessed" by one full degree. Over the course of 2,160 years, the recession would amount to thirty degrees, or an entire zodiacal sign.[3] It is the completion of thirty degrees of precession that is called an Age. At the time of Jesus, the Piscean Age was just beginning, meaning that the spring equinox was oriented to the sign of Pisces. By the same principle, we are now at the threshold of the Aquarian Age, since this is the sign that would coincide with the spring equinox after it precesses out of the sign of Pisces.

With this as background, Jesus's statement about coming not to repeal the law of Moses but to amplify it tells us that the end of one age and the beginning of another does not call for the abolition of old precepts that were given to aid our spiritual development.

EIGHT

SPIRITUAL PRACTICES FOR RELEASING BLOCKED ENERGY AT THE CHAKRAS

OVERVIEW

In this chapter, we turn our attention to the second segment, or layer, of instructions in Mathew—those found in the Sermon on the Mount. Recall from chapter 7 that the instructions given in Matthew 5:21–48 deal with two challenges relating to the transformation of consciousness: (1) strengthening the intellect through the acquisition of values and (2) stopping the misapplication of energy at the emotional level. In the second segment, covered in this chapter, Jesus addresses human shortcomings that can lead to a hardening or crystallization of the life force as it seeks to express itself through us. These shortcomings relate to murder, adultery, divorce, the making of oaths, reciprocal violence (i.e., an eye for an eye), and the social status quo (e.g., loving one's friends and hating one's enemies).

Except for two of the offences—murder and adultery, which are included in the Ten Commandments—the list does not exactly parallel anything found in the Old Testament, but adheres to a new formulation. In addition, the selection of shortcomings and the order in which they are presented in Matthew conform to the concept of the sevenfold nature of our being, which finds expression in the chakra system. Using our understanding of chakras, we can now examine the program presented by Jesus for enabling us to overcome such shortcomings by first identifying their sources within. When our inner nature is changed for the better, outer observances can then become a spontaneous outflowing from within. Observances of the spirit of the law and of the letter of the law then become unified.

CONSCIOUSNESS AS "ENERGY"

The work involved in changing our nature can be understood in terms of refining the manner in which we express the energy of life. This idea of energy as it relates to expressions of human consciousness takes on a different meaning than the ordinary one, which generally relates to some kind of force. When we think of energy in the context of Consciousness, we need to think more in terms of spaciousness, expansiveness, boundlessness, etc. As individuals, we each have access to this primordial energy of Consciousness, which we appropriate and express in our own fashion. In describing how this notion of energy relates to our efforts to transform our consciousness, author and transformation facilitator Dr. Richard Moss, eloquently writes:

> We can think of energy as occupying a range of expressions across a spectrum. At one end of the spectrum is Pure Energy or Consciousness. This is energy not yet particularized into the familiar and identifiable. It is unconstrained beingness, a primordial field of being out of which particular forms emerge. At the other end of the spectrum, energy becomes crystallized or held captive by the rigid boundaries with which we perceive aspects of reality. Because energy is the basis for life, it is also experienced directly. Most basically, energy is vitality, sexuality, feeling, intensity, but it is also a felt presence or current in and around the body. It is important to be able to directly sense and move energy as a stage in developing awareness. To be able consciously to shift

our level of energy allows us to move from focusing only on the content of consciousness to appreciating more subtle dimensions that tend to determine the quality and type of psychic content. *Higher energy refers to a more inclusive, universal awareness, while lower energy refers to a denser, more personalized consciousness. Higher energy is increased sensitivity. At higher energies, more formlessness and ambiguity can be accommodated in an individual's consciousness, and there is more fluidity between subject and object, less rigidity between what is habitually considered to be self and not-self.*[1] (emphasis added)

In the discussions to follow, we need to keep this understanding of energy in mind as we match up various teachings of Jesus in the Sermon on the Mount with the different chakras. After all, these teachings are really instructions aimed at getting us to put an end to the misuse of the energy of Consciousness that flows and manifests through each chakra.

We can also apply the notion of blockage to the idea of misusing energy since any improper usage of the primordial energy of Consciousness means that we are not deriving the benefit we can from its proper utilization. Consequently, any action we can take to stop the misuse or misapplication of this energy results in releasing or unblocking it. In chapter 9, we will encounter additional instructions from the Sermon on the Mount that are directed at facilitating the flow of this primordial Energy.

UNBLOCKING THE FLOW OF ENERGY AT THE MULADHARA CHAKRA

It is to correct the way we express the primordial energy of Consciousness at the first chakra, the Muladhara, that the instructions in Matthew 5:21-26 are addressed:

[21]You have heard that it was said to those of old, 'You shall not murder; and whoever murders will be liable to judgment.' [22] But I say to you that everyone who is angry with his brother will be liable to judgment; whoever insults his brother will be liable to the council; and whoever says, 'You fool!' will be liable to the hell of fire. [23] So if you are offering your gift at the altar and there remember that your brother has something against you, [24] leave your gift there before the altar and go. First be reconciled to your brother, and then come and offer your gift. [25] Come to terms quickly with your accuser while you are going with him to court, lest your accuser hand you over to the judge, and the judge to the guard, and you be put in prison. [26] Truly, I say to you, you will never get out until you have paid the last penny.

Here, Jesus is portraying the law against murder as a smaller aspect of a greater spiritual law. That greater law speaks to cooperation, which, when violated, leads to anger and enmity, its ultimate expression being the act of murder. To get rid of the seeds of disunity, we must abstain from holding grudges. As well, we must endeavor not to give another cause to hold a grudge against us.

In terms of the chakra concept, we are dealing with the energy of Consciousness as expressed through the first chakra. This first chakra, the Muladhara, transforms the biological life impulse into the instinct for survival. This instinct, when exaggerated, can lead to the law of the jungle, or "survival of the fittest." To unblock the life impulse at the Muladhara Chakra, we must learn cooperation and coexistence. It is only when we incorporate this consciousness of cooperation and coexistence into our mode of being that we will be able to rid ourselves of the emotional causes of violence, namely anger and malice.

UNBLOCKING THE FLOW OF LIFE ENERGY AT THE SVADVISHTHANA CHAKRA

In explaining how to unblock the flow of life energy at the second chakra (Svadvishthana), Jesus gives a reinterpretation of the law against adultery:

> [27] You have heard that it was said, 'You shall not commit adultery.' [28] But I say to you that everyone who looks at a woman with lustful intent has already committed adultery with her in his heart. [29] If your right eye causes you to sin, tear it out and throw it away. For it is better that you lose one of your members than that your whole body be thrown into hell. [30] And if your right hand causes you to sin, cut it off and throw it away. For it is better that you lose one of your members than that your whole body go into hell. (Matt. 5:27–30)

First, Jesus presents the traditional interpretation of infidelity, and then he proceeds to give an updated one. His characteristic "but I say to you" introduces an update from one of greater authority. It's as if he is saying, "Forget what you've been told; here are your new orders." As a representation of the Principle of Life, Jesus was able to review the Mosaic Code of behavior from a dynamic perspective rather than a statutory one. From this higher perspective, infidelity begins in one's heart, in the place where desires begin. For it is only because we desire something that we seize an opportunity to acquire it. If we do not find an opportunity, however, we are no better than someone who did find it and take advantage of it.

As a whole, this passage describes how we can control the tension of polarity and stop the misappropriation of life energy at the second chakra. It is this tension in the being that expresses itself as the desire for sexual gratification. The instructions, "If your right eye causes you to sin, tear it out and throw it away" and "if your right hand causes you to sin, cut it off and throw it away" suggest that we use all practical means available to counter the automatic mode of mental functioning that draws us into entanglements, whether of the mind or of the body. This practice is of particular benefit to the individual who may not know how to deal with desires and impulses which, though "natural," may be a hindrance to his spiritual advancement.

The second chakra is sometimes referred to as the sex center, but only because sex is the most characteristic way in which the tension created by polarity seeks release. Here, the misdirection of the energy of life has other manifestations such as pride, liking and disliking, attachments and aversions, feelings of superiority and inferiority—in short, psychological complexes.

Unblocking the Flow of Life Energy at the Manipura Chakra

In the instructions directed at unblocking the flow of life energy at the Manipura or third chakra, Jesus took up the subject of divorce.

> [31]It was also said, 'Whoever divorces his wife, let him give her a certificate of divorce.' [32] But I say to you that everyone who divorces his wife, except on the ground of sexual immorality, makes her commit adultery, and whoever marries a divorced woman commits adultery. (Matthew 6:31–32)

Jesus was not talking about divorce as it exists in the twentieth and twenty-first centuries, but as it existed in a social system where the woman was clearly the victim. In Jewish society, in Old and New Testament times, the rules about divorce required that a man give a woman documents proving that she was divorced from him. This was to offer her minimum protection from being accused of adultery and undergoing the associated penalty, which was death by stoning. What was instituted as a minimal condition of divorce, however, became a satisfying condition. Therefore, Jesus's intent was to impress upon us not to abuse the power of having authority over another. This principle is applicable to marriage and any other situation in which an individual, male or female, may have the upper hand. Jesus's warning that a man who unjustifiably rejects his wife would cause her to commit adultery is, in essence, a warning to those who would twist agreements and laws to suit themselves.

The misdirection of life energy at the Manipura Chakra takes the form of one-upmanship, exploitation, and abuse of power and authority. Just like the husband, whom Jesus required to act responsibly toward his wife, anyone in a position of authority must learn to act in fairness and consideration for all parties involved.

UNBLOCKING THE FLOW OF LIFE ENERGY AT THE ANAHATA CHAKRA

The teaching directed at unblocking the flow of life energy at the Anahata Chakra focuses on the issue of making oaths and swearing (i.e., calling God to witness):

> [33]Again you have heard that it was said to those of old, 'You shall not swear falsely, but shall perform to the Lord what you have sworn.' [34] But I say to you, Do not take an oath at all, either by heaven, for it is the throne of God, [35] or by the earth, for it is his footstool, or by Jerusalem, for it is the city of the great King. [36] And do not take an oath by your head, for you cannot make one hair white or black. [37] Let what you say be simply 'Yes' or 'No'; anything more than this comes from evil. (Matthew 5:33–37)

This teaching is related to the fourth or Anahata Chakra, because this center is concerned with forming associations and cultivating a sense of at-homeness. When the expression of life is thwarted at this point, the result is an approval complex. We may go to any length to win approval from our fellowman, even to the extent of invoking God as an arbiter in petty human transactions. It is against such presumptuousness that we are told not to swear at all—and the reason behind such an instruction is that we should be able to stand on our own reputation. Our word should be sufficient in whatever commitments we undertake, and if we cannot convince others of our capacity to complete an undertaking, we should, in all humility, accept the consequences. It is better for us to endure being held in low esteem than to try to win approval by making invocations.

For the energy of life to have an unobstructed flow through the Anahata Chakra, then, we should not allow the urge toward unity and camaraderie engendered at this level to degenerate into a compulsive need for approval and acceptance.

Unblocking the Flow of Life Energy at the Vishuddha Chakra

This section addresses the misuse of life energy at the fifth or Vishuddha Chakra. This chakra is concerned with exposing the hidden principles of nature and expressing them in practical terms. However, when there is a misinterpretation of the energy flow here, we become a slave to formula, blind to the fact that natural "laws" are but partial reflections of higher, spiritual principles. In tackling this problem, Jesus said:

> [38] You have heard that it was said, 'An eye for an eye and a tooth for a tooth.' [39] But I say to you, Do not resist the one who is evil. But if anyone slaps you on the right cheek, turn to him the other also. [40] And if anyone would sue you and take your tunic, let him have your cloak as well. [41] And if anyone forces you to go one mile, go with him two miles. [42] Give to the one who begs from you, and do not refuse the one who would borrow from you. (Matthew 5:38–42)

Jesus was showing, in unequivocal terms, that the so-called law of blind retribution, "An eye for an eye and a tooth for a tooth," must be superseded by the higher spiritual principle of nonresistance. This idea of nonresistance has a lot more significance to it than being a willing victim, or allowing others to take advantage of one, whether it be physical, legal, or emotional advantage. The full reasoning behind this teaching is best understood in the context of the Eastern idea of karma.

The concept of karma is that every human act will bring its own recompense, whether good or bad. Karma is seen as an inviolable law. In popular understanding, it operates mechanically—the murderer will be murdered, the thief will suffer material loss, etc. The formulation of this law in its simple form seems to satisfy mankind's thirst for vengeance as well as the idea that, reciprocating hurt for hurt, we are acting as an instrument for the expression of Divine Will.

Jesus's message is that man must not play God. When an individual takes the law into his own hands and insists on vengeance or recompense, he is perpetuating "the wheel" of karma. First, the one from whom recompense is exacted may not change his way. Second, the one doing the punishing has no guarantee that similar acts by different individuals will not be committed against him in the future. In essence, after the law of karma is satisfied, tit for tat, the world remains basically the same.

The higher spiritual law that Jesus is propounding to renovate our idea of karma (as popularly understood) is one that stops, once and for all, the vicious cycle of injury and retribution, assault and counterassault. Just because an act of violence goes unreciprocated does not mean it goes unpunished. When we accept an injury without resistance, we set forces in motion that ensure the offender comes to terms with his problem. The conscience and higher aspects of his being ultimately create an internal source of pressure for change that might not have been, had he met with resistance.*

Nonresistance also facilitates a net change in the world for good. When we voluntarily assume higher obligations than those demanded of us, we

---

*This does not apply to the punishment of crimes at the level of society. But it does suggest that an injured party not use such occasions as an opportunity for triumph.

are invoking the living spirit of Christ on our behalf. Since Christ symbolizes the Principle of Life, we are, in so doing, each allowing ourselves to become a larger receptacle and eventually a conduit for a greater flow of life. The misdirection of life energy at the fifth chakra is thus corrected when we can discern higher spiritual laws and place them ahead of lower, shortsighted ones.

UNBLOCKING THE FLOW OF LIFE ENERGY AT THE AJNA CHAKRA

In addressing the misdirection of the flow of life energy at the Ajna Chakra, Jesus said:

> [43] You have heard that it was said, 'You shall love your neighbor and hate your enemy.' [44] But I say to you, Love your enemies and pray for those who persecute you, [45] so that you may be sons of your Father who is in heaven. For he makes his sun rise on the evil and on the good, and sends rain on the just and on the unjust. [46] For if you love those who love you, what reward do you have? Do not even the tax collectors do the same? [47] And if you greet only your brothers, what more are you doing than others? Do not even the Gentiles do the same? [48] You therefore must be perfect, as your heavenly Father is perfect. (Matthew 5:43–47)

The proper expression of life energy here is in the form of objective love, or love as a principle. Such an expression of love does not require an object to make it operable. When the proper expression of life is thwarted at this stage, the effect is narcissism. Instead of love as a principle, there is self-love—we love those who love us and hate those who hate us. The true test of impersonal or objective love is that we can relate to someone from his or her own center of awareness. This center is occupied by the self-love that each of us has for him or herself. Thus, to truly love someone we must be able to identify with that person's self-love. And this is not easy. But it is only then that we can fully relate to how someone sees the world. That way, we can love even our enemies and seek divine favor for those who curse and abuse us. But of course, we do not pray for those who abuse us in order for them to be able to continue their abusive behavior.

One of the mysteries of prayer is that when we pray for others, the energy we direct towards them in prayer acts to promote their own spiritual advancement. Jesus says that by living in this manner, we emulate the father in heaven who "makes his sun rise on the evil and on the good, and sends rain on the just and on the unjust." In other words, impersonal, objective love is the property of God, and the surest path for man to reach God is to take on some of his attributes.

In the East, the uninhibited expression of the energy of life at the Ajna Chakra is equated with a state of enlightenment. An enlightened person is said to have realized his true Self. With this realization comes the power to awaken others to greater awareness of the purpose of life. By letting life have uninhibited flow, we become imbued with the mind of Christ.

ALLOWING LIFE TO HAVE UNBRIDLED EXPRESSION AT THE SAHASRARA CHAKRA

When the flow of life becomes unblocked through the other six chakras, we become the embodiment of Life as a principle. It is this unbridled expression of life that Jesus was encouraging when he said, "You therefore must be perfect, as your heavenly Father is perfect" (Matthew 5:48).

The sense in which Jesus indicated that we become perfect is that of a process. The Greek word that was translated to perfect was teleios, actually meaning "complete" or "ended." Here, we are dealing with a perfection that suggests fruitfulness—achieving a process rather than just arriving at a certain fixed state.

Another example where the term perfect was used in this sense is in Matthew 19:21. The context finds a man asking Jesus what he must do to get eternal life.* Jesus said to him: "If you would enter life, keep the commandments." When the man asked him to name the commandments he should keep, Jesus specified the following: "You shall not murder, You shall not commit adultery, You shall not steal, You shall not bear false witness, Honor your father and mother, and You shall love your neighbor as yourself" (Matthew 19:18–19). At this point the man replied, "All these I have kept. What do I still lack?" Jesus's final answer to him was, "If you would be perfect, go, sell what you possess and give to the poor, and you will have treasure in heaven; and come, follow me" (Matthew 19:20–21). Here again, we get the sense of process. The man was given certain requirements, and when it was disclosed that he had fulfilled them, he was given yet more. In other words, perfection is ongoing. It is related to the process of bearing fruit continuously.

The Sahasrara Chakra is often referred to as the "thousand-petaled lotus." This is really meant as metaphor, as no specific number is intended. In ancient times, when this image was formulated, a thousand was a sufficiently large number to give the impression of plentitude, especially when associated with the petals of a lotus. The imagery it conjures is of a flower that goes on blooming and blooming—an apt description of the unbridled expression of life.

---

*This incident was previously discussed in Chapter 3 in the context of applying esoteric interpretation to New Testament scripture.

NINE

STOKING THE FIRES OF TRANSFORMATION THROUGH SPIRITUAL EXERCISES

THE ROLE OF VIRTUES IN FACILITATING A TRANSFORMATION OF CONSCIOUSNESS

After correcting the misapplication of life energy at each chakra, we must take proactive measures to ensure the continued upward flow and refinement of that energy. This upward movement of energy constitutes the ascent of Kundalini in the Eastern tradition. While in the Eastern approach, however, Kundalini is pursued through the practice of specific techniques, in the biblical approach, Kundalini is the end product of a process of whole-life changes.

As such, what we have in the Sermon on the Mount is a program aimed at enhancing our entire life; we commit to a way of life that, in turn, engages a certain process, the end result of which is the activation of Kundalini. It bears emphasizing here that Kundalini activation is the fruit of a *transformational process*, not the fruit of technique. An analogy could be made in which an individual is depositing funds into a savings account at a bank. He has committed himself to a particular savings target, but because the funds already committed earn interest, he may exceed his initial target. Just as interest is regarded as the fruit of the saving process, rather than the goal of saving, the Kundalini experience must be regarded as the fruit, rather than the goal, of a particular life orientation.

Given their role in the advocacy of virtuous behavior, the instructions found in the sixth and seventh chapters of Matthew have merit on their own, and it is not necessary for one to be aware of the structure or design behind them. However, such awareness can help individuals see these instructions as objective principles, and therefore as psychology, rather than as just the personal approach of one religious teacher. In these instructions, Jesus deals with seven classes of exercises. Three of these he assumes are already part of our religious practice, but he offers us advice for making them more effective. These exercises are the following:

(1) Giving alms
(2) Praying
(3) Fasting

By looking at these three exercises in depth, we get a clearer idea of their psychological value. More specifically, practicing them is the equivalent of moving energy through the first, second, and third chakras, successively to the fourth.

The fourth through seventh exercises are then added, provided that the necessary groundwork has been established in the practice of the first three.

(4) The fourth exercise concerns the cultivation of trust. We are encouraged to pursue our transformative work with unwavering confidence and must not let worldly concerns distract us.

(5) The fifth exercise concerns the cultivation of humility. Here, we must learn the bounds of relationships, a task satisfied by an appreciation of the proper use of knowledge. We are not to use our knowledge to criticize others, for example, or to flaunt it before unappreciative audiences.

(6) The sixth exercise concerns the cultivation of creativity, which

comes through the ability to recognize and respond to the needs of others. In this capacity, we must become divine emissaries, learning to ask without fear and to give without grudge.

(7) Finally, in the seventh exercise, we must learn to practice discernment. We must exercise caution within and without as we try to sort the false teacher from the true.

We will now look into these exercises in more detail, showing how each one takes the individual successively closer in the direction of a union with the Divine.

FIRST EXERCISE: SHARING

The exercise of sharing is described as giving alms, or, to use a more modem concept, giving to charity. The principle behind sharing is that the very act affirms the cooperation that should exist between individuals. No longer are we living at the level of the first chakra (Muladhara), in which competition and survival of the fittest are predominant. Instead, we are realizing that the brotherhood of man is an ideal to be striven for, and we are willing to give of our resources to bring this goal about. In showing us how to share without making a show of it, Jesus said:

> [1]Beware of practicing your righteousness before other people in order to be seen by them, for then you will have no reward from your Father who is in heaven.
>
> [2] Thus, when you give to the needy, sound no trumpet before you, as the hypocrites do in the synagogues and in the streets, that they may be praised by others. Truly, I say to you, they have received their reward. [3] But when you give to the needy, do not let your left hand know what your right hand is doing [4] so that your giving may be in secret. And your Father who sees in secret will reward you. (Matt. 6:1–4)

It is important to note that the merits of making the act of sharing part of our spiritual practice is not addressed as an issue, as it is assumed that we're already doing it. The real lesson here is what constitutes a true sacrifice. Someone who parts with some of his resources to help others is only truly sacrificing if he is doing it for the benefit of the other, and expects nothing in return. If he does expect a return, no matter how subtle (even praise or esteem), then it is not a sacrifice, but an exchange—just as any ordinary commercial transaction.

This is why Jesus said that whoever gives his possessions to receive praise from others already has a reward. In contrast, the one who does not "let his left hand know what his right hand is doing" will receive his reward from the Father.

There seems to be a contradiction here, in that a reward is a reward. If we expect heavenly rewards, we are not entering into the spirit of giving any more than if we expect earthly ones. But not to let our left hand know what our right hand is doing simply refers to the idea that we do not associate cause and effect when it comes to giving to charity. This is because the right hand is associated with cause and the left hand with effect. Further, to be rewarded by the Father does not mean that we get compensation for our acts of charity. It means that we learn the lesson that this action is intended to teach, and add this newly acquired knowledge to the contents of our consciousness. It is from this expanded consciousness that we are ultimately rewarded by the Father.

SECOND EXERCISE: CONSCIOUS ATTUNEMENT, OR PRAYER

Again, Jesus took it for granted that prayer is part of the transformative work each individual is engaged in. But in his instructions on the proper mode of prayer, we get an idea of the true purpose of this activity. It is an exercise in attunement; it brings us to a remembrance of our divine heritage. For this attunement to succeed, however, we must ensure that there is no carryover from the first chakra imbalances—namely, the inability to forgive.

Complete attunement requires us to be free from feelings of hate because to realize our divine heritage as a reality, we must exercise one of the attributes of the Divine—forgiveness. We must do this because the validity of our divine heritage is contingent upon the validity of the divine heritage of our fellowman. In presenting this lesson, Jesus said:

> [5] And when you pray, you must not be like the hypocrites. For they love to stand and pray in the synagogues and at the street corners, that they may be seen by others. Truly, I say to you, they have received their reward. [6] But when you pray, go into your room and shut the door and pray to your Father who is in secret. And your Father who sees in secret will reward you.
>
> [7] And when you pray, do not heap up empty phrases as the Gentiles do, for they think that they will be heard for their many words. [8] Do not be like them, for your Father knows what you need before you ask him. [9] Pray then like this:
>
>> "Our Father in heaven, hallowed be your name. [10] Your kingdom come, your will be done, on earth as it is in heaven. [11] Give us this day our daily bread, [12] and forgive us our debts, as we also have forgiven our debtors. [13] And lead us not into temptation, but deliver us from evil.
>
> [14] For if you forgive others their trespasses, your heavenly Father will also forgive you, [15] but if you do not forgive others their trespasses, neither will your Father forgive your trespasses. (Matthew 6:5–15)

We also have, in this teaching, the well-known Lord's Prayer. Although much has been written and preached about this prayer, we still have something to learn from it, particularly when we realize that its aim is to facilitate transformation through the second chakra. The second chakra, if you recall, polarizes the generic life impulse so that we experience and relate to life as an interplay of opposites: male and female, good and bad, self and not-self, etc. The idea of this prayer is to counter that impulse, seeding our consciousness with the reality of the unity of all of creation.

The prayer begins by addressing "Our Father in heaven" to entrench in our awareness that we all share a common point of origin; we are all children of God, brothers and sisters in one spiritual family. It follows that we should all desire that the Kingdom of God be established on Earth and that its rule direct the affairs of humankind.

Next comes a request, as from a child to a father, that God ensure our necessary sustenance (daily bread).

The second request, for God to forgive us our debts, establishes a *quid pro quo*, or an exchange of equal value. The question of forgiveness is thrown back at us. It becomes a matter of whether we can forgive our fellowman. If we can, our forgiveness is assured; if not, no forgiveness can be forthcoming.

The subject of forgiveness is of special importance in the context of the transformation required at the second chakra. This is because the second chakra represents an opportunity to settle grievances resulting from frictions generated through first chakra preoccupations of survival and competition. Forgiving others by surrendering our accumulated grievances is the best way for us to lever ourselves out of such first-chakra entanglements.

Our failure to forgive others means that we cannot be forgiven of God, but not because God holds enmity, or because he takes personal offense when we sin. Failure to obtain forgiveness from God means that we have cut ourselves off from the everlasting, effervescent stream of Life that flows from God and back to God. Recall that in chapter 2, sin, in the context of the transformation of consciousness, is akin to blockage, stagnation, encrustation, and recoiling from the stream of Life. Forgiveness of sin, then, is the dissolution of these blockages, thus facilitating a reabsorption into the stream of Life. Indeed, forgiveness of others is the only way to obtain forgiveness by God, for in granting forgiveness to others, we are in effect granting it to ourselves.

Please refer to Appendix IV for additional insights on how the Lord's Prayer can be utilized for spiritual attunement.

THIRD EXERCISE: TEMPERING THE WILL (BY DEVELOPING PATIENCE)

This exercise deals with gaining the proper attitude to fasting. In Jesus's instructions, fasting appears to be more than a simple demonstration of piety. As with the instructions on sharing (giving of alms) and attunement (prayer), the spiritual aspirant must treat this activity as one between him and God alone. Only then will the person experience its benefit in full. It should be noted also that, once again, Jesus takes it for granted that fasting is part of the individual's spiritual practice.

> [16] And when you fast, do not look gloomy like the hypocrites, for they disfigure their faces that their fasting may be seen by others. Truly, I say to you, they have received their reward. [17] But when you fast, anoint your head and wash your face, [18] that your fasting may not be seen by others but by your Father who is in secret. And your Father who sees in secret will reward you. (Matthew 6:16–18)

The spiritual value of fasting is found in breaking the chain of causation in the stimulus-response mechanism in us. This mechanism ensures that every time a need arises, efforts are made to bring about its satisfaction. A delay in the need-fulfillment cycle helps to free us from the power that our appetites may have over us. In this regard, our will is strengthened—and with this will comes patience, for what is patience but the ability to wait?

The uninhibited flow of the life force through the third chakra marks an important point in transformation. After this stage is achieved, the individual reaches a significant milestone. He now changes his motivations to act from negative influences to higher principles, such as cooperation with others, a sense of purpose, and love. It is only when one acts from such higher motivations that one is living up to his capabilities as a human being. How else do we distinguish ourselves from the rest of the animal kingdom than through our ability to act out of principles and higher motivations?

The experiences of Jesus after his baptism by John the Baptist, recorded in Matthew 4, were an enactment of this life force flowing unimpeded through the three lower chakras. After his baptism, Jesus fasted for forty days and nights in the desert. At the end of this fast, he was tempted (i.e., tested) by the devil. Jesus was subjected to three tests:

The first temptation concerned the use of spiritual powers to satisfy physical needs:

> "If you are the Son of God, command these stones to become loaves of bread." (Matthew 4:3)

The second temptation dealt with the assertion of one's own specialness:

> "If you are the Son of God, throw yourself down, for it is written, 'He will command his angels concerning you,' and 'On their hands they will bear you up, lest you strike your foot against a stone." (Matthew 4:6)

The third test addressed the ever-present danger of falling under the spell of a power complex.

---

* The idea of a power complex relates to someone who sees himself as special and therefore not subject to the universal laws to which everyone else is subject.

> Again, the devil took him to a very high mountain and
> showed him all the kingdoms of the world and their glory.
> ⁹ And he said to him, "All these I will give you, if you will
> fall down and worship me." (Matthew 4: 8–9)

On each occasion, Jesus refuted the temptation to eventually triumph over the devil. After the devil left him, we are told that "angels came and ministered to him" (Matthew 4:11).

The underlying lesson of these temptations is this: Before we can claim sonship with God, we must triumph over first-, second-, and third-chakra issues. As illustrated in Figure 3, it is the combined influences of these three lower chakras that constitute the lower self. The devil, whom Jesus allowed to test him, can be interpreted as our lower nature—the source of all of our personal weaknesses and self-doubts. As such, this scene is the enactment of an identity crisis of a spiritual nature. It is also a birthing process. The birth pertains to the realm of true humanity, or fourth-chakra functions. It must be remembered that all this began with fasting, which facilitates the rebirthing process through the precipitation of a crisis in one's being. When this crisis abates, one is able to draw upon a larger pool of resources than was previously available to him to further his God-ordained purpose in life.

FOURTH EXERCISE: THE CULTIVATION OF TRUST

Conducting the life force through the fourth chakra is accomplished by cultivating trust in the transformation process. There are two aspects to this trust. The first is acquiring unwavering commitment to the process, an attitude fashioned by a singleness of purpose. The second aspect is acquiring the unshakable confidence that, by ordering our priorities so that things of the Spirit take precedence over things of the world, all will be well. The logical extension of this confidence is that we banish from our minds all those fretful anxieties concerning the practical needs of life.

Figure 3: Regions of the Higher and Lower Self

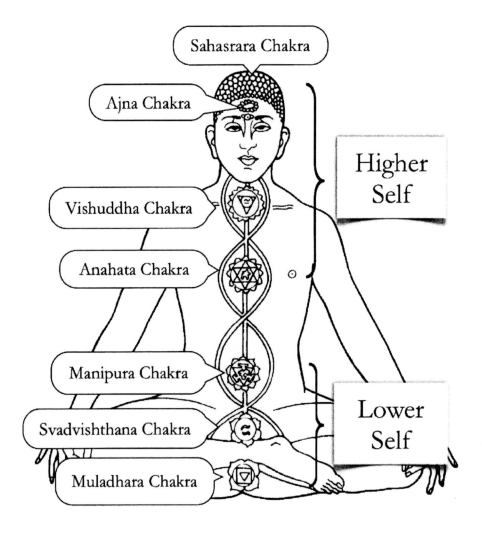

To address these two aspects of trust, Jesus's instructions in the sixth chapter of Matthew can be divided into two segments. The first segment extends from the nineteenth to the twenty-fourth verse:

> [19] Do not lay up for yourselves treasures on earth, where moth and rust destroy and where thieves break in and steal, [20] but lay up for yourselves treasures in heaven, where neither moth nor rust destroys and where thieves do not break in and steal. [21] For where your treasure is, there your heart will be also. (Matthew 6: 19–21)
>
> [22] The eye is the lamp of the body. So, if your eye is healthy, your whole body will be full of light, [23] but if your eye is bad, your whole body will be full of darkness. If then the light in you is darkness, how great is the darkness!
>
> [24] No one can serve two masters, for either he will hate the one and love the other, or he will be devoted to the one and despise the other. You cannot serve God and money. (Matthew 6: 22–24)

In this first segment, singleness of purpose is underscored by the saying that "No man can serve two masters," particularly when those masters are God and money (or wealth). The idea of polarizing God and money and presenting them as irreconcilable alternatives is based on the principle stated earlier in the excerpt that where one's treasures are, that is where his heart will be. Said another way, the question of whether we can outgrow the magnetic pull of the material world depends on how much vested interest we have in it. Since the type of existence that characterizes life at the fourth chakra is one of compassion and brotherhood, its expression here will be obstructed if we are satisfied with playing the existing state of affairs in the world to our personal advantage. We would have no interest in changing the existing order for one that reflects the values of brotherhood and compassion.

For the second segment of Jesus's teaching, we have the following:

> [25] Therefore I tell you, do not be anxious about your life, what you will eat or what you will drink, nor about your body, what you will put on. Is not life more than food, and the body more than clothing? [26] Look at the birds of the air: they neither sow nor reap nor gather into barns, and yet your heavenly Father feeds them. Are you not of more value than they? [27] And which of you by being anxious can add a single hour to his span of life? [28] And why are you anxious about clothing? Consider the lilies of the field, how they grow: they neither toil nor spin, [29] yet I tell you, even Solomon in all his glory was not arrayed like one of these. [30] But if God so clothes the grass of the field, which today is alive and tomorrow is thrown into the oven, will he not much more clothe you, O you of little faith? [31] Therefore do not be anxious, saying, "What shall we eat?" or "What shall we drink?" or "What shall we wear?" [32] For the Gentiles seek after all these things, and your heavenly Father knows that you need them all. [33] But seek first the Kingdom of God and his righteousness, and all these things will be added to you.
>
> [34] Therefore do not be anxious about tomorrow, for tomorrow will be anxious for itself. Sufficient for the day is its own trouble. (Matthew 6:25–34)

A popular interpretation of the second segment is that if we seek the kingdom of God, our material needs will be met. Such an interpretation runs the danger of turning spiritual seeking into just another commercial transaction. As long as we view things this way, spiritual seeking becomes just another ego-directed strategy to get what we want out of life, no different from any other method we may employ to secure material benefits.

With that in mind, it becomes clear that this exhortation is not to be interpreted as an enticement into spiritual pursuits for material gain, especially since the exhortation also adds the requirement that we ought to seek God's righteousness. God's righteousness is really God's standard of excellence for us, which is much higher than our own. Whereas our own standards of righteousness are based on our conscious understanding of ourselves, which is itself constructed upon our individual experiences, God's righteousness is based on what he knows our potential to be. Submitting ourselves to the righteousness of God, then, is to accept the standard of training that he sees fit for us. It is the same idea that Paul expresses here in his letter to the Hebrews:

> "My son, do not regard lightly the discipline of the Lord,
>   nor be weary when reproved by him.
> 6 For the Lord disciplines the one he loves,
>   and chastises every son whom he receives." (Hebrews 12:5–6)

The "discipline of the Lord," to use Paul's terminology, can be likened to an Olympic-level athletics coach taking on a high-school level athlete who has a significant amount of natural talent. Left to his own devices, the talented athlete might have measured success by his own personal-best performances. However, in the hands of the Olympic-level coach, he must broaden his sights, as his performances will be measured against a much higher standard of competition. The trainer must push the athlete beyond his self-perceived limits. Such is the situation in the life of the spiritual seeker who submits to God's standards of excellence.

FIFTH EXERCISE: THE CULTIVATION OF HUMILITY

Facilitating the life force through the fifth chakra is achieved by cultivating humility. As with the cultivation of trust at the previous chakra, nurturing humility is bounded by two observances. The first is to refrain from criticizing others and the second is not to indiscriminately disseminate the knowledge that we have acquired. In simple terms, we must be neither a self-appointed critic nor a self-appointed teacher.

In his instructions on how the life force can wind its way through the fifth chakra, Jesus had the following to say:

> [1] Judge not, that you be not judged. [2] For with the judgment you pronounce you will be judged, and with the measure you use it will be measured to you. [3] Why do you see the speck that is in your brother's eye, but do not notice the log that is in your own eye? [4] Or how can you say to your brother, 'Let me take the speck out of your eye,' when there is the log in your own eye? [5] You hypocrite, first take the log out of your own eye, and then you will see clearly to take the speck out of your brother's eye.
>
> [6] Do not give dogs what is holy, and do not throw your pearls before pigs, lest they trample them underfoot and turn to attack you. (Matthew 7:1–6)

It was earlier said that the Vishuddha Chakra is concerned with the discovery of the laws of nature. Here, we can broaden that definition to include the practical application of those laws. This is the essence of relationships—the capacity for perceiving similarities and dissimilarities between various phenomena. The danger of imposing abstract systems or laws on concrete situations is that premature conclusions can be drawn from an incomplete understanding. When it comes to the spiritual aspect of things, the problem is multiplied. The human mind cannot always grasp spiritual laws in their fullness, thus hasty attempts to draw hard and fast conclusions in a physical setting could be misguided. This is the reasoning behind the warning of Jesus that one should not judge another.

When we judge another, we overlook the fact that we cannot make another person responsible for our level of knowledge. When we acquire knowledge, it is to be used for ourselves, not to establish standards for others to follow. Another point worth mentioning is that not even the one who judges is capable of putting into practice all the knowledge he or she has acquired all of the time. Thus, when we judge another, we expect from them what we cannot accomplish in ourselves. This is indeed being hypocritical.

The second observance that rounds out the quest for humility is discretion with regard to esoteric knowledge. Jesus cautions that one should not "give that which is holy unto the dogs" (King James Version) nor "cast pearls before swine." In esoteric literature, there is a well-known principle that if information is imparted to another before that person is ready, more harm than good is done, as life lessons must be assimilated in steps. When we display our knowledge indiscriminately before another is ready, then we interrupt that person's progressive awakening.

A popular misconception about Jesus's caution is that his imagery casts aspersions on those who are not yet ready. Actually, if there is any aspersive intent, it is toward the one who tries to satisfy his own ego by indiscriminately displaying his knowledge. To "give that which is holy unto the dogs" or to "cast pearls before swine" portrays the one so doing as ignorant of the true value of the knowledge he has gained. It is not the fault of the swine that pearls have no aesthetic appeal, but it is certainly the fault of the one casting them not to know this.

SIXTH EXERCISE:
THE CULTIVATION OF CREATIVITY

The instructions Jesus gave relating to the sixth chakra concern the awakening of latent creativity. This is, however, not creativity in the sense of artistic expression, but in the sense of discerning and filling human needs, which is another expression of facilitating the flow of the life force in others.

As we examine the instructions given, we see two aspects to this creativity. The first is confidence and the second is a sense of stewardship. We thus find the following instructions directed at fostering these qualities:

[7] Ask, and it will be given to you; seek, and you will find; knock, and it will be opened to you. [8] For everyone who asks receives, and the one who seeks finds, and to the one who knocks it will be opened. [9] Or which one of you, if his son asks him for bread, will give him a stone? [10] Or if he asks for a fish, will give him a serpent? [11] If you then, who are evil, know how to give good gifts to your children, how much more will your Father who is in heaven give good things to those who ask him!

[12] So whatever you wish that others would do to you, do also to them, for this is the Law and the Prophets. (Matthew 7:7–12)

From these instructions, we see that the essential ingredient of creativity is confidence, or faith.* Aspiration, knowledge, and experience will accrue to us proportionate to our amount of faith. Further, our sense of certainty will determine the extent to which we believe that all barriers in our external life can be overcome. It follows that if barriers can be eliminated simply by asking God that they be removed, they only existed in the first place to coax this faith out of us.

In addition to faith and the confidence that goes with it, the individual must exercise stewardship to become a channel for bridging needs with the necessary resources. From the experience of filling needs in his own life, he can now turn to fill needs in the lives of others around him. The rule enunciated here that "whatever you wish that others would do to you, do also to them" constitutes the Golden Rule.

---

*In a spiritual sense, faith is a different kind of knowing, born from our orientation to the larger Reality of which our physical reality is only a small portion. To live a life of faith, we need to live at our "human possibility frontier," which is to be in contact with that which is highest in us and therefore closest to the Divine. Our level of faith is determined by our capacity to be in rapport with the subtle, the ineffable, and the inexpressible. This is where we make contact with the hidden principles of the Universe.

"Whatever you wish that others would do to you" includes situations in which we experience a need that can be satisfied by the initiative of someone else. The other part of the principle, "do also to them" suggests that instead of waiting for someone else to take the first step, we should realize that we are not unique, and that the very same need we experience exists in others. The task for us, then, would be to help others in the same way that we desire to be helped.

SEVENTH EXERCISE: THE CULTIVATION OF DISCERNMENT

Discernment is a quality that affects the transformation of one's whole being, which is why it is associated with the seventh chakra, the center identified with striving itself. In Jesus's instructions for facilitating the flow of the life force at this chakra, we see a couple of different facets of this discernment. First, it is discernment that enables us to choose the way of life (i.e., precepts to follow that are appropriate for us). It is also the expression of discernment that enables us to sense the consequences of not taking appropriate action to advance the transformational process when opportunities present themselves. On the subject of discernment, Jesus said:

> [13] Enter by the narrow gate. For the gate is wide and the way is easy that leads to destruction, and those who enter by it are many. [14] For the gate is narrow and the way is hard that leads to life, and those who find it are few.
>
> [15] Beware of false prophets, who come to you in sheep's clothing but inwardly are ravenous wolves. [16] You will recognize them by their fruits. Are grapes gathered from thorn bushes, or figs from thistles? [17] So, every healthy tree bears good fruit, but the diseased tree bears bad fruit. [18] A healthy tree cannot bear bad fruit, nor can a diseased tree bear good fruit. [19] Every tree that does not bear good fruit is cut down

and thrown into the fire. [20] Thus you will recognize them by their fruits. (Matthew 7:13–20)

As with most imagery in the New Testament, the precept that a narrow roadway represents the *way of life* and a wide road the *way of destruction* seems so apt that we may be lulled into a false sense of understanding this discourse. Indeed, we can derive benefit from relating to the way of life and its opposite in physical terms. But to understand the substance of what is being taught, we must go beyond the physical symbols.

The narrow gate and the narrow way symbolize a life lived by principles. If we live a life in which we stick to principles, our choices have already been made for us, in a manner of speaking. The opposite is a life where the rules are made up as one goes along, leaving plenty of room for one to maneuver, to negotiate compromises. The destruction at the end of this (wide) road results because a life lived without principles does not contribute to a transformation of personal consciousness or to a growth of Higher Consciousness.

The warning against false prophets also applies at various levels. First, it cautions against taking instruction from someone who is inept—a charlatan. Second, it deals with aspiring teachers who are deceptive, who want to attract a following for personal motives rather than spiritual ones. Such individuals pose no problem for sincere seekers of Truth because sincere seekers can discern the pretenders. Sincere seekers are never without some level of spiritual understanding to begin with, and when they seek a teacher, they are really looking for someone in the flesh who embodies the ideals they already hold for themselves. Thus, when teachers fail to meet the expectations of the sincere seeker, he or she knows it's time to move on. The third level of interpreting the warning against false prophets applies to discernment that concerns one's own internal processes. As such, it does not apply to others, but to oneself.

Those who have consciously embarked on the path of transformation may find, once the higher chakras are affected, that their ability to influence others naturally increases. They may find themselves with the power to animate and motivate others, thus influencing the choices they make for their lives. However, the existence of such power in our life is not sufficient evidence that we are ready to be a spiritual teacher. This task requires that one's life is in order, since part of the responsibilities of being a spiritual teacher is that the example of our personal life should provide inspiration to others. This is the true fruit of anyone's teaching. It is not how well one speaks, but how well one lives. Should the one serving the function of a spiritual teacher lack the faith or the will to trust his outer life to the ideas he is propounding, then instructing others would be nothing but a sham. Anyone who feels the call to teach must make the effort to prove within himself that which he asks others to accept.

THE ULTIMATE TEST—PRACTICAL APPLICATION

All of the above exercises are meaningless, however, if we do not try to integrate them and put them into practice. In this respect, a system is only as good as the extent to which it is applied. It is this reality that provided the impetus for the parting words of Jesus in the Sermon on the Mount:

> [21] Not everyone who says to me, 'Lord, Lord,' will enter the Kingdom of Heaven, but the one who does the will of my Father who is in heaven. [22] On that day many will say to me, 'Lord, Lord, did we not prophesy in your name, and cast out demons in your name, and do many mighty works in your name?' [23] And then will I declare to them, 'I never knew you; depart from me, you workers of lawlessness.'
>
> [24] Everyone then who hears these words of mine and does them will be like a wise man who built his house on the rock. [25] And the rain fell, and the floods came, and the winds blew and beat on that house, but it did not fall, because it had been founded on the rock. [26] And everyone

who hears these words of mine and does not do them will be
like a foolish man who built his house on the sand. [27] And
the rain fell, and the floods came, and the winds blew and
beat against that house, and it fell, and great was the fall of
it. (Matthew 7:21–27)

The message here is that the attainment of the Kingdom of Heaven,
meaning the completion of transformation, is a matter of process; it is not
enough to simply desire it. Further, a crucial step in this process is submitting our individual will to the Divine will. It is important that we
understand that this submission is only achieved through our commitment to let our individual actions be guided by higher principles. Transformation of consciousness occurs as we lose the impetus to live for
ourselves.

Since the Kingdom of Heaven represents a stage of being in which our
individual will is open and receptive to the influence of the Divine will, it
is tautological to say that only those who do the will of the Father will
enter the Kingdom. Why? Because doing the will of the Father *is* the vehicle that transports one into the Kingdom.

Jesus likens those who hear his words and do them to a wise man building his house on rock. In chapter 3, we looked at how building a house on
a foundation of rock translates to rooting our consciousness in ideas that
are proven by experience, rather than those based on theory or hearsay.

Hearing the words of Jesus has to be understood in other than the literal sense, otherwise they would only apply to those persons who were
within physical earshot of them. In the context of transformation, hearing
the words of Jesus should be interpreted as being attuned to the Higher,
or Christ Self, which exists in everyone, and which Jesus symbolized.

Jesus's emphasis on doing ("Everyone then who hears these words of
mine and does them") is in stark contrast to a spiritual outlook that treats

doing as optional, rather than a primary requirement. Of course, it's easy to understand how this position garners support, since it is based on the idea that the aim of a spiritual engagement in life is to be saved and go to heaven, rather than to participate in the process of transforming consciousness. Once we understand and accept that it is a change in consciousness toward which Jesus is calling us, then the notion of believing being a substitute for doing becomes indefensible.

TEN

PARABLES OF THE KINGDOM I: INITIAL FRUITS OF TRANSFORMATION

THE KINGDOM OF HEAVEN

As previously discussed, the process of transforming consciousness is what Jesus refers to as "the Kingdom of Heaven," or, sometimes, "the Kingdom of God."

Christians have historically made the error of thinking of the Kingdom as a place of abode, whether in this world or some unknown realm. This error is understandable, since we have difficulty conceiving of a personal existence in other than a physical reality. Lacking such understanding, we make projections based on our lived experiences. Even when we admit that some form of existence other than the physical may be a necessary condition to inhabit our notional sense of a heavenly realm, we still hold on to the idea of some sort of place. We use expressions such as, "He's gone to a better place" to comfort someone who has experienced the death of a loved one.

First of all, a "place" of abode—as we understand the concept of place—is only relevant to physical beings who occupy three-dimensional space, but not to nonphysical beings. For according to scripture, to inherit the Kingdom of Heaven, we have to change into something else, since "flesh and blood" cannot make the journey.*

---

*1 Corinthians 15:50: "I tell you this, brothers: flesh and blood cannot inherit the kingdom of God, nor does the perishable inherit the imperishable."

Further, apart from simply expressing a sentiment for a satisfactory spiritual outcome to one's life, it is not very meaningful to talk about "going to heaven." Biblical references to such should be treated as allegorical—not unlike the journey to the "Celestial City" by Christian, the main character in John Bunyan's *The Pilgrim's Progress*.[1]

Acknowledging that something is allegorical is not the same as saying it is not real at some level. It is only that its reality exists on a different level than the literal one. I can recall the profound disappointment I felt as a child when I learned from my father that the Celestial City of Bunyan's masterpiece was not a real place we could go to. This book had a major impact on my childhood imagination as it was the first book I learned to read. I could not have been older than six or seven when I was enticed to tackle, on my own, the richly illustrated large-print edition my father, a preacher, often read to us. The world of *The Pilgrim's Progress* was therefore very alive for me, reinforced by my father's practice of using examples from it in discussions with church members who sought him out for advice. I was so moved by the adventures of the characters Christian and Faithful that I felt that our family should also set off on their quest. This was when I asked my father why our family was not taking a journey to the Celestial City!

More meaningful than thinking of the Kingdom of Heaven as a place, then, is thinking of it in terms of a state of being that is attainable through the transformation of our consciousness. The human situation in relation to the Kingdom of Heaven is not unlike that of a caterpillar trying to imagine what its life will be like when it becomes a butterfly. Nothing upon which the caterpillar could draw from its lived experience can prepare it for this radically new life, since in its present condition, it lacks any understanding of what it is like to be a butterfly. This is acceptable for caterpillars, since nature takes care of the transformation process for them. But unlike caterpillars, we do not automatically transform from our caterpillar-equivalent state into our butterfly-equivalent potential. To achieve this passage requires nothing less than our leaving our present ego-centered consciousness and way of being. To accomplish this task, we need both a vision of what our transformational possibilities are and detailed directions on how to live up to our potential. These instructions are exactly what we receive in the thirteenth chapter of Matthew.

Here, we find six parables, each one using a different dynamic, a mental image, to portray the Kingdom. Each of these parables begins with the words, "The Kingdom of Heaven is like ..." indicating the need to get a sense of the Kingdom at an emotional level, rather than an intellectual one. Jesus's use of this approach to acquaint us with the Kingdom enables us to sense the dynamism involved, so that we are not lulled into thinking about the Kingdom in familiar, static terms.

The parables compare the Kingdom to various processes—weeds invading a planted field, the life cycle of a mustard seed, the workings of leaven in dough, hidden treasures that are accidentally found, a pearl ardently sought after, and the act of landing and sorting a net full of fish. Another parable precedes these to set the stage for their proper interpretation. This is the parable of the sower. It is important to note that it's not these objects by themselves which exemplify the Kingdom, but rather the events surrounding them.

The Parables of the Kingdom build on the instructions conveyed in the Sermon on the Mount, which are directed at assisting us in cultivating higher consciousness. With the assumption that this higher consciousness has taken hold in the being, the Parables of the Kingdom go one step further, revealing the fruits of this cultivation.

In the parables, as with most of the lessons in the Sermon on the Mount, the unfoldment of consciousness* is viewed in the context of the

---

*The term consciousness is spelt in this book with both a lowercase c and a capital C. When capitalized, we are referring to Consciousness as a principle—as a cosmic and universal force or presence. When lowercased, (e.g., human consciousness), we refer to our collective capacity for awareness, thinking, feeling, interaction, and consideration of others. Our human consciousness can be understood as an apportionment of Consciousness, or the universal presence. The idea of the transformation of human consciousness refers to the increase of our human capacity to allow the universal presence to flow into and conduct itself through our awareness. I might also use the phrase "unfoldment of Consciousness" to refer to the progressive revelation of the cosmic presence called Consciousness in our being.

seven-tiered model represented by the chakra concept. Each parable, including the tone-setting one of the sower, shows what happens in a person's life when a chakra is fully active and functioning. The parables are therefore an unveiling of the progressive refinement of human consciousness as it expresses itself through the various chakras. In a way, they tell a story about the adventure of Consciousness itself—the individual being a venue for its expression.

THE TONE-SETTING PARABLE OF THE SOWER

In this parable, the entire schematic of the Kingdom as a dynamic process is revealed. Here, we find not only the structure that connects the various parables, but also the clues needed to uncover the insights the parables contain regarding how the unfolding of Consciousness expresses itself.

> ³ And he told them many things in parables, saying: "A sower went out to sow. ⁴And as he sowed, some seeds fell along the path, and the birds came and devoured them. ⁵Other seeds fell on rocky ground, where they did not have much soil, and immediately they sprang up, since they had no depth of soil, ⁶ but when the sun rose they were scorched. And since they had no root, they withered away. ⁷ Other seeds fell among thorns, and the thorns grew up and choked them. ⁸ Other seeds fell on good soil and produced grain, some a hundredfold, some sixty, some thirty. ⁹ He who has ears, let him hear. (Matthew 13:3–9)

This parable contains a fundamental law of expansion. In regard to consciousness, however, expansion happens not on the same plane, but on successively higher ones. Its growth is geometric as opposed to arithmetic (i.e., multiplicative as opposed to additive). However, since this parable was given outside of any particular context, the disciples asked Jesus for an explanation, and he gave them the following:

[18] Hear then the parable of the sower: [19] When anyone hears the word of the kingdom and does not understand it, the evil one comes and snatches away what has been sown in his heart. This is what was sown along the path. [20] As for what was sown on rocky ground, this is the one who hears the word and immediately receives it with joy, [21] yet he has no root in himself, but endures for a while, and when tribulation or persecution arises on account of the word, immediately he falls away. [22] As for what was sown among thorns, this is the one who hears the word, but the cares of the world and the deceitfulness of riches choke the word, and it proves unfruitful. [23] As for what was sown on good soil, this is the one who hears the word and understands it. He indeed bears fruit and yields, in one case a hundredfold, in another sixty, and in another thirty. (Matt. 13:18–25)

This explanation to the parable of the sower is also, in itself, a parable. This means that a full understanding of it can only come with a deepening of our awareness;* that is, as our awareness deepens, the meaning of this explanation will also deepen. Still, it is a step toward clarity, and once we have properly interpreted phrases such as "the word of the kingdom," "the wicked one," and "bears fruit," we can arrive at a final intellectual explanation to the parable.

Let us begin with the concept "word of the kingdom." This can be understood as something with the power to ignite within the breast—the feeling center—a certain sense of wonderment, a sense of the Numinous.

---

*I'm using the phrase "deepening of our awareness" in the general sense only. We deepen our awareness when we bring more of our critical and intellectual faculties to bear on a situation. For example, when information is given to us, we can accept it at face value, or evaluate it against everything we have already proven to be true. This evaluation would then either confirm or contradict this new bit of information, allowing us to add to our knowledge base with confidence.

As discussed in chapter 1, the Numinous is a moment of insight, a break-through of understanding in the individual into the true nature of Real-ity. It may also be referred to as a sense of the Sacred. This sense, ignited within us, is a representative "piece" of the Kingdom itself. It represents the reproductive power of the Kingdom, of Consciousness, to expand itself.

The sower symbolizes our ever-present potential to experience the Numinous, to awake to the glory of Being or the wonder of existence. It does not refer to a physical agent, or even to a specific action on the part of someone. And it definitely does not refer to missionaries or preachers. The Kingdom of Heaven is the process of Consciousness contemplating and becoming conscious of itself. This process of Consciousness receiving knowledge of itself breaks through into our human awareness, and when this occurs, there are many alternative outcomes.

At the densest levels of being—the most unappreciative functioning of human life—there is little possibility of a sense of wonderment. Every-thing is taken for granted. There is no awe at anything. Consequently, no contact is made with the beauty that is life. This level of existence is like two tunnels running side by side for their entire length, without ever con-necting. A "seed" of the Kingdom would refer to points along these tun-nels where the wall separating them is thinnest; it speaks to the potential of two otherwise separate realities to unite.

In this light, the seeds that fell on the path, the pavement, or roadway are opportunities missed. At this level, our human consciousness is just too preoccupied with life at one level of its manifestation that awareness of other levels escapes us. Here, we take life totally for granted, deny any opportunity to explore the purpose of life, in terms of how we can find per-sonal meaning in it. The principle being demonstrated is that of the impos-sibility of the Kingdom of Heaven penetrating our consciousness, without our lending our cooperation to the process.

In terms of the chakra system, life lived at this level is ruled entirely by first-chakra (Muladhara) impulses. Under the influence of the first chakra, we find the "wicked one" always snatching the word—the awe, or the

Numinous—out of life. Here, we see only hardship, necessity, toil, practicality, and thus, competition. When there is no awe, there is also no gratitude, since we do not perceive the necessity for it.

As for the seeds that fell on stony ground, this is a level of life in which some breakthrough of the Numinous into consciousness has taken place. Such a breakthrough may first happen by accident. We may inadvertently come upon some knowledge that we cannot apply, at which point we realize that there is something more to life—that there is "something out there." Because we are unprepared to use this knowledge, however, we lapse back into a state of unawareness, that state where things are taken for granted.

An example of this phenomenon is the death of someone close to us. We may, for a short while, contemplate the mystery of life and its purpose, but then soon lapse back into complacency. Whenever the mystery of life intrudes into consciousness, there is a cessation of normal functioning, just long enough for us to acknowledge its presence. But unless we know how to hold on to this sense of the profound, it quickly dissipates, like a vapor. To make use of such opportunities to expand consciousness, we must be prepared.

In terms of the chakra system, stony ground represents the second or Svadvishthana Chakra. Consciousness is only able to express itself at this chakra through the principle of polarization. This polarization can give rise to psychological complexes in our personal consciousness. It is these complexes that constitute "the rocks in the soil" mentioned in the parable. Psychological complexes exist because we have not yet learned the lessons of our various experiences. Integration is thwarted due to the many isolated pockets of experiences that dominate our attention. Under such conditions, we may acknowledge the existence of the Numinous for a while, but its ultimate disappearance is certain.

When seeds fall among thorns, there is an opportunity for some sense of wonderment, awe, or reverence to be part of the normal expression of life. This does not preclude our carrying on our ordinary affairs of life independently of this awareness. We may call this approach to the Numinous the "side-by-side method," since we've made no adjustment in the rest of our life for this sense of the Numinous to grow.

In the words of the parable, as the seeds grow up, they are choked by the thorns and fail to reach maturity. Here, we are dealing with a situation of lack of selectivity, or lack of commitment. Such a condition is found when we are not prepared to exchange the mundane for the Numinous, but instead wish to graft the Numinous onto the mundane. Needless to say, this does not work, since the Numinous, to survive—or to continue impressing upon one's consciousness—must have room to grow. Unless the sense of wonder and awe that characterizes the seed of the Kingdom germinates into activities that give longevity to the sense of wonder, the result is a petering out.

The reason for failure here is that we may feel that it is not practical to live a life dedicated to the preservation of the Sacred Space necessary for the long-term survival of the seeds. Expediency wins out over sacrifice, as we perceive the Numinous only as something to be taken advantage of, to be possessed on our terms.

This describes what happens when Consciousness tries to establish itself at the third or Manipura Chakra. In the words of the parable, the word is choked by thorns; in other words, an attempt is made to subordinate the Numinous to the materialistic nature. Although when our consciousness is arrested at the Manipura Chakra, we are initially moved to give place in the heart to wonder and awe, the possessive side of our nature soon takes over. We start wondering, "How can I make a commercial success of this? How can I benefit socially?" In short, there is no commitment to the Numinous for its own sake, and in such circumstances, the Numinous ceases to be.

Finally, we encounter seeds that fall on good ground and result in varying levels of productivity. Here, we have all the ingredients that are lacking in the previous cases. We have receptivity, such that there is recognition of the seeds (the opportunities to experience the Numinous). We have preparedness, such that we know a good thing when we see it. The soil, or the experience within which the Kingdom takes hold, is rich. There are no lumps, or no complexes in the psyche. Next, there is commitment. We know that the kingdom will become manifest in proportion to the room we create for it in our heart and life; that is, in our aspirations and daily activities.

Good ground is symbolic of the fourth or Anahata Chakra. When the Numinous becomes entrenched here, we can actually let it become an integral part of our being, because this center is the seat of our aspirations. Such a possibility is not present at lower centers of expression of consciousness, since this is the first level where the aspirations can be changed. It marks the level at which we can adjust our lifestyle so that reverence can be entertained on a permanent basis.

From this point on, different levels of output (e.g., thirty-, sixty-, and one-hundred-fold) become possible. These levels relate to higher chakras— the Vishuddha, the Ajna, and the Sahasrara respectively. Therefore, the fourth chakra, the Anahata, is the point of "inflection" in the organization of Consciousness. It is a relay station, marking the zone between where Numinosity ceases to be either a novelty or something intermittent, and where it becomes the very stuff of life, or the "bread of life."

Beyond this level, we become a facilitator, hosting Numinosity in our own life and inciting it in the lives of others, a state symbolized by the germinating seeds growing to maturity, bringing forth fruits thirty-, sixty-, and a-hundred-fold.

The overriding lesson of this parable of the sower is twofold. The first part of the lesson deals with *the universal availability of the Kingdom.* Superimposed upon this is the second aspect, regarding the principle of *changing relative efforts.*

The first aspect is rather straightforward and is represented in the concept of a sower scattering seeds indiscriminately. This means that everyone has an opportunity to participate in the expansion of his or her consciousness.

The second aspect is more complex and must be looked at in more detail. In regard to the second part of the lesson, when we take the seeds in various environments to represent the various levels of expression of Consciousness, we find that the success of the entire transformation process in each of us depends upon the degree of our participation.

- At the first chakra, where, as previously stated, we find a total lack of appreciation of the beauty and profundity of existence, we can say that God alone carries the burden of world sustenance.
- At the second chakra, where we partially recognize the wonder of life, but sense no responsibility for its maintenance, we share a minuscule bit of the burden. We may want to help, but lack of preparedness prevents us from doing so in a meaningful way; in other words, we cheer from the sidelines.
- At the third chakra, our effort is stronger, but we still do not fully share the burden. There is preparation, but commitment is lacking. That is, we are prepared to act, but on our own terms.
- From the fourth chakra on, we find greater willingness to take on some of the burden. This is what it means for the mature tree to yield thirty-, sixty-, and one-hundred-fold. The process of Consciousness coming into some awareness of itself is easier at higher levels; special effects are not needed. From here on, we can see the sublime in the very ordinary, and opportunity in every obstacle.

THE PARABLE OF THE WEEDS— THE PRINCIPLE OF COMPETING REALITIES

The psychological substance of the second parable, the parable of the weeds, can be fully realized only in the context of the tone-setting parable of the sower. The parable of the weeds covers the first stage of the manifestation of the kingdom. Its psychological message is similar to that in the part of the previous parable in which the seeds fell on stony ground. In fact, we are confronting the same material, since we are dealing with the

Svadvishthana Chakra, which is the second level of the expression of Consciousness. We take up the parable in the twenty-fourth verse of the thirteenth chapter.

> [24] He put another parable before them, saying, "The Kingdom of Heaven may be compared to a man who sowed good seed in his field, [25] but while his men were sleeping, his enemy came and sowed weeds among the wheat and went away. [26] So when the plants came up and bore grain, then the weeds appeared also." [27] And the servants of the master of the house came and said to him, "Master, did you not sow good seed in your field? How then does it have weeds?" [28] He said to them, "An enemy has done this." So the servants said to him, "Then do you want us to go and gather them?" [29] But he said, "No, lest in gathering the weeds you root up the wheat along with them. [30] Let both grow together until the harvest, and at harvest time I will tell the reapers, 'Gather the weeds first and bind them in bundles to be burned, but gather the wheat into my barn.'"(Matthew 13:24–30)

Jesus waited until he had given the disciples several more parables before explaining this one. However, just as the explanation given to the parable of the sower also contained a parable, so too does the explanation here:

> [36] Then he left the crowds and went into the house. And his disciples came to him, saying, "Explain to us the parable of the weeds of the field." [37] He answered, "The one who sows the good seed is the Son of Man. [38] The field is the world, and the good seed is the sons of the kingdom. The weeds are the sons of the evil one, [39] and the enemy who sowed them is the devil. The harvest is the close of the age, and the

reapers are angels. [40] Just as the weeds are gathered and burned with fire, so will it be at the close of the age. [41] The Son of Man will send his angels, and they will gather out of his kingdom all causes of sin and all law-breakers, [42] and throw them into the fiery furnace. In that place there will be weeping and gnashing of teeth. [43] Then the righteous will shine like the sun in the kingdom of their Father. He who has ears, let him hear. (Matthew 13:34–47)

Our task is now to seek deeper explanations to this parable beyond the ones given. We approach this by zeroing in on the overriding principle and then finding suitable explanations to the symbols used in it. The principle here is the eternal paradox of competing realities—good and evil, positive and negative, black and white, light and darkness. In other words, it is again the principle of polarity.

The first element in this explanation is the concept of "good seeds," which are sown by the man. The interpretation of these seeds matches that in the parable of the sower: it refers to Numinosity. More specifically, the good seeds would consist of "units," or moments of Numinosity. Such units, or *numinosum** need not be homogeneous and can represent various things—an instantaneous flash of insight that cannot be explained, an intense feeling of awe, a feeling of joy, an inexpressible sense of the unity of all things, an appreciation of beauty, etc. It is this numinosum that is a child of the Kingdom. Similarly, a child of the "devil" is the opposite of Numinosity—hate, anger, despair, ignorance, greed, etc. Each person has within him both good and bad seeds, both children of the Kingdom and children of the devil.

---

* Carl Jung says of the numinosum: "The numinosum—whatever its cause may be—is an experience of the subject independent of his will…The numinosum is either a quality belonging to a visible object or the influence of an invisible presence that causes a peculiar alteration of consciousness." Vol .11 of the Collected Works, para. 11.

Jesus explained that the good seeds are the children of the Kingdom and that the man who planted them is the "Son of Man." If we fail to see that Jesus was speaking symbolically, we create implications for his words that contradict some of his other teachings. For example, if we ignore the symbolism and interpret "children of the kingdom" at the surface level, we are left with the unacceptable conclusion that individuals are either predestined to be children of God or children of the devil. Such an explanation would suggest that destiny is predetermined. Individuals would have their destinies already sealed for all of eternity.

In the context of the growth of consciousness, the Son of Man, who planted the good seeds, represents a reality that is already perfected and lies somewhere in mankind's collective future. This reality seeds itself in the human heart and mind with the hope that it can ignite something there and accelerate the process redeeming the human reality unto itself. The Son of Man represents a new order of humanity.

In contrast to this reality of the future, there is this other reality of mankind's collective past. This reality is that of inertia, stagnation, pain and suffering, containment, fear, distrust, ignorance, separativeness, and indulgence. These are the seeds sown by the evil one.

However, contained within this parable of the weeds, of these bad seeds, is a resolution to the drama of these competing realities. We saw that the good seeds were sown first, and only after that were the weeds sown in the same field. We are told that the weeds were sown "while his men were sleeping." This statement refers to lapses in our attention or resolve, or more particularly, to a fall back to a condition where our consciousness is more comfortable with what is habitual and effortless, as in a moment of sleep.

As soon as the good seeds were sown, or the Numinous had invaded the awareness and taken hold, the opposite of the Numinous, its shadow, if you will, was also attracted. That's because when the expression of Consciousness is limited to the second chakra, the Svadvishthana, little is experienced without polarization. One loves what is deemed to be good, but only in the context of condemning something or someone else as evil; one is drawn to the beautiful and the aesthetic, but only in the context of avoiding and repudiating what is deemed ugly; one loves, but only in the context of possessing and confining the object of one's affection. It goes on and on, contrast and pairs of opposites calling the tune to the expression of the Numinous.

We have the reassurance that this does not have to be, however, for it was only while "his men were sleeping," or while we are unconscious and not watchful, that polarity is manifested. Good does not need to exist only as a contrast to evil, nor beauty to ugliness, nor the moral to the immoral, nor joy to sorrow, because each of these elements has the power to stand up by itself. But we are not always watchful, and each time an inroad is made by the Numinous into our individual consciousness, the potential is created for its opposite to take hold. This potentiality is only energized from the part of our nature that asserts itself during moments of unawareness—that part said to belong to the subconscious.[2] The subconscious is a reservoir of stored experiences in their unassimilated form; a hotbed of complexes formed from our past traumas, disappointments, fears, unexpressed ambitions and motives, and the like.

This phenomenon can also be demonstrated at the social level. Sometimes when a group of people is infused with a vision of a better world, that vision, if not thoroughly understood and thought out, leads to actions that are diametrically opposite to the principles behind the vision. We have had societies founded upon the religious ideals of love and brotherhood, only to have them resorting to the persecution of nonconformists a short time thereafter. People have thrown off the cloak of an oppressive political system only to put in its place a system that is even more tyrannical. It seems an inviolable law that the high ideals that give birth to reform, be they religious or political, become downgraded and cheapened in just a matter of time. This is due to the insufficiency of Being that is manifest when the expression of Consciousness is arrested at the second chakra.

The reason for such duality is not that the good cannot exist independently of the bad, for example, or that happiness cannot exist independently of sorrow, or whatever dualistic combination we may examine. This duality becomes inescapable only when there is an attempt made to lay personal claim to the virtues—goodness, knowledge, righteousness, wisdom, etc. These virtues must be seen to exist as principles, as impersonal states of being, in the same way that personalities exist. We must see that it is not possible to be good independent of actions that express goodness. The same goes for many other virtues.

When we have incorporated this lesson into our being, we will no longer allow evil seeds to be sown in us, because we are always "awake" in the sense of being conscious and aware. It is only when we are blind to the power of polarity that "sleep" ensues.

Returning to the parable, we are told that the servants approached the landowner and suggested they pull up the weeds and destroy them. His response was that they do no such thing, since there was a chance that, while they pulled up the weeds, the wheat would be damaged also. His orders were that everything sown be allowed to grow until harvest, when the weeds would be pulled up and burned, and the wheat would be gathered into his barn.

The suggestion of the servant is a typical human response when we're confronted with the polar opposites of the values we've appropriated unto ourselves: "Why does there have to be so much unhappiness? Why does God permit evil?" and so on. We do not realize that at a lower level of awareness, we only experience things by contrast. At this lower level, if the bad is taken away, the good will also cease to exist. Or if the negative is taken away, the positive will cease to be perceptible. The bad, therefore, has its place in the world as much as the good, even if it is only to ensure that the good is not taken for granted.

THE PARABLE OF THE MUSTARD SEED— THE PRINCIPLE OF OVERCOMING LIMITATIONS

With the parable of the mustard seed, we come to the third level of the expression of Consciousness. Its message is about the proper awakening of another psychic center in the body, the Manipura Chakra.

[31] He put another parable before them, saying, "The King-dom of Heaven is like a grain of mustard seed that a man took and sowed in his field. [32] It is the smallest of all seeds, but when it has grown it is larger than all the garden plants and becomes a tree, so that the birds of the air come and make nests in its branches." (Matthew 13:31–32)

It should be pointed out that this parable is not simply comparing the Kingdom to a grain of mustard seed, but rather to the entire process by which the grain expands itself. Specifically, the Kingdom is similar to the process by which a mustard seed goes from being a thing of insignificance to a thing of great significance. Through this process, the mustard seed is lifted from "personal" near-nonexistence to being a support for the existence of others, in this case, birds.

This process is quite likely the same one to which Jesus alluded on another occasion, when he said to his disciples that if they had faith as a grain of mustard seed, they would be able to move mountains (Matthew 17:20). It is easy to misinterpret this saying and the parable of the mustard seed, and consequently miss the common lesson they contain. In both instances, Jesus was referring not to a small portion of faith, but to faith *as the mustard seed demonstrates it.* There is a major difference here, for in the latter sense, we are dealing with quality as opposed to quantity.

Faith, as expressed by a mustard seed, is a process of rising beyond limiting factors, beyond insignificance, beyond oblivion, to regions of expansion, strength, and purpose. Such faith is therefore another facet of the Kingdom—another mechanism by which Numinosity grows.

As we saw in the parable of the sower, when Numinosity expresses itself at the third chakra, we come upon a point of inflection, a point of change. At this point, our focus needs to change from the personal to the transpersonal; from concerns about self to group concerns; from self-pity and inferiority complexes to compassion and service.

We previously saw that the Manipura Chakra is the center of self-will and of all desires to display power, and that it also correlates with the adrenal glands of the endocrine system. The adrenals are known as the "fight-or-flight" glands. They deal with what seem to be polar functions of aggression and fear. These responses are expressions of what is, in reality, the same psychological state. This state results from the need for self-protection and self-preservation. A preoccupation with self-protection and self-preservation crystallizes into an inferiority complex. Therefore, when we become aggressive and enjoy displaying personal power, we may really be protecting a fragile self-image.

The parable of the mustard seed is telling us that for Numinosity to continue to expand, it must go through this point of inflection. It must survive the certain death that comes with all natural systems and put new life into itself. The secret of self-regeneration must be learned, and such knowledge cannot be gained by defending a fixed position. If the Numinous, as expressed at this level, is properly understood by our conscious mind, the sensitivity that it stimulates will not be translated into self-pity and feelings of inferiority. Instead, it will be interpreted as an awareness of needs as they exist everywhere, not just in oneself. From this awareness of the universality of needs will spring the urge to reach out and attend to the needs of others, which counters the initial impulse to fill needs only in ourselves, an impulse that may have previously culminated in aggression. The impulse to fill needs then culminates in compassion and outreach in service.

The lesson that must be gained from this parable is that though the mustard seed is small, it cannot be associated with what smallness normally signifies. It is not related to self-pity or stinginess. The mustard seed has learned to use what little it has to secure not only its own existence, but also the existence of others. It has learned to transcend neediness, and therein lies the secret of its survival and growth.

The message of the mustard seed can also be expressed in terms of the law, or principle, of obligation. This is the principal law of life. It says that our personal power will grow in direct proportion to the obligations we have assumed. With this principle in mind, we see that all disproportionate possessions of power are equalized by the obligations associated with each level of power. The flipside of this principle is that failure to undertake obligations limits the amount of power that we can achieve. The mustard seed is a symbol of what happens when we overcome a small self-image, fear, inferiority complexes, and the touchiness to which these give rise.

The experience of life from the Manipura Chakra is just another of the many ways that Numinosity is experienced. The expression of Consciousness at this chakra, like with all the others, has both a spontaneous or unconscious mode of expression and a conscious or creative mode. Spontaneously or unconsciously expressed, the result is sensitivity, self-pity, and inferiority complexes. But expressed consciously, or with awareness, we get concern for others, kindness, and service.

Ironically, when we experience Numinosity and fail to realize that the experience should not be taken as an occasion for personal triumph, the result is a feeling of being different or special. It is only when we allow the Numinous free reign in our being, and not lay personal claim to it, that it, and therefore the Kingdom, can be saved from falling under the influence of entropy.

This act of giving free reign to the Numinous is accomplished when we put the shoe on the other foot, when we see the other's side in every situation of offence. We then learn that the Numinous, and therefore the Kingdom, is best served if sensitivity is regarded as a common human experience and not just a personal trait. It is only then that the lesson of the mustard seed can be assimilated.

ELEVEN

PARABLES OF THE KINGDOM II: ADVANCED STAGES OF TRANSFORMATION

THE PARABLE OF THE LEAVEN— THE PRINCIPLE OF INTEGRATION

The fourth parable in the series on the Kingdom correlates with the seeds that fell on good soil in the parable of the sower. Remember, the good soil represents the following psychological conditions, which manifest in this particular order:

- Awareness of the Kingdom
- Desire for the Kingdom
- Commitment to the Kingdom

The parable of the leaven demonstrates what happens when the natural momentum of Numinosity to expand itself meets with our conscious effort. Here is that parable:

> [33] The Kingdom of Heaven is like leaven that a woman took and hid in three measures of flour, till it was all leavened. (Matthew 13:33)

Again, in this parable, we see what happens to Numinosity after we commit to facilitating its expansion; that is, after we have given the Numinous the cooperation of our will.

The psychic center described by this parable is the fourth or Anahata Chakra. Little can go wrong when Consciousness expresses itself here, because most of the opportunities to misrepresent the Numinous have already been surmounted. If anything does go wrong, it is only that we do not go far enough.

At the Anahata Chakra, the Numinous is allowed to expand and touch the lives of others. At first, this reaching out, or "jumping the gap" between self and others, might occur only among members of a select group, such as those bound by contract and obligation (e.g., family, friends, spouses, children, parents). Later, interpersonal bridging of gaps occurs in response to a good deed done to or in memory of someone.

The picture of the Kingdom within this parable is one in which the dynamic expansion of Consciousness has become autonomous. Said another way, the Numinous has become so entrenched in our life that nothing can stop its growth. There are several pertinent insights in this parable that instruct us on the mechanics of the unfolding of the Kingdom at this level. These insights are contained in the imagery of the working of leaven in flour, or in dough.

The first insight we can glean is that the Kingdom works initially beneath the surface and against apparently insurmountable odds. By likening the Kingdom to the working of leaven, Jesus is saying that the dynamic process of the expansion of the Numinous is explosive in its potency. This potency is released when the Numinous finds the right medium within which it can grow, just as the potency of leaven is released only after it is placed in the proper medium, such as dough. In the right environment, the Numinous never looks back, and its growth is unstoppable. In the corresponding human reality, the leaven is represented by our ideals and the yearnings of our innermost being. In many of us, these yearnings are not realized due to a lack of the proper medium within which they could find expression.

Another lesson from this parable is that the expression of the Numinous at the Anahata Chakra is without pomp and hoopla. After being told that the woman placed the leaven in three measures of flour, the next thing we know, the whole was leavened. We never see the step-by-step process that promotes the leavening of the whole; all we are told is that leavening does take place. This aspect of the parable tells us that once the Numinous is given free reign—that is, once it is given a medium within which it can grow effectively—the results of its working may not be obvious from the surface. We won't be able to make a daily notch on some yardstick of progress, because no knowledge of the inner working of the Numinous is available to us.

We can learn something here about the way in which consciousness grows. It grows from the inside out, from the core of our being to areas of exterior observation. When its work is completed, only then is it revealed, and not before. The lesson here is that once we have committed ourselves to our ideals and provided these ideals with a medium within which they can grow—this medium being our daily activities—we should not be impatient for results. Proof that the principles we've engaged in our life are working will come in its own time.

Another insight from this parable is the thoroughness with which the Numinous permeates the whole being. One is no longer compartmentalized. Just as the distinction disappears between leaven and flour, so too does it disappear between the ideal and the real, the Numinous and the mundane, the conscious and the unconscious.[1] One does not possess beliefs that have not been personally put to the test; neither does one express some aspects of oneself to intimate associates and different ones to others. Just as integration with respect to leaven and flour creates a transformation involving both leaven and flour, integration in the being creates something that involves both ideal and real. Truly, this is the thought also captured in the following discourse from the *Gospel of Thomas*,[2] in which Jesus is reported to have said:

When you make the two one, and when you make the inner
as the outer and the outer as the inner and the above as the
below, and when you make the male and the female into a
single one, so that the male will not be male and the female
not be female, when you make eyes in the place of an eye,
and a hand in the place of a hand, and a foot in the place of
a foot, and an image in the place of an image then shall you
enter the Kingdom. (Log 21, pp. 17–18)

In this discourse, the work of integration is emphasized and is shown
as a necessary condition for the Kingdom making a permanent home for
itself within a human framework.

In the yogic tradition, the Anahata Chakra is the target of many religious practices and rituals. This is because it is intuitively understood that
Yoga (i.e., the union of the conscious and unconscious) is completed when
this center is opened up, meaning that when the expression of Consciousness is raised up to this level, it becomes autonomous. This is not to
say that there is not anything else for the individual to do, however. What
it does mean is that the work of transformation has reached an accelerated
tempo. In society, it is equivalent to a child reaching the age of majority.

If we look carefully, we also see that the Anahata Chakra, or heart center, is the target of much of Christian doctrine, as taught by the apostles.
Paul talks of this center in one of his Epistles:

[26] The Spirit helps us in our weakness. For we do not know
what to pray for as we ought, but the Spirit himself intercedes for us with groanings too deep for words. [27] And he
who searches hearts knows what is the mind of the Spirit,
because the Spirit intercedes for the saints according to the
will of God. (Romans 8:26–27)

Here, Paul is describing what has been called the "automatic prayer of the heart." This occurs because the opening up of the heart center represents unceasing contact with the Spirit, or with pure Consciousness. After all, if, as Paul says, the Spirit itself is the agency that reaches out and yearns for perfection, the work of transformation has become autonomous indeed.

Paul further tells us that this Spirit intercedes according to the will of God. This means that these yearnings are not sporadic, nor are they the sights of a burdened mind. Rather, they are the systematic and structured spurrings of the Soul, aligned with God's overall plan for us. In other words, these inner yearnings of the Spirit, or this automatic prayer of the heart, is conducted with wisdom.

Finally, the workings of the Kingdom expressed at the heart center are conducted with conviction. At this level, vows and promises are unnecessary. All we must do is be very clear on what we seek from life. We do not need to make announcements and proclamations and vows, though they may be helpful for those of us in need of courage. In short, when the impersonal work of the Kingdom has taken hold, we should attempt only to become a faithful witness to the underlying current of change that is taking over and restructuring our life.

THE PARABLE OF THE HIDDEN TREASURE— THE PRINCIPLE OF JOYOUS SACRIFICE

In this fifth parable, we see the Kingdom likened to a series of images coming together in a definite sequence:

> 44 The Kingdom of Heaven is like treasure hidden in a field, which a man found and covered up. Then in his joy he goes and sells all that he has and buys that field. (Matthew 13:44)

The interpretation of this parable must take all the images in the sequence into consideration, both individually and collectively. But let's start with the first image, which is that of riches hidden in a field. This is an apt description for the nature of the fifth psychic center, or Vishuddha Chakra, for the expression of the Numinous here is in "gems" of wisdom.

The Vishuddha Chakra, or speech center, as it is sometimes called, is credited with giving us the power to express the contents of our own mind. It is intimately connected with our ability to communicate and to create simple formulas to express inherently complex relationships (e.g., $E=mc^2$). When this center is opened up, we recognize that we are in possession of a virtual treasure chest, complete with the ability to not only gain knowledge of the hidden processes at work in nature, but also to give articulation to this knowledge. Individuals who have had this center opened are the traditional mystics and geniuses.

Thus, this parable is telling us how we can bring such faculties under full control of the Kingdom, adding our labor to what comes naturally to advance the cause of the Kingdom.

Before we delve deeper into the parable, however, we need to realize that when we speak of the "opening up" of the centers, we are speaking in a relative sense. For example, an individual whose natural abilities tend toward fifth-chakra functions may still have expressions characteristic of lower chakras. Thus, the purpose of the Kingdom involves a process of lifting the expression of consciousness from wherever one is at. Therefore, the individual who is lifting the expression of his personal consciousness from second to third, or from the third to the fourth, etc., may be more in step with the idea of the Kingdom than someone who is naturally at a higher level, but is not doing anything to advance himself.

As we look at the more dynamic aspects of this parable, we are presented with the images of a man finding this treasure and taking the necessary precautions to secure it. It is obvious that the man found this treasure unexpectedly and that he had no previous knowledge of its existence or its location. However, his response is forthright: he immediately goes off to sell all that he had to buy the field. By this act he becomes the legal owner of the treasure. All of these images relate to conscious effort at directing the faculties of the fifth center to the service of the Kingdom, of the dynamic process of Consciousness expanding itself.

We will examine more closely each of the three aspects to the real-life psychological process that the images in this parable represent. These are:

- Finding the treasure
- Acknowledging its value
- Taking the necessary steps to secure and legitimize the claim

Finding the Treasure

As mentioned, the man's discovery of the treasure was serendipitous, meaning that it was not only unexpected, but also likely made while he was busy looking for something else. The nature of this discovery is in line with the mode of mental functioning at the fifth center. Serendipity is quite well known to scientists. In fact, it is the way in which many major scientific discoveries are made, the discovery of penicillin being a case in point. Usually, the one whose fifth center is functioning gets flashes of insight that may instantaneously give the solution to a long-standing problem. The individual has no control over these flashes (sometimes attributed to intuition); they just come and go as they please, dropping a jewel here, and one there.

Acknowledging Its Value

The one so gifted as to chance upon these gems of insight may be left with a problem. He may lack the rational explanations for his discoveries necessary to convince both peers and laymen of their validity. What is needed here is a way for the individual finding "the treasure" to legitimize his claim to it and make it his own.

Taking the Necessary Steps to Secure and Legitimize the Claim

Third, the man who found the treasure "joyfully went and sold all that he had," so that he would have the means to purchase the field. He did not take the easy way out, which would have been to extract the treasure and take it away. But he realized that this was not a proper course of action; it would have involved theft on top of trespassing. Instead, common sense told him that the rightful owner of the treasure was the one who owned the field.

At the psychological level, this part of the parable is telling us that we must not be satisfied with the sporadic functioning of intuition. Rather, we must develop it into a conscious faculty. By so doing, we legitimize our role as a progenitor of Numinosity.

At the spiritual level, what this part of the parable is showing us is that, first, the Kingdom of Heaven is a reality in its own context. This means that we have to meet it on its own terms, rather than expect it to adapt to ours. When the Numinous has begun to express itself through the fifth chakra, we can, quite spontaneously, become host to many supernatural and mystical experiences. Should we be satisfied with these experiences as they come, however, without seeking the underlying principles that inspired them, we would be "robbing the field of its treasure." Consequently, if this entire parable is to be summed up in one thought, it is this: The true value of religious or mystical experiences lies not in the experiences themselves, but in what they are calling us toward. The true purpose behind receiving such experiences is to help us gain a greater sense of certainty about the merits of what we have been seeking, along with a stronger commitment to our search.

In adapting this approach, we would do what many mystics-turned-scientists do as a matter of course: to create a point of contact with peers and laymen alike for the transfer of Numinosity. We do this by making the expression of the Kingdom—of the Numinous—as natural as possible. This is accomplished by attempting to give the principles that underlie the harmonious workings of the Universe expression in our being. In so doing, we set new standards for others to copy.

Another aspect of the Kingdom expressing itself here is that of true sacrifice. It is noteworthy that the man who found the treasure realized its value to the point that he did not mind parting with everything he owned to legitimize his claim. After finding the treasure, he went and sold all that he had to be able to purchase the field. In parting with his possessions, he is performing an act of sacrifice that is not recognized as a loss. He simply conducts himself in the manner of one carrying out an exchange. He knows opportunity when he sees it and is bent on taking advantage of it. This is also how we should receive the treasures of the Kingdom—with diligence and sacrifice.

Finally, applying these lessons need not be restricted to the aspiring mystic. The parable holds instructions for ordinary consciousness as well. When the Numinous has expressed itself in our life, we should work to elevate the quality of the rest of our life up to a standard where the experience becomes "normal" for us. This implies that the major outer effect of an experience of the Numinous should be on our lifestyle or on the way we live on a day-to-day basis.

THE PARABLE OF THE PEARL OF GREAT VALUE— THE PRINCIPLE OF BECOMING AN EMBODIMENT OF TRUE LIFE

In the sixth parable on the Kingdom, the principle that is being demonstrated is that of embodying our higher understanding of the purpose of life.

> [45] Again, the Kingdom of Heaven is like a merchant in search of fine pearls, [46] who, on finding one pearl of great value, went and sold all that he had and bought it. (Matthew 13:45)

There is a great deal of difference between this parable and the others. The major difference is that in the previous parables, the process of unfolding of Consciousness, or the Kingdom, was likened to an inanimate object and the story surrounding it. For example, in the parable dealing with the second chakra, the story was about the good and bad seeds; in the parable dealing with the third chakra, the tale was about the mustard seed; in that dealing with the fourth chakra, it was about leaven; and in that dealing with the fifth, a hidden treasure. Here, in the sixth parable, the story is about a person actively engaged in the process of seeking, and about his response when confronted with the object of that search.

In each of the other parables, the point of focus is the employment of a principle that facilitates the growth of Numinosity. In this one, however, the process being represented is somewhat reversed. We are dealing not with a principle being absorbed into one's being, but with committing all of one's being to a principle. More will be said about this later, but for now, note that whereas the other parables deal with expansion, this one deals with concentration.

The important symbols in this parable are the merchant and the object of his search; namely, pearls. These are symbols of universal significance. By making the merchant the point of focus, this parable is dealing with the mechanics of conscious seeking. In the fifth parable, the man who found the buried treasure just happened upon a good thing, although, to his credit, he was conscious enough to recognize value when he saw it. With the merchant, however, seeking is a conscious activity, such that it engages all of his attention.

Here on display, at this chakra, is a fine demonstration of "professionalism" and its application to the task of spiritual seeking. As such, the merchant is an apt symbol for conscious seeking, because a merchant is an expert at the determination of value. He is in the import/export business, and is more than likely also well acquainted with the customs and cultures of many lands. His search for fine pearls is therefore likely to be a worldwide one. His vision of what has value is not constrained by the conventions of the society into which he was born. Neither is he bound by man-made divisions, whether familial, tribal, national, racial, or ideological. So he is the epitome of broad-mindedness and professionalism all in one. At this advanced level of spiritual seeking, distinctions between traditions—between East and West, for example—become irrelevant, and more than likely a hindrance to our search for Truth. (Spiritual seekers sometimes forget that the Spirit does not divide and parcel itself out into different traditions and customs. When we say, "This belongs to the Western spiritual tradition," or "That belongs to the Eastern spiritual tradition," we are not speaking for the Spirit, but only reflecting our own cultural biases.)

For the symbol of the "fine pearls," let us look at the biological process that brings real pearls into being. A pearl is the outcome of the incredible effort of an oyster to soothe an irritation. When a grain of sand invades the confined quarters of an oyster's shell, the oyster applies coats of lubricants around the grain to buffer itself. The result is a pearl. It is the oyster's answer to living with an irritation.

A comparable process specific to humans results in "pearls" of a different kind. It is the process of trying to place all of the irritations of our life into perspective, developing explanations that help make life livable despite its difficulties. Sometimes, many layers of these explanations form a coherent system called a philosophy. Espousing such a philosophy of life empowers us to live comfortably with various irritations. And since the difficulties that each of us encounters are not identical, our diverse experiences give rise to various philosophies, each meaningful in its own context.

By seeking out "fine pearls," our merchant, or global seeker, is examining various cultural traditions to find the philosophy, or the system of explanations, that rings true with his own individual pattern of unfolding. And he wants to use this system, not so much to put his past into perspective, but to structure his future actions. For indeed, the higher, more important aspect of a philosophical system is that it allows one to commit oneself with confidence. When we find a philosophical system that rings true and commit ourselves to its use in guiding our future actions, it is as if we were parting with all else for this one system. In the words of the parable, the merchant sold all that he had to own that pearl of great value.

In terms of the Ajna or sixth chakra, the parable is saying that to fully harness the powers of this center for the cause of the Kingdom—the unfolding of Consciousness—we must demonstrate commitment.

The Ajna Chakra is related to the pineal gland, which lies deep within the brain in line with the spot directly between the eyebrows. Because of this location, and because the gland is thought to play a part in the expression of clairvoyance and the like, the pineal gland has been called "the Third Eye." When the Third Eye is opened, the individual is supposedly able to relate to the essences of things directly, as opposed to being constrained to dealing with them on the surface. The pearl of great value therefore signifies that the Third Eye is working to foster the ultimate in self-understanding because it enables the individual to see beyond outer symbolism into the real nature of things.

Only when self-understanding is achieved can we formulate the specific purpose of our life. That is why the merchant in the parable is willing to part with everything he owns to acquire this pearl. In reality, we must remove every shackle that prevents us from fully actualizing our life purpose. It is also significant that the price of the pearl is relative to the merchant's worth. This tells us that when we have found life's purpose—the pearl that we have been looking for—all of our previous life becomes a prelude to this moment.

Now let's move to a second level of interpretation of this parable. The second level is obtained when we equate the merchant with the Numinous itself as it seeks to express itself in a human reality. There is a certain reversibility found in this process that is not found at the previous chakras. By the time Consciousness has been able to express itself through the facilities of the Third Eye, or the Ajna Chakra, it is hard to tell from which direction the efforts of striving are coming. From the outside, the individual may be striving to give a faithful expression to a philosophy of life, while from the inside, a certain divine principle is striving to give itself embodiment in human form.

Because of this reversibility, we can also say that the Numinous, with the same degree of intentionality that we saw in the merchant, is seeking that perfect pearl—that Third Eye of someone who is prepared—on which to concentrate all of its efforts. When this acquisition is made, the Numinous and the Kingdom, synonymously, are able to limit themselves to one function. For example, the expression of the Numinous at the lower chakras is accomplished in ways that can be called miraculous, or unconventional. These modes of expression are designed to assist us to awaken to the wonder of being, to the adventure that is life. However, miracles are not necessary when we are conscious enough to regard life in all its manifestations as a wondrous, miraculous event. This realization becomes possible when the Third Eye is open, and, to the Numinous, this is the pearl of great value that it seeks. For when this stage of the expansion of human consciousness has been reached, it can be said that Consciousness has become conscious of itself.

Finally, in order to demonstrate the universality of this experience, we shall look at another way of articulating the principle of the reversibility of the direction of effort in striving. It is expressed here in the form of a dilemma posed by the ancient Taoist sage, Chuang Tzu:

> Once upon a time, I, Chuang Tzu, dreamt I was a butterfly, fluttering hither and thither to all intents a butterfly. I was conscious only of following my fancies as a butterfly, and was unconscious of my individuality as a man. Suddenly, I awoke and there I lay, myself again. Now I do not know whether I was then a man dreaming I was a butterfly, or whether I am now a butterfly dreaming I am a man.[3]

Like Chuang Tzu, the issue for the individual working at mastering the Third Eye, the pearl of great value, is whether he is trying to embody

Consciousness, or whether Consciousness is using him as a vehicle to express itself.

THE PARABLE OF THE DRAGNET OF FISH— THE PRINCIPLE OF CONSOLIDATION AND ASSIMILATION

The final of the Parables of the Kingdom deals with how the process of the expansion of Consciousness expresses itself at the seventh or Sahasrara Chakra:

> [47] Again, the Kingdom of Heaven is like a net that was thrown into the sea and gathered fish of every kind. [48] When it was full, men drew it ashore and sat down and sorted the good into containers but threw away the bad. [49] So it will be at the close of the age. The angels will come out and separate the evil from the righteous [50] and throw them into the fiery furnace. In that place there will be weeping and gnashing of teeth. (Matthew 13: 47–50)

The underlying meaning of this parable has to do with the process of judgment that is taking place in the human psyche. On the surface, it seems to deal with the final judgment and the determination of individual destinies, but this impression was derived from the expression "the end of the world" in the Kings James version. A more up-to-date translation, such as that in the English Standard Version we've been using, has rendered this expression "the close of the age."

As such, in this parable, we are dealing with the conclusion of a cycle of human experiences, or an "incarnation," from the point of view of the soul. Although there are different ways of understanding the reincarnation process, the more sophisticated explanations credit the process of rebirth not to the human mind or ego, but to the soul.[4] This level of reality, the soul, is connected to the individual in the earthly life, and when death of the biological organism ensues, the soul assimilates the experiences of that life into itself. Then, depending on what additional lessons it needs in an earthly environment, it becomes drawn back to the earth in another body. The circumstances within which the soul is born are determined by the lessons it still needs to acquire in order to balance the experiences already assimilated. It is said, however, that when the Sahasrara Chakra is awakened, the individual becomes free of the need to take rebirth. Such an individual becomes liberated, or *mukta,* as it is called in Sanskrit. This liberation from repeated cycles of life and death is called *mukti,* and the one so blessed with it realizes his unity with the Eternal Spirit, or God.

It is within this doctrinal context that we find explanations to this parable. But first let me emphasize the fact that, though reincarnation is often thought of as alien to what is traditionally taught as Christian doctrine, it does not mean that there is no support for it in the New Testament. As we have already seen, many Eastern concepts and doctrines have heretofore gone unrecognized in the teachings of Jesus; the principle of reincarnation (at least some version of it) is no exception.

Turning now to the parable, we will unravel its meaning by tackling some of its key symbols. The symbols of the sea and fish are quite universal in religious mythologies of various cultures. They therefore belong to the class of symbols called archetypes, of which we spoke earlier. The sea, within which the net was cast, represents what Carl Gustav Jung labeled the collective unconscious.[5] It is from this collective level of psychic urges, promptings, and mental and emotional patterns that the individual ego is configured. The ego, thus configured, is given expression in the earthly life and daily activities of the individual.

The fish represent individual identities, or lives, experienced throughout various incarnations. The net represents an aggregation of these fish, or lives, and therefore stands for the soul. The sorting of the fish represents the process of judgment in which the soul engages. This process entails the selection and rejection of life experiences from the soul's many incarnations. After this process is complete, that part of the soul that is in harmony with the Principle of Unity becomes one with God. The rest goes back to the collective unconscious.

The concept of the "end," whether that be of the world, or of a time, represents the end of an era for the soul. When the end comes for the soul, it must integrate itself through the medium of an individual earthly life, and, if necessary, drink the bitter cup of sorrow as it deals with any inharmonious or unassimilated experiences that exist.

TWELVE

KUNDALINI SYMBOLISM IN THE MIRACLES—AS RECORDED IN JOHN AND MATTHEW

THE ACTIVATED KUNDALINI AT WORK

It is probably not unreasonable to speculate that if someone were to engage in a spiritual practice utilizing the exercises outlined in the Sermon on the Mount and the Parables of the Kingdom, he or she could experience a release of the pent-up psychic energy of Kundalini. Of course, there are no guarantees, since many factors—conscious and unconscious—play a part in determining whether someone is ready for this life-altering event.

As stated in the Introduction, I believe that the New Testament disguises the preparation for Kundalini awakening by exhorting Christians to prepare themselves for the Second Coming of Christ. Furthermore, this preparation was to be engaged in with total commitment, since no one knew the hour or the day when Christ would return. I see an equivalent open-endedness here in the attitude required for the spiritual seeker to awaken Kundalini, because it, like the returning Christ, does not operate on our agendas, but on its own.

One of the chief manifestations of an activated Kundalini is its power to "heal" and purify the body, lifting the entire bodily consciousness in the process. When this energy is sufficiently liberated from the restrictions imposed by patterns of our individual thinking, feeling, and acting, it begins to have free reign in our life, removing whatever barriers that remain. This aspect of Kundalini is expressed in the symbolism of two serpents entwining a staff or some other vertical axis. Variations of this symbolism can be found in the myths of diverse cultures. According to Joseph Campbell,[1] it can be found as early as 2350–2150 BCE in Akkad, ca. 2025 BCE in Sumer, and all the way down to our time as the emblem of the medical profession in the Western world. In tracing some of the modifications that this symbol has undergone, Joseph Henderson, in his individual contribution to the collective work *Man And His Symbols* states:

> [T]he snake, as represented by the therapeutic symbol of the Roman god of medicine Aesculapius…has survived to modem times as a sign of the medical profession. This was originally a nonpoisonous tree snake; as we see it, coiled around the staff of the healing gods, it seems to embody a kind of mediation between earth and heaven.
>
> A still more important and widespread symbol of chtonic transcendence is the motif of the two entwined serpents. These are the famous Naga serpents of ancient India: and we also find them in Greece as the entwined serpents on the end of the staff belonging to the god Hermes…
>
> Originally in Egypt Hermes was known as the ibis-headed god Thoth, and therefore was conceived as the bird form of the transcendent principle. Again, in the Olympian period of Greek mythology, Hermes recovered attributes of the bird life to add to his chthonic nature as serpent. His staff acquired wings above the serpents, becoming the caduceus or winged staff of Mercury, and the god himself became the "flying man" with his winged hat and sandals.[2]

The association of the serpent with healing is not restricted to the sphere of mythology, but pervades religions as well. It can be found in Hinduism, Jainism, Buddhism, and Mithraism, to name a few.

It can also be found in the Old Testament, where, despite a total

Figure 4: Serpent Symbolism

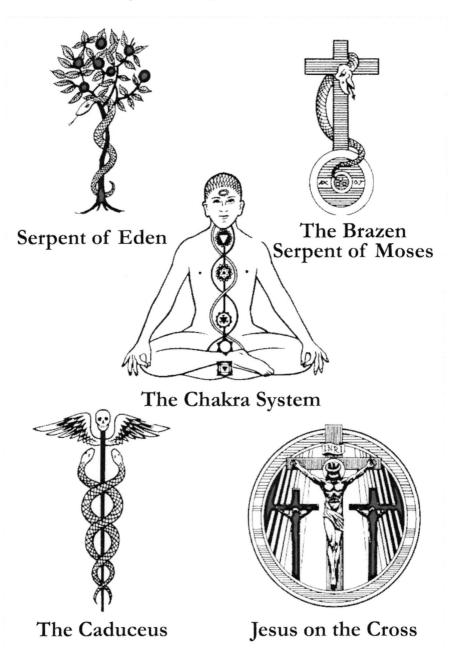

Serpent of Eden

The Brazen
Serpent of Moses

The Chakra System

The Caduceus

Jesus on the Cross

disdain for the serpent as something evil (as seen in the Eden episode), it shines forth on one occasion to confer life instead of death. In the incident of the brazen serpent, recorded in the Book of Numbers, the Israelites were in the wilderness, on their way from a military engagement on Mount Hor, when vigorous dissension broke out among them. We are informed that, because of this dissension, "the Lord sent fiery serpents among the people, and they bit the people, so that many people of Israel died." The people beseeched Moses, and after making intercession to God in prayer, he was instructed by God to make "a fiery serpent and set it on a pole, and everyone who is bitten, when he sees it, shall live." Moses did as he was instructed, with the result being that "if a serpent bit anyone, he would look at the bronze serpent and live" (Numbers 21:8–9).

It is significant that in the Gospel of John, Jesus highlighted this incident as a foreshadowing of his crucifixion, saying, "as Moses lifted up the serpent in the wilderness, so must the Son of Man be lifted up, that whoever believes in him may have eternal life." (John 3:14, 15).

Jesus's comparison suggests a further parallel between himself and the process of the activated Kundalini, which is symbolized by the erect serpent of brass. This three-way relationship, first between the serpent and Kundalini, second between Kundalini and healing, and third between Jesus and Kundalini, helps us to gain a better perspective on the wonder-working aspect of Jesus's ministry, particularly that aspect related to healing.

THE SYMBOLISM OF THE MIRACLES

When seen esoterically, the miracles of Jesus are not actual events, but symbolic representations of the flow of Life in its unbridled expression. As a representation of the activated Kundalini, Jesus became the emissary of healing in its physical, emotional, and spiritual aspects. This view of the miracles is consistent with the underlying theme of transformation in the New Testament.

It is apparent that the authors of Matthew and John made every effort to give due representation to Kundalini in the miracles by showing sequences of miracles whose particulars match up with the characteristics of the seven major chakras. However, the relationship is not an exact one, as there are many more miracles mentioned than can be aligned with the chakras. As with the presence of esoteric information in the New Testament generally, there is enough seeming arbitrariness to many of the miracles to obscure the underlying relationship with the chakras.

The symbolic status of the miracles is reinforced by the writers of the Gospels showing different initial or first miracles. The Gospel of John goes so far as identifying a specific miracle, the wedding in Cana, as Jesus's first, stating "this beginning of miracles did Jesus in Cana of Galilee, and manifested forth his glory; and the disciples believed on him" (John 2:11).

In Matthew, the first mention of miracles occurs after the story of the temptations and the calling of the twelve disciples: "And he went throughout all Galilee, teaching in their synagogues and proclaiming the gospel of the kingdom and healing every disease and every affliction among the people." (Matthew 4:23) However, the first of a series of individualized miracles for which the chakra association can be established occurs only after the Sermon on the Mount:

> [1] When he came down from the mountain, great crowds followed him. [2] And behold, a leper came to him and knelt before him, saying, "Lord, if you will, you can make me clean." [3] And Jesus stretched out his hand and touched him, saying, "I will; be clean." And immediately his leprosy was cleansed. [4] And Jesus said to him, "See that you say nothing to anyone, but go, show yourself to the priest and offer the gift that Moses commanded, for a proof to them." (Matthew 8:1-4)

In both Mark and Luke, the healing of a man with an unclean spirit was Jesus's first recorded miracle, and occurred after he had called the twelve disciples:

> [21] And they went into Capernaum, and immediately on the Sabbath he entered the synagogue and was teaching. [22] And

they were astonished at his teaching, for he taught them as one who had authority, and not as the scribes. [23] And immediately there was in their synagogue a man with an unclean spirit. And he cried out, [24] "What have you to do with us, Jesus of Nazareth? Have you come to destroy us? I know who you are—the Holy One of God." [25] But Jesus rebuked him, saying, "Be silent, and come out of him!" [26] And the unclean spirit, convulsing him and crying out with a loud voice, came out of him. [27] And they were all amazed, so that they questioned among themselves, saying, "What is this? A new teaching with authority! He commands even the unclean spirits, and they obey him." [28] And at once his fame spread everywhere throughout all the surrounding region of Galilee. (Mark 1:21-28)

Luke also records this healing almost word for word as in Mark:

[31] And he went down to Capernaum, a city of Galilee. And he was teaching them on the Sabbath, [32] and they were astonished at his teaching, for his word possessed authority. [33] And in the synagogue there was a man who had the spirit of an unclean demon, and he cried out with a loud voice, [34] "Ha! What have you to do with us, Jesus of Nazareth? Have you come to destroy us? I know who you are—the Holy One of God." [35] But Jesus rebuked him, saying, "Be silent and come out of him!" And when the demon had thrown him down in their midst, he came out of him, having done him no harm. [36] And they were all amazed and said to one another, "What is this word? For with authority and power he commands the unclean spirits, and they come out!" [37] And reports about him went out into every place in the surrounding region. (Luke 4:31-37)

The Correlation of Miracles and Chakras

In the Gospel of John, there are only seven miracles chosen for high profile. By examining their characteristics, we see that each miracle represents the result of energization or healing at one of the chakras, progressing from the first chakra to the seventh. In Matthew, that relationship also holds for the first eleven* high-profile miracles occurring immediately after the Sermon on the Mount.

John's Record of the Miracles

First, let us examine the relevance of the seven miracles of John in terms of Kundalini awakening. Those seven miracles are as follows:

- Turning water into wine
- Healing a nobleman's son from a distance
- Healing a paralytic man at the Pool of Bethesda
- Feeding the five thousand
- Walking on water at the Sea of Galilee
- Making a blind man see
- Raising Lazarus from the dead

Turning Water into Wine

This miracle described in John 2:1–10 relates how Jesus turned six pots of water into wine during a wedding celebration at Cana. This miracle corresponds to the Muladhara Chakra and the glands of generation in the endocrine system, otherwise known as the gonads: the testes in males and the ovaries in females.

Turning water into wine symbolizes the energy transformation that must accompany a change in consciousness. In Yoga literature, it is maintained that for transformation to take place, we must convert the urge for physical, biological continuation to a comparable urge for spiritual advancement. It is also said that *retas* (sexual fluids) must be converted into *ojas* (higher forms of energy).

---

* The eleven miracles are distributed over nine chakras, with two of the major seven covered twice.

Figure 5: The Miracles in John

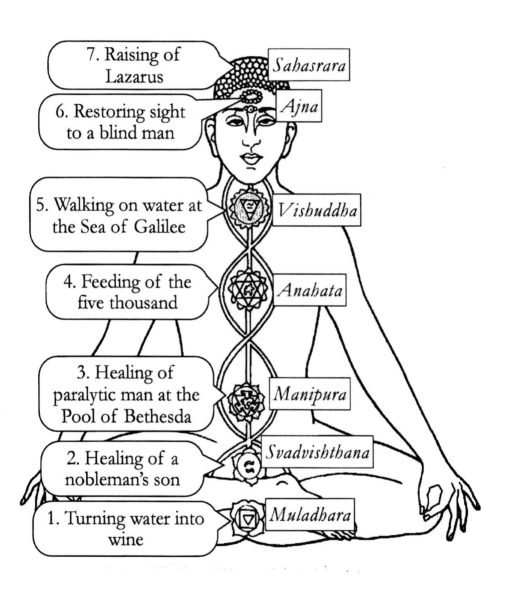

7. Raising of Lazarus — *Sahasrara*

6. Restoring sight to a blind man — *Ajna*

5. Walking on water at the Sea of Galilee — *Vishuddha*

4. Feeding of the five thousand — *Anahata*

3. Healing of paralytic man at the Pool of Bethesda — *Manipura*

2. Healing of a nobleman's son — *Svadvishthana*

1. Turning water into wine — *Muladhara*

In *The Bases of Yoga*, Sri Aurobindo explains the relationship between the sexual impulse and the transformation of consciousness:

> To master the sex-impulse—to become so much master of the sex-centre that the sexual energy would be drawn upwards, not thrown outwards and wasted—it is so indeed that the force in the seed can be turned into a primal physical energy supporting all the others, retas into ojas. But no error can be more perilous than to accept the immixture of the sexual desire and some kind of subtle satisfaction of it and look on this as a part of the sadhana. It would be the most effective way to head straight towards spiritual downfall and throw into the atmosphere forces that would block the supramental descent, bringing instead the descent of adverse vital powers to disseminate disturbance and disaster. This deviation must be absolutely thrown away, should it try to occur and expunged from the consciousness, if the Truth is to be brought down and the work is to be done.[3]

This is certainly not a concept alien to the teachings of Jesus. For the individual with an awareness of these matters, his statement about one's sexual status and the Kingdom of Heaven can be seen as addressing the same subject:

> [T]here are eunuchs who have been so from birth, and there are eunuchs who have been made eunuchs by men, and there are eunuchs who have made themselves eunuchs for the sake of the Kingdom of Heaven. Let the one who is able to receive this receive it. (Matthew 19:12)

Further, the fact that this miracle involved six water pots suggests a symbolic relationship to the other six chakras, in which the latent Kundalini becomes energized and ascends from the Muladhara to enliven them.

Healing the Nobleman's Son from a Distance

In this miracle described in John 4: 46–54, Jesus heeded the intercession of a nobleman and healed his sick son in Capernaum. Meanwhile, Jesus was in Cana, a distance of eighteen miles. The relationship of the miracle to the Svadvishthana Chakra hinges on the underlying principles common to both. The salient feature of this miracle is that Jesus did not have to be in physical proximity to the sick individual in order to transfer healing power. Also, the act of healing was done at the request of a third party, further emphasizing the factor of intermediation.

Healing the Paralytic Man at the Pool of Bethesda

This miracle in John 5:1–9 deals with the healing of a paralytic who was unable to receive healing by reason of his inability to move. After inquiring whether the man desired healing, Jesus healed him when he replied in the affirmative. The healing took place on the Sabbath and therefore incurred the disapproval of the people.

This healing clearly demonstrates a relationship to the Manipura Chakra and the affiliated endocrine gland. The Manipura Chakra is described as the seat of the will, and is reinforced by the function of the adrenal glands. These glands produce one of the hormones recognized as the chief source of the power complex in humans. The man at the poolside had been affected for thirty-eight years and was no nearer now to taking advantage of the healing that had always been just outside his grasp. He is symbolic of individuals who are ineffectual because they cannot gather the necessary energy to put their plans into action.

Although the abuse of power is a more prevalent form of Manipura Chakra malfunction, failure here could also be expressed as a lack of true effectiveness in pursuing things that are truly worthwhile.

Feeding the Five Thousand

This miracle is found in John 6:1–14. It describes the occasion when Jesus, taking only five loaves and two fish, multiplied them to feed five thousand people. Twelve baskets of fragments remained after all had eaten. The principle behind this miracle is the provision of spiritual sustenance from a divine source and the distribution of this nourishment to all areas of need. Such a principle is expressed through the medium of compassion. The Anahata Chakra with which this miracle is linked, also relates to the distribution of both nutrients and compassion. It is connected to the circulatory system of the body, which, in turn, is responsible for the distribution of nutrients throughout the body.

The endocrine gland associated with the Anahata Chakra is the thymus. Its function has to do with the maintenance of the immune system of the body, which really boils down to ensuring the homogeneity of the body system as a functioning unit.

Walking on Water at the Sea of Galilee

In this miracle, described in John 6:16–21, the disciples were taking a trip on the Sea of Galilee, from Tiberias to Capernaum, when Jesus approached them, walking on the water. This miracle seems to depart from the pattern of the others in that it does not represent a healing or some other beneficial act. The principle that this miracle portrays is one of mastery over the "elements." It demonstrates the ability of the illuminated mind to rise above mass consciousness, symbolized by the water. The symbol of water is quite apt, for it represents life situations that would engulf us should we not make the effort to rise above them.

The Vishuddha Chakra, with which this miracle is linked, is related to the thyroid gland in the throat. The function of this glands is associated with respiration and overall body metabolism. It also has an effect on mood, so much so that it has been called the Dr. Jekyll and Mr. Hyde gland because of the wide mood swings caused when it malfunctions. Walking on the water symbolizes the total control we can achieve over mood and emotion when the active Kundalini is united with the principle of Consciousness in the Vishuddha Chakra.

Making a Blind Man See

In John 9:1–12, we find Jesus giving sight to a man blind since birth. The report of this event includes certain concepts that reinforce the association between the miracles and the chakras. Before healing the blind man, Jesus was asked by his disciples whether the man's blindness was the result of sin by him or his parents. Jesus replied that the man was born blind, not because of sin, "but that the works of God might be displayed in him." Jesus then went on to declare himself as "the light of the world."

This miracle stands for the activation of the Ajna Chakra or the opening of the Third Eye. It was said earlier that in various esoteric literature, the opening of the Third Eye relates to the activation of the pineal gland, which medical science has now confirmed to be light-sensitive. It is held in esoteric circles that the activation of the pineal gland is what constitutes the process known as enlightenment. When the consciousness is enlightened, we becomes capable of discerning the real from the symbolic, and the eternal from the temporal.

Raising Lazarus from the Dead

The raising of Lazarus in John 11:1–46 represents the resurrection in consciousness that occurs when Kundalini reaches the Sahasrara Chakra. When this occurs, the individual becomes "dead to the world," but alive in the Spirit, meaning that he takes his cues and directions from things that pertain to the spiritual, as opposed to the material.

The awakening of the Sahasrara Chakra also implies our mastery over death and the fear of dying. Indeed, it is only then that we can truly be said to be born again.

The Miracles in Matthew

The relationship of the miracles to the chakras in Matthew is somewhat looser than that found in John, but not because the association is any less valid. The authors of Matthew and John simply selected different ways to represent the healing of each chakra.

The format used to convey the chakra association in each Gospel also differs. Whereas John covers seven high-profile miracles, Matthew deals initially with eleven. The first nine of these can be associated with the seven major chakras, plus two minor ones found between the fifth and sixth, and sixth and seventh, chakras respectively.[4] The final two miracles relate again to the sixth and fifth chakras, in a descending pattern. The resulting pattern embodied in Matthew is representative of the Kundalini ascending through the seven major and two minor chakras, and then after awakening the Sahasrara Chakra, flowing back down as far as the throat center.

The miracles that establish the above pattern are as follows:

- Healing the leper
- Healing the centurion's servant from a distance
- Healing Peter's mother-in-law
- Healing many evil spirits and other illnesses
- Calming the stormy sea
- Healing two men possessed with devils
- Healing a man sick with palsy by forgiving his sins
- Healing a hemorrhaging woman
- Raising the ruler's daughter from a coma
- Restoring sight to two blind men
- Restoring speech to a man made dumb because of demonic possession

Healing the Leper

The details of this miracle are found in Matthew 8:14. Jesus healed a leper by touching him after the leper requested that Jesus make him clean. This miracle parallels the miracle of turning water into wine in John, but both symbolize different characteristics of the Muladhara Chakra. This miracle embodies the function of the Muladhara to anchor the spirit in matter.

It was said earlier that the Muladhara Chakra is related to physical survival and therefore the satisfaction of physical needs. Disease and destruction of body tissue, such as occur with leprosy, undo the anchoring function of the Muladhara Chakra. The idea at this point is for the spirit in man to outgrow its material home and not for that home to be wrecked. No disease is more symbolic of physical destruction than leprosy. This disease manifests itself as a degeneration of bodily tissue such that the leper

Figure 6: The Miracles in Matthew

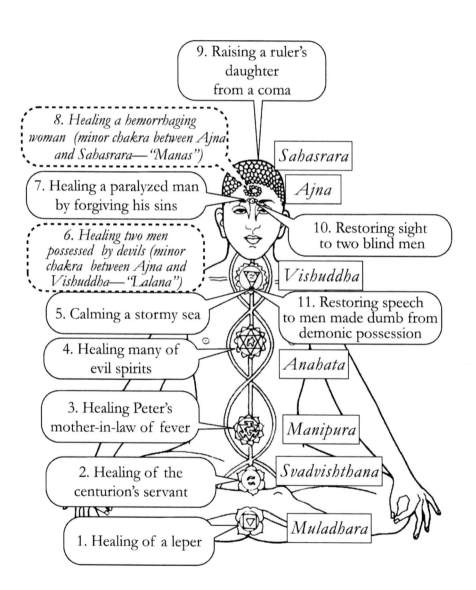

9. Raising a ruler's daughter from a coma

8. *Healing a hemorrhaging woman (minor chakra between Ajna and Sahasrara—"Manas")*

7. Healing a paralyzed man by forgiving his sins

6. *Healing two men possessed by devils (minor chakra between Ajna and Vishuddha—"Lalana")*

5. Calming a stormy sea

4. Healing many of evil spirits

3. Healing Peter's mother-in-law of fever

2. Healing of the centurion's servant

1. Healing of a leper

10. Restoring sight to two blind men

11. Restoring speech to men made dumb from demonic possession

Sahasrara

Ajna

Vishuddha

Anahata

Manipura

Svadvishthana

Muladhara

eventually becomes disfigured. The healing that Jesus performed symbolized the restoration of contact between the body and the spirit.

Healing the Centurion's Servant from a Distance

In this miracle, found in Matthew 8:5–13, Jesus was asked by a centurion
to heal his trusted servant, who was critically ill with paralysis. When Jesus
agreed to go and heal the servant, the centurion replied that it was not
necessary for Jesus to go to his home; he said that just a word from Jesus
would suffice. After praising the centurion for possessing such a high level
of faith, Jesus healed the servant from where he was.

This healing is similar to that of the nobleman's son in John, where a
person of status was interceding on behalf of someone with whom there
was a strong bond of affection. Here, the intercession was made by someone of rank interceding for someone under his authority. Also, the healing was performed at a distance. This miracle again demonstrates the role
of mediation in bringing about healing at the Svadvishthana Chakra.

There is also some significance in the nature of the disease being healed.
The paralysis that the servant suffered is characterized by a lack of ability
to move or to exercise full bodily functions, likely as a result of damage to
the central nervous system. The Svadvishthana Chakra, through its association with the sex function, is related to the ability to feel sensations,
and the servant's healing symbolizes a return of this ability.

Healing Peter's Mother-in-Law

This miracle is found in Matthew 8:14–15. The incident describes how
Jesus went with Peter to his home and found his wife's mother in bed with
fever. Jesus healed her, and she got up to minister to him and Peter. This
miracle contrasts with the healing of the paralytic in John. It would relate
to the Manipura Chakra.

Healing Many of Evil Spirits and Other Illnesses

These are really many miracles, but the way they are presented suggests
that they symbolize one principle only. In Matthew 8:16–17, Jesus was

brought many who were possessed with devils and cast the evil spirits out with his word. Then he healed all that were sick in order to fulfill the word of Isaiah the prophet:

> That evening they brought to him many who were oppressed by demons, and he cast out the spirits with a word and healed all who were sick. This was to fulfill what was spoken by the prophet Isaiah: "He took our illnesses and bore our diseases." (Matthew 8:16–17)

The way these miracles are related, i.e., as the fulfillment of a prophecy in Isaiah, suggests they reflect healing of the Anahata Chakra, the heart center, or the center of compassion and empathy. The miracle that corresponds to this chakra in John was the feeding of the five thousand—another act with a spontaneous, empathetic flavor.

Calming the Sea

In this miracle, related in Matthew 8:17–23, we find Jesus with his disciples in a boat, when a storm broke. Jesus was asleep, and disarray over the storm broke out among the disciples. They woke him, and he immediately "rebuked" the sea to restore calm. This relates to the fifth Vishuddha Chakra and symbolizes mastery of the awakened consciousness over the elements of life, be they physical, emotional, or mental. It also symbolizes the power of consciousness to restore order out of chaos.

It is significant that this miracle compares almost exactly with John's miracle of Jesus walking on the water. In both cases, power was demonstrated over physical expressions of nature.

Healing Two Possessed with Devils

This miracle, found in Matthew 8:28–33, concerns the healing of two men who were under the influence of demons. The demons were driven out by Jesus and entered a herd of swine. The characteristics of this miracle also qualify it as one that relates to the fifth chakra. However, it should instead relate to one of the minor chakras found between the Vishuddha and the Ajna, or fifth and sixth chakras. This has been called, by certain classical sources, the *Lalana* chakra.[4]

Healing a Palsy Victim by Forgiving His Sins

This miracle, found in Matthew 9:1–9, involves the healing of a man who was paralyzed. Upon seeing the man, who had been brought to him, Jesus told him that his sins were forgiven. The significance of this miracle is that it links the existence of health problems to the existence of sin. This contrasts to the miracle of the healing of the blind man in John, in which the man's handicap had nothing to do with sin.

It is significant that both the miracle in John and this one relate to the Ajna Chakra. In John, however, the relationship is rather straightforward, with restoration of sight symbolizing the opening of the Third Eye. In this miracle, the relationship is merely implied.

The "forgiveness of sins" is also a symbol for enlightenment and the Ajna Chakra. This is because when we experience "enlightenment," we are able to see how all that we have ever been and all that we have ever done, whether good or bad, could be used to benefit others. We therefore become "forgiven," as there are no carryovers in the form of guilt and the like. We use our energies for constructive purposes instead.

Healing the Hemorrhaging Woman

This healing is reported in Matthew 9:20–22. Jesus was on his way to perform another healing, the raising of the young woman in a coma, which we will cover next, when his garment was touched at the hem by a woman who had been hemorrhaging for twelve years. No additional details of the woman's condition are given; however, Jesus perceived that someone had touched him, and upon seeing the woman, assured her that her faith had made her whole. This miracle relates to the chakra between the Ajna and the Sahasrara, the *Manas*.[5]

Raising a Young Woman in a Coma

This miracle, detailed in Matthew 9:18 and 23–26, involves the daughter of a nobleman, who was near death. The report says that the people attending her had given her up for dead, but Jesus assured them she was just "asleep."

Whether she was indeed dead or just in a coma is immaterial for the underlying principle portrayed by this miracle. This principle is the awakening of the individual from unconsciousness to full consciousness. This miracle therefore relates quite clearly to the Sahasrara Chakra, as does the miracle of the raising of Lazarus in John.

Restoring Sight to Two Blind Men

Matthew 9:27–31 tells us that after Jesus performed the miracle of raising the nobleman's daughter, two blind men approached him and requested healing. He asked them if they believed he could heal them, to which they replied in the affirmative. Jesus then healed them.

This marks the point in the series of miracles in which the energy begins to flow downward through the chakras. After the Kundalini reaches the Sahasrara Chakra and we become spiritually awakened (symbolized by the raising of the nobleman's daughter and Lazarus), the energy flows down to the Ajna. The opening of the blind men's eyes here relates to the Third-Eye symbol of the Ajna Chakra.

Restoring Speech to a Man Made Dumb by Demonic Possession

This miracle is recorded in Matthew 9:32–33 and relates to the Speech Center, or the Vishuddha Chakra.

Although Jesus did many other miracles, those works were just alluded to, both by John and Matthew. For example, Matthew 9:35 said, "And Jesus went about all the cities and villages, teaching in their synagogues, and preaching the gospel of the kingdom, and healing every sickness and every disease among the people."

THIRTEEN

THE DESTINY OF THE SAVED

BENEATH THE SYMBOLISM OF HEAVEN

Among the many questions that arise when we interpret Jesus's life and teachings psychologically is that of the future destiny of the "saved." Under traditional interpretations of the New Testament, the saved are thought to inherit the Kingdom of Heaven, which, also traditionally interpreted, is seen as a place of unsurpassable and neverending joy. This inheritance is regarded as just reward for present-life righteousness and sacrifices.

Upon acknowledging the views of this book, however—namely, that Jesus represents a universal principle to be assimilated into consciousness and that the Kingdom of Heaven is *the process* of the expansion of Consciousness itself—we must rethink the destiny of the saved. Indeed, a destiny that harmonizes with this way of looking at Jesus and his teachings is one that also addresses the question of how the process of the expansion of Consciousness ultimately resolves itself.

To properly pursue this question, we must return to the seven-tiered model of Man that provided the framework for understanding the work of consciousness expansion to be undertaken at the individual level. This model has the ability to contribute to our understanding of mankind's collective future, as well as the flexibility to accommodate traditional views of Man's destiny. It fits all these roles by explaining the underlying symbolism of the New Testament on the subject (particularly those of Paul).

The particular aspect of the seven-tiered model that is important to us here is that which links each chakra above the first (the Muladhara) with a level of reality beyond the physical one. With the inclusion of the first chakra, which relates to the physical body, our human reality has the potential of being in tune with seven interpenetrating levels of reality, or "worlds."[1]

The first world is the physical one, which we inhabit with the physical body. As for the other six "worlds," these are of a higher order and are not readily discernable to ordinary human consciousness. We are connected to them through higher "bodies," of which we may not have any tangible perception. Actually, we may experience connections with these bodies through such phenomena as dreams, hallucinations, visions, intuitions and revelations, astral travel, and the like. A clear example of an individual experiencing himself in a higher body and world is found in Paul's account of a man who was "caught up to the third heaven." This person is generally acknowledged to be the apostle Paul himself. About this experience, he wrote:

> [2] I know a man in Christ who fourteen years ago was caught up to the third heaven—whether in the body or out of the body I do not know, God knows. [3] And I know that this man was caught up into paradise—whether in the body or out of the body I do not know, God knows—[4] and he heard things that cannot be told, which man may not utter. (2 Corinthians 12:2–4)

The fact that Paul talks around the incident suggests that, apart from his own sense of modesty, he found it quite difficult to find familiar terms of reference to relate it to ordinary experience. His disclosure that this man "heard things that cannot be told" should not be taken literally, in the sense of physical hearing of audible words being involved. What it does suggest is that the capacity was not there to express the heightened level of consciousness to which this individual was exposed, in the constricted terms of ordinary language. In other words, there were no terms of reference to guide one in the translation of the intelligence that characterized such a high order of reality in terms pertinent to the mundane, physical one.

It is for this very reason that different realities can coexist with the physical one, without our having so much as an inkling of this reality, that self-transformation through the expansion of consciousness is necessary. By striving to expand our consciousness, we are establishing stronger and more stable connections with our higher bodies and the higher worlds of which they are a part. The strength of these connections would be inversely related to how much our understanding of reality is dominated by physical sensations. This is one of the reasons austerities and asceticism form such an important part of the observances of many religious groups. Paul himself expressed his concern that Christians not be overwhelmed by the sensations of the bodily consciousness, but instead to "put to death" both the body and its deeds:

> [13] For if you live according to the flesh you will die, but if by the Spirit you put to death the deeds of the body, you will live. (Romans 8:13)
>
> Put to death therefore what is earthly in you: sexual immorality, impurity, passion, evil desire, and covetousness, which is idolatry. (Colossians 3:5)

The aim of the transformation of consciousness from the perspective of the seven-tiered model of Man would find support from the discoveries of theoretical physics. Theoretical physicists have confirmed what the mystics of antiquity were contending—that what we perceive as reality on the physical level is only just a special case of a larger reality. We now know that our perception of materiality through various manifestations—form, density, and weight, for example—is a consequence of the limiting nature of our senses.

There was a time when the molecule was considered the basic constituent of matter, but then that "basic constituent" changed to the atom and eventually to even finer "particles." We are now at the point where it is scientifically illiterate to talk of a constituent "particle" of matter. Instead, research has confirmed that the constituent of matter is better explained in terms of a wave rather than a particle. What scientific research has done is to take us further and further from the authority of our physical senses, to the point where the very matter of which our bodies are composed "disappears," to reappear as waves, or better still, "vibrations."

In Eastern thought, the nonpermanent nature of reality as perceived through the senses is routinely recognized. They label the physical world and its trappings as *maya,* meaning illusion. From such a perspective, our spiritual duty is not to try to fly off to heaven, but to try to liberate ourselves from a state of illusory existence. This aim of liberation is pursued through the discipline of Yoga, which comprises separate practices aimed at strengthening the body (Hatha Yoga), the mind (Raja Yoga), and the will (Karma Yoga).[2] It is believed that if one is successful at Yoga, he or she can achieve union with the higher aspects of his or her being while yet in the physical life.

REINCARNATION

Another important aspect of the seven-tiered model that helps clarify the destiny of the "saved" is the idea of reincarnation. Although there are various interpretations of this idea, its basic thrust is that what we see and experience as an individual life in the physical world is only one of the many attempts of the soul to perfect itself in divine virtues. As the process of perfection advances, the soul becomes progressively capable of impressing the consciousness of a higher reality in the mind of the individual to whom it is connected in time-space. When the process of perfection of the soul reaches a level where earthly experiences are no longer necessary for it, it becomes liberated. Such a soul would no longer be subject to rebirth, except as a deliberate act of sacrifice for the purpose of enlightening and liberating the rest of humanity. In terms of the chakra concept, a liberated soul would correlate with the consciousness anchored in the seventh, or Sahasrara, chakra.

One of the implications of reincarnation is that the physical death of the individual is just the closing of one chapter of experience from the point of view of the soul. When a physical life is concluded, the experiences of that lifetime are evaluated and judged. This judgment is made from the perspective of how the events of the life have contributed to making the soul more conscious of the underlying unity of purpose of existence. As a result of this evaluation, the decision has to be made as to what further earthly experiences, if any, are necessary to round out an incomplete experience or counterbalance inappropriate attitudes.

In contrast to traditional Christian attitudes, advanced practitioners of Yoga do not require the enticement of heaven to live conscientiously. They recognize that just as their current abilities are the accumulated experiences of the soul acquired through past incarnations, present effort will increase the soul's ability to express itself in a future life.

SUPPORT FOR A PROCESS-ORIENTED VIEW OF SPIRITUAL DESTINY IN THE NEW TESTAMENT

As a careful study shows, all the doctrinal elements necessary for us to construct a scenario of Man's future destiny that is consistent with the seven-tiered model of Consciousness are contained in the New Testament. All we need do is take account of the special perspective from which the destiny of Man is viewed and make allowances for it. For example, whereas the seven-tiered model operates in terms of process, the New Testament's perspective is in terms of time and the things that we can accomplish in time. In so doing, the New Testament addresses itself to the matter-bound mind. It tries to impress upon us the transitory nature of existence at the level of the material, and the need to take advantage of opportunities for awakening that, in this context, are infrequent and fleeting.

It is this special perspective of the New Testament that accounts for the individual's destiny being viewed against the two reference points of the death of the individual and the Second Coming of Christ. In contrast to the Eastern teaching of reincarnation, the apostle Paul does not treat destiny as a process, but as something that takes place in two discrete stages: At death, the individual's fate becomes sealed, or "locked-in," and at the Second Coming of Christ, he receives his final reward.

While contributing to making his work of communicating complicated metaphysical processes to ordinary individuals easier, Paul's special perspective from which the destiny of Man is presented creates problems for us. For one thing, his teachings on death lack the theoretical rigor and logical consistency of a philosophical system. It is only when these teachings are evaluated against the more complete system of the seven-tiered model that the inconsistencies evident in them become reconciled.

With respect to his teachings on the finality of death, Paul says: "…it is appointed for man to die once, and after that comes judgment" (Hebrews 9:27). This gives the impression that the individual's fate is sealed at death for all of eternity. Paul's teachings on the fate of Christians who have died reinforce this idea that death is the time of final accounting. In the passage to follow, he suggests that death presents an opportunity for the Christian to be reunited with Christ, his Savior:

> So we are always of good courage. We know that while we are at home in the body we are away from the Lord, [7] for we walk by faith, not by sight. [8] Yes, we are of good courage, and we would rather be away from the body and at home with the Lord. (2 Corinthians 5:6–8)

The idea of death being a time of reward is, however, contradicted by Paul himself, as he tries to describe how the final reward of salvation—the resurrection of the body at the Second Coming of Christ—would be orchestrated. On many occasions, he refers to those who have died as being asleep in Christ. For example, in the quote to follow, he tries to reassure those who are bereaved in the church at Thessalonica that anyone who is already "dead in Christ" will not miss out on their reward:

> [13] But we do not want you to be uninformed, brothers, about those who are asleep, that you may not grieve as others do who have no hope. [14] For since we believe that Jesus died and rose again, even so, through Jesus, God will bring with him those who have fallen asleep. [15] For this we declare to you by a word from the Lord, that we who are alive, who are left until the coming of the Lord, will not precede those who have fallen asleep. [16] For the Lord himself will descend from heaven with a cry of command, with the voice of an archangel, and with the sound of the trumpet of God. And the dead in Christ will rise first. [17] Then we who are alive, who are left, will be caught up together with them in the clouds to meet the Lord in the air, and so we will always be with the Lord. (1 Thessalonians 4:13–17)

When viewed against the background of the seven-tiered model, Paul's pronouncements concerning the fate of the "dead in Christ" are highly symbolic. For example, his idea that the dead in Christ are asleep until the Second Coming becomes just another way of talking about reincarnation. This is not too obvious on the surface, until we recognize that, in contrast to Eastern thought, in which the life process is viewed from the vantage point of higher levels of being (that is, from the levels of soul and spirit), the teachings of Paul view life in terms of the narrow interval of time between birth and death of the individual. From the perspective of this narrow interval, for someone alive at present, a previous incarnation of the soul would not be any different from sleep, since we do not, as a rule, retain any memory of past lives.

Further doctrinal support for the presence of reincarnation in Paul's teachings can be found in the concept of "predestination," which he elucidates in his Romans Epistle. Here, Paul puts forward the idea that individuals could be destined for salvation by reason of being predestinated by God:

> 28 And we know that for those who love God all things work together for good, for those who are called according to his purpose. 29 For those whom he foreknew he also predestined to be conformed to the image of his Son, in order that he might be the firstborn among many brothers. 30 And those whom he predestined he also called, and those whom he called he also justified, and those whom he justified he also glorified. (Romans 8:28–30)

In the above excerpt, this process of "predestination" is shown to involve five different stages. The individual is said to be–

- foreknown by God
- predestinated by God
- called by God
- justified by God, and
- glorified by God.

It is possible that Paul introduced this doctrine because, first, it was confirmed by his own experience, and, second, it gave him the chance to deal with the problem of unequal distribution of opportunity amongst individuals. But he deals with this through the back door. However, not knowing his specific intent, it is difficult to tell if he was fully aware of the link that predestination establishes with reincarnation. The evidence for the equivalence of these two concepts is hardly a matter for contention:

- Reincarnation says that an individual's present-life situation is determined by the past-life experiences of the soul;

- Predestination says that some individuals are destined for salvation by virtue of being foreknown by God.

Recalling that Paul was using the special vantage point of the narrow interval of time comprising birth to death of the individual, foreknowledge of the individual by God simply means that the individual is just continuing a previous conscious effort directed at the awakening of Consciousness.

THE SECOND COMING OF CHRIST

As for the Second Coming of Christ, this became for Paul and the other apostles an "event" against which the final redemption of the individual is referenced. The possibility must be entertained that this "event" served as a metaphor for the final outcome of transformation at the collective level. The distinction between personal and collective salvation is not always made clear in Christian doctrines, even though it forms a basic underpinning to New Testament teachings. Also, the identification of the Second Coming of Christ with salvation at the collective level does not preclude the position taken in the Introduction that the individual can reunite with Christ as a Principle and thus experience the Second Coming in the consciousness. The difference between a personal experience of the Second Coming and that of which the apostles speak is that they were referring, in part, to an occurrence at the collective level.

In terms of personal salvation, this is satisfied by a change of personal consciousness. This is recognized in esoteric circles as "the First Work" or "the Lesser Work." Collective salvation, on the other hand, will be satisfied by a change in the very nature of what we presently acknowledge as "reality." Such a change is "the Greater Work" of the transformation of Consciousness. When it occurs, the result will be a new "reality," which will be just as tangible as the present, material one. In short, the relationship between personal and collective salvation is a cause-and-effect one. Personal transformation is a precondition for collective transformation, for it is only when sufficiently large numbers of people transform consciousness individually that a new "consensus reality" occurs.

The whole process can be likened to the action of a teeter-totter: when the balance shifts in favor of Consciousness over un-Consciousness, in the collective sense, the whole thing tips. This is the action Paul so eloquently describes as that for which "the whole creation has been groaning together in the pains of childbirth until now" (Romans 8:22). As we have already acknowledged, our present material reality is just a special and very limiting case of all possible realities. * It is real to us, because we are all involved in a "conspiracy" that has us continuously reinforcing the illusion of reality to one another. In discussing this change in reality that will be the lot of transformed individuals, Paul says:

> 51 Behold! I tell you a mystery. We shall not all sleep, but we shall all be changed, 52 in a moment, in the twinkling of an eye, at the last trumpet. For the trumpet will sound, and the dead will be raised imperishable, and we shall be changed. 53 For this perishable body must put on the imperishable, and this mortal body must put on immortality. 54 When the perishable puts on the imperishable, and the mortal puts on immortality, then shall come to pass the saying that is written:
> Death is swallowed up in victory. (1 Cor. 15: 51–55)

In another discourse, Paul refers to this change in reality as the adoption and redemption of the body. The implication is that the very material substance of which our bodies are composed will be changed. He said:

> 19 For the creation waits with eager longing for the revealing of the sons of God. 20 For the creation was subjected to futility, not willingly, but because of him who subjected it, in hope 21 that the creation itself will be set free from its

---

*To explore this idea further, I strongly recommend the documentary movie *What the Bleep Do We Know?*

bondage to corruption and obtain the freedom of the glory of the children of God. [22] For we know that the whole creation has been groaning together in the pains of childbirth until now. [23] And not only the creation, but we ourselves, who have the firstfruits of the Spirit, groan inwardly as we wait eagerly for adoption as sons, the redemption of our bodies. (Romans 8: 19–23)

It is now possible to explain the paradox of the noble biblical characters enumerated by Paul, of whom he said, "the world was not worthy," and who died without receiving "the promise." He placed Abel, Enoch, Noah, Abraham, Sarah, Isaac, Jacob, Joseph, Moses, Rahab (the harlot), Gideon, Barak, Samson, Jephthah, David, Samuel, and others in this category, saying this about them:

These all died in faith, not having received the things promised, but having seen them and greeted them from afar, and having acknowledged that they were strangers and exiles on the earth. [14] For people who speak thus make it clear that they are seeking a homeland. [15] If they had been thinking of that land from which they had gone out, they would have had opportunity to return. [16] But as it is, they desire a better country, that is, a heavenly one. Therefore God is not ashamed to be called their God, for he has prepared for them a city. (Hebrews 11:13–16)

As he continues his eulogy, he adds this:

[33] [T]hrough faith [they] conquered kingdoms, enforced justice, obtained promises, stopped the mouths of lions, [34] quenched the power of fire, escaped the edge of the sword, were made strong out of weakness, became mighty in war,

put foreign armies to flight. [35] Women received back their dead by resurrection. Some were tortured, refusing to accept release, so that they might rise again to a better life. [36] Others suffered mocking and flogging, and even chains and imprisonment. [37] They were stoned, they were sawn in two, they were killed with the sword. They went about in skins of sheep and goats, destitute, afflicted, mistreated—[38] of whom the world was not worthy—wandering about in deserts and mountains, and in dens and caves of the earth.

[39] And all these, though commended through their faith, did not receive what was promised, [40] since God had provided something better for us, that apart from us they should not be made perfect. (Hebrews 11: 33–40)

In other words, these individuals, having completed the First Work, must wait for the outcome of the Greater Work. In this scheme, Paul cites Jesus Christ as a prototype, the first off the assembly line of this transmutation process. That is why Paul assured his followers that if [11] "the Spirit of him who raised Jesus from the dead dwells in you, he who raised Christ Jesus from the dead will also give life to your mortal bodies through his Spirit who dwells in you" (Romans 8:11).

AN EASTERN ANALOGUE

The vision that Paul held out that this transmutation would take place is shared by the Eastern model also. According to the Indian mystic-philosopher and scholar, Sri Aurobindo, (whose works were previously cited) the holy men who compiled the Indian scriptures called the Vedas some six thousand years ago, referenced their discoveries regarding the destiny of matter and Man. Aurobindo used these writings to corroborate his own discovery that "Matter is a form of veiled Life" and "Life a form of veiled Consciousness."[3] He saw this Life in Matter as a force that would eventually unveil itself, propelling humankind into a more complete realization of our eternal destiny of being a fit vehicle for the embodiment of the Spirit.

Like Paul, who saw the body as an indispensable part of mankind's destiny of playing host to "the manifestation of the sons of God" (Romans 8:19), Aurobindo declared:

> The body could become a revealing vessel of a supreme beauty and bliss, casting the beauty of the light of the spirit suffusing and radiating from it as a lamp reflects and diffuses the luminosity of its indwelling flame, carrying in itself the beatitude of the spirit, its joy of the seeing mind, its joy of life and spiritual happiness and thrilled with a constant ecstasy.[4]

This new "body," with its enlarged consciousness, would indeed be the basis of the "new heavens and a new earth in which righteousness dwells" that another apostle, Peter, spoke about (II Peter 3:13).

The new heavens, according to Aurobindo, would comprise not places of enjoyment and repose, but ever higher planes of Being, toward which everyone, even "the new man," must strive. The new earth, likewise, would represent a state in which matter obeys higher laws, obscurity gives way to clarity, and ignorance gives place to awareness. In this new earth, even death will be abolished.

In elaborating on this type of emergence and the organizational structure that the new, "supramental" manifestation of Spirit on Earth would take, Aurobindo says:

> It may well be that, once started, the (supramental) endeavor may not advance rapidly even to its first decisive state; it may be that it will take long centuries of effort to come into some kind of permanent birth. But that is not altogether inevitable,

for the principle of such changes in Nature seems to be a long obscure preparation followed by a swift gathering up and precipitation of the elements into the new birth, a rapid conversion, a transformation that in its luminous moment figures like a miracle. Even when the first decisive change is reached, it is certain that all humanity will not be able to rise to that level. There cannot fail to be a division into those who are able to live on the spiritual level and those who are only able to live in the light that descends from it into the mental level. And below these too there might still be a great mass influenced from above but not yet ready for the light. But even that would be a transformation and a beginning far beyond anything yet attained. This hierarchy would not mean as in our present vital living an egoistic dominance of the underdeveloped by the more developed, but a guidance of the younger by the elder brothers of the race and a constant working to lift them up to a greater spiritual level and wider horizons. And for the leaders too this ascent to the first spiritual levels would not be the end of the divine march, a culmination that left nothing more to be achieved on earth. For there would be still yet higher levels within the supramental realm, as the Vedic poets knew when they spoke of the spiritual life as a constant ascent.... [5]

It is remarkable, to say the least, that such a similar understanding existed between men of such diverse backgrounds as the apostle Paul and Aurobindo. For example, in the above quotation, Aurobindo sees this change as "a rapid conversion, a transformation that in its luminous moment figures like a miracle." Likewise, Paul wrote, "in a moment, in the twinkling of an eye, we shall be changed."

Another example of their similar visions of humanity's future: Aurobindo sees the resulting transmutation organizing humankind according to the inner qualities fostered by each individual's work at transforming his consciousness. He said, "There cannot fail to be a division into those who are able to live in the light that descends from it into the mental level," and so on. In a similar vein, Paul intimated,

> ^{23} Whatever you do, work heartily, as for the Lord and not for men, ^{24} knowing that from the Lord you will receive the inheritance as your reward. You are serving the Lord Christ. ^{25} For the wrongdoer will be paid back for the wrong he has done, and there is no partiality.

Paul also said,

> "^{10} For we must all appear before the judgment seat of Christ, so that each one may receive what is due for what he has done in the body, whether good or evil. (2 Corinthians 5:10)

Yes, the "supramental" manifestation, using the terminology of Aurobindo, or the "resurrection," according to the New Testament tradition, will work itself out according to an inviolable law. And as in Jesus's parable of the talents (Matthew 25:14–30), it will be the quality of consciousness that will determine the "body" and the authority that each person will receive—"each according to his own labor." This is the only salvation that the transformation of individual consciousness would offer—the opportunity for ever higher attainments of manifesting the divine spirit in Man.

It is only in the pursuit of a transformed consciousness that we will be able to find the treasure that lies hidden within. After all, it is only when our gaze is changed from seeking salvation without to finding it within that we can share in the realization of Paul, that we,

> with unveiled face, beholding the glory of the Lord, are being transformed into the same image from one degree of glory to another. For this comes from the Lord who is the Spirit (2 Corinthians 3:18).

AFTERWORD

In the Preface, I made reference to a body of literature covering over a century of research that has surfaced concerning the evidence for and against the historicity of Jesus, i.e., whether Jesus existed as a real person, or whether he was myth made flesh by the early architects of the Christian movement. In this regard, researchers Timothy Freke and Peter Gandy, in their best-selling book, *The Jesus Mysteries* (1999), proffered the intriguing thesis that the Gospel story of Jesus was not a literal biography of a historical Messiah, but a Jewish adaptation of the Pagan Mysteries in terms attractive to a Jewish audience and in a context relevant to local Jewish spiritual and political aspirations. The centerpiece of these Pagan Mysteries was the story of a dying and resurrecting God-Man, known by various names in the ancient world—Osiris in Egypt, Dionysus in Greece, Attis in Asia Minor, Adonis in Syria, Bacchus in Italy, Mithras in Persia. The oldest evidence of this God-Man idea is Osiris, whose myth dates back more than 2,500 years before the time of Jesus.

In recognition of the universal and composite nature of the God-Man idea, Freke and Gandy used the combined name, Osiris-Dionysus, in their discussion of the Pagan Mystery traditions. According to them, initiates into the Mysteries "could become aware that, like Osiris-Dionysus, they were also 'God made flesh.' They too were immortal Spirit trapped within a physical body. Through sharing in the death of Osiris-Dionysus initiates symbolically 'died' to their lower earthly nature, while through sharing in his resurrection they were spiritually reborn and experienced their eternal and divine essence. This was the profound mystical teaching that the myth of Osiris-Dionysus encoded for those initiated into the Inner Mysteries, the truth of which initiates directly experienced for themselves." (*The Jesus Mysteries*, p.24)

Thus, say Freke and Gandy, "In the Jewish adaptation, Jesus is Osiris-Dionysus thinly disguised as the Jewish Messiah in order to make the Pagan Mysteries accessible to Jews. His composite nature is particularly clear from the contradictory accounts of his birth, which portray him both as the Messiah in the line of David and Osiris-Dionysus the Son of God." (p. 206)

Like the Pagan Mysteries from which they were adapted, the Christian Mysteries were intended to be offered at different levels, the Outer Mysteries, which contained the story of Jesus, set in Palestine, was for the newcomers, while the progressive, Inner Mysteries, were available as members advanced in spiritual development. This inner, higher level of the Mysteries became identified as Gnosticism, while the Outer Mysteries became solidified as Literalism, otherwise known as institutional Christianity. Eventually, political and demographic disruptions intervened to cause a rupture to this arrangement: In 70 CE, when the Romans destroyed Jerusalem, Jews became scattered throughout the Roman Empire as slaves and refugees. Those who had been initiated into the Outer Mysteries, with only limited ideas of what Christianity was all about, had little more than what they believed to be the "biography" of Jesus, the Messiah, to guide them. Those in the western part of the Roman Empire, cut off from the established centers of the Jesus Mysteries in Alexandria and the eastern areas of the Empire, were unable to complete their initiation into the full Mysteries. Within decades, the Outer Mysteries became identified with a literalist movement, geographically and spiritually cut off from the Gnostic inner core.

However, through an ironic twist, the Jesus Mysteries failed to take off within the Jewish community, and "Within 100 years the Pagan godman disguised as the Jewish Messiah, who was designed to introduce the Pagan Mysteries to the Jews, was actually bringing Jewish traditions to Pagans!"*

---

* *The Jesus Mysteries*, p. 202

It is the literalist movement that we have inherited as the institutional church. Eventually, with the political clout of Rome behind it, the institutional, literalist church anathematized Gnosticism and went to extreme and ruthless lengths to eradicate all links to its Pagan roots. This also meant that in anathemizing Gnosticism, the church cut itself off from its own mystical heritage, becoming wholly reliant on a literalist interpretation of the Christian Gospels.

For the many Christians for whom the historical reality of Jesus is the center pole holding up their figurative tent of faith, the work of Freke and Gandy, and similar offerings, such as *The Pagan Christ* by Tom Harpur— which shows the Gospel story of Jesus to be a retelling, in minute detail, of the myth of the Egyptian god Horus—would be regarded with skepticism, if not hostility. Not only would they see such works as a frontal attack on many cherished beliefs, but also on their only hope for salvation, which they have come to believe is dependent on their acceptance of a historical Jesus as the only begotten son of God, sent by the Father to die on the cross so that humanity can be saved from sin.

However, as *Hidden Treasure* shows, such a rendition of God's plan of salvation is flawed, and that by reason of our inability to uncover the deeper meaning of the Christian message that lies beneath its outer, doctrinal shell. As was shown in our exploration of the transformational psychology of the Gospels, the plan of salvation has always been about the process of transformation that we must become engaged in if we are to progress toward our God-endowed potential. As stated in the Preface, the role of Jesus in the Gospels was to be a scaffold for this psychology. Once we understand and submit to the psychology, we're no longer dependent on the historical drama; it would have served its function in the same way that we are able to remove the outer scaffold when a building has been successfully constructed. It is in the application of the psychology that we awaken and grow the Christ presence in ourselves. And it is by virtue of this growing inner presence of Christ that we can be transformed and, consequently, become saved.

As we become familiar with this psychology, the more we will come to appreciate how estranged the Christianity with which we are familiar is from this underlying esoteric current of transformation. We will also begin to appreciate that the more distant Christian churches are from this underlying esoteric current, the less they are an expression of God's will and more the product of our human machinations.

My assurance to Christians who are apprehensive about these revelations about Jesus is that whether we see him as historical or mythical does not affect the efficacy of the transformational psychology in the New Testament, or, for that matter, God's plan of salvation for humanity. As a matter of fact, it is counterproductive to believe that God has taken on human form only once in human history and that we need to believe in the historical fact of this doctrine in order to be saved. In many respects, the Jesus of the Gospels fulfilled a role of outlining and demonstrating a psychology that is designed to awaken the Christ presence in each of us. The more we become fixated on a historical Jesus, the more we lose sight of our responsibility to give birth to Christ.

My sense is that despite its potential for precipitating a crisis of faith within Christianity, much of this research into Christianity's true beginnings will ultimately be helpful to the practice of true Christianity—by which I mean Christianity as a transformative discipline—by forcing it to make a correction in its focus from Jesus to Christ. For example, Freke and Gandy began *The Jesus Mysteries* with the dedication, "To the Christ in you" and make the declaration in the final chapter:

> Our desire is not to attack Christianity, but to point to the possibility of it regaining something it has lost—the Inner Mysteries which reveal the secrets of Gnosis. We do not feel that the Jesus Mysteries Thesis undermines Christianity, but rather that it reveals the ancient grandeur of the Jesus story. It truly is the 'greatest story ever told'—a story that has been thousands of years in the making.*

* *The Jesus Mysteries*, p. 256

In the same vein, Tom Harpur, an ordained Anglican priest, confesses to a strengthened Christian faith as a result of his research and discoveries. He makes the plea in *The Pagan Christ*:

> The inspiration of Jesus Christ as portrayed in the Gospels is in no way lessened by the knowledge that each of us has the potential for birthing the Christ within, and for living that out to ever fuller maturity. Quite the contrary. As Paul told the Galatians, the aim of all his efforts and teachings was that the Christ might be fully "formed in you."*

A transformational focus of spiritual practice would renovate all the institutional elements of our spiritual life. Each person would realize that he or she is a sculptor of his or her own soul, and by this craft fashion his or her own salvation, each one according to his or her labor.

---

*The Pagan Christ, p. 190

APPENDICES

I: A Meditation on the Unforgivable Sin

II: A Meditation Workshop on the Beatitudes

III: Working with the Parables of the Kingdom as Spiritual Exercises

IV. The Lord's Prayer and the Chakras

V. Astrological Symbolism in the Relationship between Jesus
    and His Twelve Disciples

APPENDIX I

A MEDITATION ON THE UNFORGIVABLE SIN

To understand what the unforgivable sin is, we must look at the context concerning its first emergence as a subject of discussion. This is given in Mark 3:22–29:

> [22] And the scribes who came down from Jerusalem were saying, "He is possessed by Beelzebub," and "by the prince of demons he casts out the demons." [23] And he called them to him and said to them in parables, "How can Satan cast out Satan? [24] If a kingdom is divided against itself, that kingdom cannot stand. [25] And if a house is divided against itself, that house will not be able to stand. [26] And if Satan has risen up against himself and is divided, he cannot stand, but is coming to an end. [27] But no one can enter a strong man's house and plunder his goods, unless he first binds the strong man. Then indeed he may plunder his house. [28] Truly, I say to you, all sins will be forgiven the children of man, and whatever blasphemies they utter, [29] but whoever blasphemes against the Holy Spirit never has forgiveness, but is guilty of an eternal sin."

Luke 12:10 repeats the citation, but without a context:

> [10] And everyone who speaks a word against the Son of Man will be forgiven, but the one who blasphemes against the Holy Spirit will not be forgiven.

Next, we need to arrive at a deeper understanding of what it means to blaspheme and what the Holy Spirit represents. As well, we need to understand why an offence against the Son of Man (Christ) can be forgiven, while one committed against the Holy Spirit cannot.

What Is Blasphemy?

Blasphemy is defined in *Young's Analytical Concordance of the Bible* as, "to speak injuriously against." Blasphemy is similar to slander: it is when someone uses speech to try to bring something exceedingly high down to a base level, or, said another way, when someone speaks of something holy in an irreverent manner.

The Holy Spirit

Christian scriptures tell us that the Father, Son, and Holy Spirit, though three distinct persons, are essentially one. How are we to understand this? The best way is to look at it is in terms of a practical example. Let's take water, which can exist in three states—liquid, solid (ice), and gas (water vapor). These three states of water are each distinct, but they are nevertheless one and the same. In similar manner, the Father, the Son, and the Holy Spirit are three different states of the Divine. These three modalities exist to maximize our access to the redemptive power of the Divine.

The Holy Spirit is understood as a "person" of the Holy Trinity. Although it is not a "thing" in the sense that we can point to it and say "there it is," we can nevertheless make reference to its effects.

If we understand salvation as a process of renewal and growth of personal consciousness toward the Universal, the role of Christ in "salvation" can be best understood as the principle of renewing life, while the role of the Holy Spirit must be understood as the reconciling principle of God that lives in each of us. In this reconciliation role, the Holy Spirit (or Holy Ghost in the King James Version) is our inner guide, awakening and leading us to the divine source that is our heritage. If, for whatever reason, we set up an opposition to this guide, then we render it of no effect.

Blasphemy against the Holy Spirit (BATHS)

When someone blasphemes against the Holy Spirit, he or she maintains an inner posture that is prejudiced against the revelation of the Spirit that can emerge from within. So, to blaspheme against the Holy Spirit is not a single act per se, but a state of consciousness. When we are in this state of consciousness, we are inaccessible to the reconciling work of the Holy Spirit.

But how can we blaspheme against an internal guide, a force that prompts us from within? We can do so by maliciously opposing the manifestations of this force, especially without justification. In the West Indies, where I grew up, people had a colloquial expression to describe the general attitude of those set against seeing anyone progress, even though they themselves had no interest in advancing. The local people called such an attitude "bad-mindedness." Bad-mindedness was also used to describe those who were opposed to your progress, even if they did not reap a benefit from their efforts or your failure. Blasphemy against the Holy Spirit could be seen as a form of bad-mindedness, but on a more serious level, in that we turn against the manifestations of God acting in us.

Recall that in Mark, after performing a miraculous healing, Jesus was accused of casting out demons and consequently of being in league with Beelzebub, the prince of demons. More than anything, this was a stupid and malicious accusation because common sense alone should have told the accuser that the statement could not be true. As Jesus retorted, "How can Satan cast out Satan?"

It is interesting, though, that this malicious accusation was not interpreted by Jesus as an attack on him personally, but as an attack on the Holy Spirit. That's because the workings of the Holy Spirit were being impugned and reviled—or spoken of injuriously. Jesus pointed out something disingenuous in the accusation: the accuser, instead of acknowledging that he had witnessed something miraculous and was in the presence of something wondrous, shut down his own perception, resorting to a bogus interpretation of what he had observed.

This same psychological dynamic occurs whenever we have insight into truth, but refrain from acknowledging it on account of what it might require of us. Such reluctance to surrender to the truth that is perceived can lead to a split between the part of us that knows (the knowing self) and the part of us that feels (the feeling self). The knowing self is aware of truth, but the feeling self refuses to go along and be won over, inventing bogus arguments to justify its refusal. Each of us knows how frustrating it is when we're engaged in a debate with someone who, at a certain point, puts up a counterargument that he knows in his heart of hearts to be false. But he makes it anyway, just to score points. This is what it means to be disingenuous.

To blaspheme against the Holy Spirit is to maliciously oppose the work of God to reconcile the world to himself, and a world that includes oneself. Indeed, the reconciliation of the world to God can only be accomplished one person at a time. The Holy Spirit is the force by which God opens our hearts and makes us each aware of the path to our divine heritage. To see this force at work, and then to marshal our cognitive faculties to repudiate and discredit it, is the equivalent of someone in a flood refusing a lifeline. When we oppose the Holy Spirit—God's agency of reconciliation—in this manner, we establish an internal, intrapsychic opposition to the single force that can draw us closer to God. This opposition then expresses itself in one becoming prejudicial against all things truly spiritual.

Ironically, opposing the work of the Holy Spirit does not necessarily mean that one is anti-religious. Indeed, we may show the outer signs of religiosity, but draw the line when the profession of religion requires sacrifices, particularly sacrifices of the old order—things that buttress our ego-bound sense of self. This old, ego-bound self is master of its universe and it does not want to surrender control to the emergent power of the Spirit. Therefore, there is an aspect of defensiveness in such opposition to the Holy Spirit. In organizing against the influence of the Holy Spirit, we are really trying to protect the status quo, not realizing that it is at the expense of something greater; because in organizing against the Holy Spirit, we're organizing our personal energies against our own best interests.

The Unforgivable Sin (UFS)

The consequence of blaspheming against the Holy Spirit is stated most dramatically in the King James Version (KJV) of the Bible. For example, while the English Standard Version simply states that BATHS is "an eternal sin," the KJV drives home the point, saying that one cannot be forgiven of the offence either in "this world or the world to come." Many other acts classified as sin in this world would not be considered sins in "the world to come" because they would become non-issues. But blasphemy against the Holy Spirit won't be forgiven because it will disallow us from being drawn to God, and forgiveness can only occur when we are open to the embrace of the Divine. We can't be forgiven in the world to come because we won't be there; our negative intra-psychic dynamic would prevent us from getting to the kind of relationship that characterizes that world.

In Matthew 13:12, Jesus speaks eloquently to the psychological dynamic that is created when we create internal barriers against our own redemption:

> For to the one who has, more will be given, and he will have
> an abundance, but from the one who has not, even what he
> has will be taken away.

If we organize our psyche to protect against awareness, not only do we not go forward, but we also fall back. Carl Jung touched upon a fundamental spiritual insight when he said that the human psyche has a natural gradient toward wholeness, which suggests that it takes definite effort to thwart the movement of the soul toward the Divine. In simpler and more religious terms, it is natural for us to want to acquire self-knowledge, and with that, knowledge of the source of our origins, which is divine;

and when we shut down this natural capacity for inquiry, we frustrate the work of the Holy Spirit.

BATHS cannot be forgiven because it is not a single act. It is not some debt that can just be written off. It is a posture in one's consciousness, or a "dynamic." A dynamic is a set of self-perpetuating and self-reinforcing actions in which one action leads to another, like some perpetual-motion machine. If we are caught up in the psychological dynamic of evading truth when confronted with it, the situation can only go from bad to worse, such that we will find it ever harder and harder to extricate ourselves from it.

At a psychological level, when we receive forgiveness for an offence, we become the recipient of more energy, which assists us in returning to a state of wholeness. However, with BATHS, even if we were forgiven, any additional energy introduced would be co-opted to serve the psychological complex of truth-avoidance. Thus, we are caught in a psychological situation that cannot benefit from having more energy introduced. It is as if the personality were caught up in a vortex from which it cannot be extricated—and this situation itself is the "unforgivable sin." Short of the old personality structure dying, it cannot be reconciled. But as long as the unhealthy dynamic persists, it will continue to block the reconciling work that the Holy Spirit is trying to accomplish in us.

Clearly, to commit the UFS is to act against our own spiritual interest. So what would prompt someone to do so? I can think of several possibilities, such as fear of the unknown or fear of change—being too heavily vested in the status quo. Essentially, we commit the UFS when we put doctrine above revelation and when we value conformity more than obedience to the inner promptings of the Spirit. We are, in effect, relying on our own righteousness. As such, we run the danger of living a form of religious life that is unable to bear spiritual fruit. And since we are not available and responsive to the Spirit, we stagnate.

BATHS is a more common occurrence than we might want to think, seeing that its consequences are so severe. However, since this sin is a dynamic in consciousness, it can be corrected—but only by the offender and not by any outside agency. That's why it is an unforgivable sin—because it is not within God's sphere of influence to end this psychic campaign against the Holy Spirit. If it were within his sphere, this would violate an individual's free will. God is all merciful, but there is one thing he cannot do, and that is to make up our minds for us.

APPENDIX II

A MEDITATION WORKSHOP ON THE BEATITUDES

The Objective of Meditation

The objective of these meditation exercises is not so much to solicit spiritual experiences as it is to gain insight into giving clearer expression in one's life to spiritual principles. When these principles begin to take root and become part of one's reality, however, extraordinary experiences may result to give confirmation and reinforcement to the outer consciousness that they are now in place.

When seen in the context of the embodiment of spiritual principles, the ultimate meditation practice is "meditation with open eyes," meaning possession of the capacity to dwell at all times at the centre of one's true self, one's Divine Self.

Prerequisite to Effective Meditation

All meditation, no matter what form it may take, derives its effectiveness from the degree of sincerity of its practitioner. This is particularly true with respect to the prayer-meditations suggested here on the Beatitudes. After all, sincerity is a prerequisite if one is to become clear, very clear, on the object of one's spiritual seeking. The practical implications of this sincerity are:

- First, we must understand that the grace of God may manifest in response to our invitation in a manner quite contrary to our expectations. The implication here is that we must be supple in our spiritual attitude. One does not dictate to God.

- Second, we must be mentally prepared to die to our conception of who we are and be willing to be born, progressively, to the true Self, which, for now, we may not even understand. Feelings of uncertainty are quite natural as we take leave of a reality that we know and seek after another that is perceived only faintly, if at all. Here, we must assume the attitude of someone who has been alerted that his house is on fire. In such a situation, our first priority would be to get to safety. It is only after we have removed ourselves from an untenable situation that we can be fussy about where we are going next.

There are several other practical aspects of sincerity that we must possess in order to derive optimum benefit from our meditation practice:

- We must be prepared to assume the responsibility commensurate with the higher level of consciousness that we seek. (For example, higher consciousness always requires greater responsibility.)

- We must learn to observe others to find and acknowledge the qualities in expression that we aspire to develop in ourselves.

- We must be willing to see ourselves as others see us and not be prone to deluding ourselves that we are already in possession of that which we are seeking.

- We must be willing to acknowledge what we are, without judgment, and without the need to blame others for any failures or shortcomings we may observe in ourselves.

Meditation Technique

(a) Setting

These exercises are best practiced before going to sleep, but can take place at any time you have a few minutes to yourself. Personally, I prefer the evening, prior to bedtime, because I found that my efforts were supplemented by dream material woven around the principles I was striving to bring into conscious expression at the time.

Also consider your location and physical posture. Find somewhere comfortable and without distractions, and be sure to keep a straight back, propping yourself up with pillows, if necessary. Some find it more conducive to meditation to lie down on their backs, with the body outstretched. The problem here is that it is easy to fall asleep before you have accomplished the task you have set out to do.

(b) Focus

Before you focus on the target values you would like to incorporate into yourself, clear yourself further by offering a prayer to the Divine. Such a prayer should be brief and audibly spoken, and it must contain the following essential elements:

i   An address to the reality you want to communicate with. You can address this reality as God, Father, Mother, Father-Mother, or something else. It doesn't really matter, as long as you do it with feeling.

ii The purpose of your communication

iii A recognition that prayer commits you to an ever-increasing expression of the complete truth of your Self (remember that we are not talking about the ego-self here)

The words of the prayer must be enunciated, and it is important that you fully deliberate on the significance of what is being uttered. Needless to say, the goal of prayer is not to get the Divine to do your bidding, but rather, to open you up to the Divine Presence that is always present and available, and willing to participate in our personal reality would we but invite It. Your prayers are therefore evocations that should act upon you to bring about an attunement in you to this Presence. Starting out, you might want to write out your prayer in the same manner you would write a letter, until eventually you feel comfortable enough to offer up prayers spontaneously.

The Meditation Exercise

The Beatitudes can be considered objective values or outer-world expressions of spiritual principles. As such, their embodiment in one's character provides points of contact between one's conscious self and the inner spiritual world of principles.

To embody the spiritual principles implied by the Beatitudes, you first have to arrive at a feeling level as to what the Beatitudes imply in a practical, everyday setting; this is really the key in this entire exercise. Just as you may have a feeling when a particular thought associated with a past event crosses your mind, so too can you experience a specific feeling from dwelling on thoughts and event scenarios associated with specific virtues.

Second, you should try to see the practical adjustments you must make in your personal life in order to establish some resonance (i.e., empathetic link) with the spiritual principles you are trying to embody. If you are trying to incorporate the principle of peace into your normal everyday expression, you must be alert to opportunities to restore harmony out of chaos in the various departments of your life. Instead of thinking of peace as just the absence of conflict, you must become a living example, an embodiment, of the state of peace.

Three Aspects of the Meditation Exercise

Each exercise in this section is therefore broken up into three parts. The first part is the specific objective you hope to achieve, or the aspect of character that you endeavor to incorporate into your being.

The second aspect is the point of focus. This is the thought that you would hold to bring you to the feeling state associated with the particular character aspect implied by the Beatitude.

The third aspect is the reinforcing scenario. For this you create a scenario in your mind of a situation that would normally overwhelm you. The task then is to find the emotion within yourself that will allow you to change the way you typically reacted to such a situation when it occurred in real life. This is almost like a rehearsal to ensure that you program new responses to old situations. Indeed, when you work through such scenarios, you will be rerouting the hormonal reaction and nerve impulse pathways habitually associated with those situations. In other words, what you are attempting is not only a mental exercise, but a tangible, material change in the being at the level of habits and instincts.

The foregoing discussion is restated below for emphasis.

Three Aspects of the Meditation Exercise: A Restatement

Objective of the Exercise: This is the aspect of character that you endeavor to incorporate into your being.

The Point of Focus: This is the thought that you would hold to bring you to the feeling state associated with the particular character aspect of a certain Beatitude. Just as you may have a feeling when a particular thought associated with a past event crosses your mind, so too can you experience a specific feeling from dwelling on thoughts and event scenarios associated with specific virtues.

The Reinforcing Scenario: This is a practical, everyday situation in which you would want to adjust your reactions. You do this by imagining a scenario while recreating a feeling state compatible with the character aspect you are trying to instill. This is almost like a rehearsal to ensure that you accustom the new responses to old situations.

The First Exercise

Matthew 5:3: *Blessed are the poor in spirit, for theirs is the Kingdom of Heaven.*

In chapter 7, this Beatitude was reinterpreted to mean that only those who lack the impulsiveness of self-will would be able to participate in the process of expanding their consciousness, which process is the Kingdom of Heaven.

Objective of the Exercise • To learn patience and humility as part of the normal expression of your being

The Point of Focus • "The Kingdom of Heaven will reveal itself in my life in direct proportion to the room I make for it." Keep this thought in your mind as exclusively as possible, until the words are replaced by a feeling state.

The Reinforcing Scenario • Consider whether you are willing to live life without expecting special treatment, content to share the fate of ordinary men and women.

The Second Exercise

Matthew 5:4: *Blessed are they that mourn, for they shall be comforted.*

Reinterpreted, this Beatitude says that those who feel alienated by the false reality of our experience will begin to be reconciled to the true, more enduring reality of our spiritual nature.

Objective of the Exercise • To learn what your attachments are and to see how you can reorient yourself to that which is eternal from that which is ephemeral

The Point of Focus • "Can I survive without my possessions, social status, relationships, and all the things that give my life importance and security?" Keep addressing this question without judging your reactions. Try to feel what it would be like to live without these trappings.

The Reinforcing Scenario • Think of all the things that are important to you and then mentally eliminate them one by one, imagining what life would be like to be without them. Consider that, in truth, you are quite naked and that nothing you identify with can add to your being.

The Third Exercise

Matthew 5:5: *Blessed are the meek for they shall inherit the earth.*

Reinterpreted, this Beatitude means that those who are even-tempered and not given to grandiosity will realize the earth in its true form, namely as a field of experience for the soul.

Objective of the Exercise • To be watchful and wakeful so that, like a little child, you can again see the wonder and magic in the expressions of life around you. This is how you would ultimately come to realize the reality or truth of Earth as a field of experience for the soul.

The Point of Focus • "What would my experience of the world be without the opinions I have been collecting about everything?"

The Reinforcing Scenario • Consider how impossible it is to understand something with the intellect alone. The intellect approaches knowledge by dissecting and categorizing and, as a result, misses out on knowing reality as it is—whole and undifferentiated.

The Fourth Exercise

Matthew 5:6: *Blessed are those who hunger and thirst after righteousness for they shall be filled.*

Reinterpreted, this Beatitude says that those who spend their energy focusing on how justness can make a difference in the world are hastening that reality into manifestation.

Objective of the Exercise • To develop an attunement to humanity's connectedness and, as a result, expand your sense of self, bringing latent faculties into expression

The Point of Focus • "What are the practical implications of the objectives of my spiritual search? Would I be able to live in a system where no one derives an unfair advantage over another?"

The Reinforcing Scenario • Consider how sensitive you are to the injustices around you. Also, consider the extent to which you derive personal benefit from a socioeconomic system based on criteria that are other than spiritual.

The Fifth Exercise

Matthew 5:7: *Blessed are the merciful for they shall obtain mercy.*

The reinterpretation of this Beatitude is that those who show compassion exercise continuity of being with others, and thereby bring themselves to the notice of the higher spiritual realm.

Objective of the Exercise • To see yourself, regarding your use of authority and privilege, as others see and experience you.

The Point of Focus • "To what extent can I claim personal credit for the successes in my life? And to what extent have I benefited from the goodwill of others, both seen and unseen?"

The Reinforcing Scenario • Bearing in mind the higher expression of the Law of Karma—namely that all tendencies toward a separative sense of self must be rectified by understanding the self-defeating nature of separativeness—imagine life situations in which you would experience being treated in the way you have treated others. Is there anything you would change?

The Sixth Exercise

Matthew 5:8: *Blessed are the pure in heart for they shall see God.*

Reinterpreted, this Beatitude says that those who are clear in their motives and emotions will be able to take heed of the presence of God. The implication is that God's presence is always there, but is obscured by hidden motives and jumbled emotions.

Objective of the Exercise • To develop an absolute sincerity with respect to your spiritual goals by always seeking out the motives that determine your actions and expressing the virtues you have already claimed as your personal attributes

The Point of Focus • "What will happen if I am suddenly confronted with the object of my spiritual search? Am I prepared to realize that which I am seeking?"

The Reinforcing Scenario • Think of what you will need to accomplish in your present life to give you the feeling that your life was well lived.

The Seventh Exercise

Matthew 5:9: *Blessed are the peacemakers for they shall be called the children of God.*

Reinterpreted, this Beatitude says that the first attribute of a child of God is the power to bring reconciliation and wholeness into situations of division and conflict.

Objective of the Exercise • Through your way of living, to bring the Earth into closer alignment with the true reality of itself

The Point of Focus • "Am I an embodiment of wholeness in the various aspects of my personal life, including my relationships?"

The Reinforcing Scenario • Consider that peace is more than the absence of conflict. It is a state that is quite dynamic and must be sustained by an ongoing personal consecration. Becoming a peacemaker in the true sense means being able to inject this dynamic sense of wholeness into any conflict situation, so that warring factions can be affected.

The Eighth Exercise

Matthew 5:10: *Blessed are they which are persecuted for righteousness' sake; for theirs is the Kingdom of Heaven.*

Reinterpreted, this Beatitude says that those who have a personal commitment to the common good, or to justness, open themselves up to the transformative process that also goes by the name "Kingdom of Heaven."

Objective of the Exercise • To generate the courage to live out your convictions and be consistent in the pursuit of what is right, even in the face of opposition

The Point of Focus • "What do I stand to lose if I dedicate myself to the causes I really believe in? What causes would I refuse to back down on, even when under the utmost pressure?"

The Reinforcing Scenario • Consider what price you would pay if you lived according to your convictions. Without judging or castigating yourself, weigh the benefits you think would come to the Earth if others with similar convictions lived them out, too. Now weigh these benefits against the costs. Think of your actions as rivulets that join other rivulets to form a brook. Then think of several of these brooks joining to form a stream, which in turn joins other streams to form a river. Think of this river flowing into the ocean to connect with all of the waters of the Earth. Reflect on how change in the world would be impossible if someone, somewhere, did not have the courage of his or her convictions to act outside the mainstream.

The Ninth Exercise

Matthew 5:11–12: *Blessed are you when others revile you and persecute you and utter all kinds of evil against you falsely on my account. Rejoice and be glad, for your reward is great in heaven, for so they persecuted the prophets who were before you.*

This Beatitude needs no reinterpretation. It is encouragement to those encountering opposition to their expressions of the Christ Principle in their lives.

Objective of the Exercise • To see victory even in defeat when you are dedicated to the cause of Christ Consciousness, which is to serve the Principle of Life as a unifying, restorative force

The Point of Focus • "Can I have compassion for people whose visions may not be as farsighted as mine, or have I been too quick to criticize those whose visions I may not have understood?"

The Reinforcing Scenario • Consider how many individuals have been rash to assume the role of prophet and visionary; the true visionary does not go about his or her work with pomp and hoopla, but quietly commits to living out his or her convictions. Note also that the main problem for visionaries is that they touch a sensitive nerve in society. The quality of their living sets too high a standard for others to follow, so we, as a society, respond negatively in an attempt to silence and decommission them.

The Tenth Exercise

Matthew 5:13: *You are the salt of the earth, but if salt has lost its taste, how shall its saltiness be restored? It is no longer good for anything except to be thrown out and trampled under people's feet.*

This is an exhortation to those who have difficulty giving expression to their understanding of life's purpose.

Objective of the Exercise • To better reflect your understanding of the purpose for your life

The Point of Focus • "What lasting impressions do I leave with others? Do I leave them better focused than before they came into contact with me?"

The Reinforcing Scenario • Consider that life may not call you to do anything dramatic, such as discover a cure for cancer. Consider also that the little incremental things you can do from day to day, hour to hour, are what shape your life's purpose. And in giving form to the purpose of your life, you can affect others who are striving for their individual realizations.

The Eleventh Exercise

Matthew 5:14–16: *You are the light of the world. A city set on a hill cannot be hidden. Nor do people light a lamp and put it under a basket, but on a stand, and it gives light to all in the house. In the same way, let your light shine before others, so that they may see your good works and give glory to your Father who is in heaven.*

This is a call to be a source of illumination to others by virtue of your inner realization of truth.

Objective of the Exercise • To become the embodiment of spiritual principles, so that others can see a working model of how those principles unwind in a terrestrial setting

The Point of Focus • "What is the ultimate truth to which this bodily form that I identify with as myself is only an outer expression?" In other words, "Who am I?"

The Reinforcing Scenario • Consider how being "the light of the world" is being a source of hope to those around you. It means withdrawing any energy used to focus on reality models that are based on old patterns of conflict and separation, and then reinvesting that energy in the embodiment of new patterns based on interconnectedness.

The Twelfth Exercise

Matthew 5:17–20: *Do not think that I have come to abolish the Law or the Prophets; I have not come to abolish them but to fulfill them. For truly, I say to you, until heaven and earth pass away, not an iota, not a dot, will pass from the Law until all is accomplished. Therefore whoever relaxes one of the least of these commandments and teaches others to do the same will be called least in the Kingdom of Heaven, but whoever does them and teaches them will be called great in the Kingdom of Heaven. For I tell you, unless your righteousness exceeds that of the scribes and Pharisees, you will never enter the Kingdom of Heaven.*

This exercise is not based on a Beatitude proper, but it acknowledges that though each age brings its own truth, each of these truths is really just another aspect of the one Truth that emerges and reemerges, time and again, from different perspectives.

Objective of the Exercise • To become aware that you cannot dismantle what exists until you have put into place that which is to supersede it

---

The Point of Focus • "How much effort am I expending to touch people at the level of reality they are in? Am I so consumed by "the new" that I have forgotten to relay what I have discovered in terms that others can understand?"

The Reinforcing Scenario • Consider that a building under construction needs scaffolding until it can stand on its own. Once the building is complete, however, keeping the scaffolding in place would be not only impractical but might also detract from the building's aesthetics and functionality. Likewise, it would be unwise to take down the scaffolding before the building could stand on its own.

APPENDIX III

WORKING WITH THE PARABLES
OF THE KINGDOM AS SPIRITUAL EXERCISES

When I think about the Kingdom of God I am struck dumb
by its grandeur; for the Kingdom of God is God
himself with all his fullness.
—Meister Eckhart

The Exercises

Each of the parables offers a seed for contemplation and the basis of a spiritual exercise. The seed for contemplation is like the core spiritual principle conveyed by the parable, with which we can familiarize ourselves at an emotional level. The objective of the contemplation is to arrive at a feeling state that is the true "meaning" of this key idea (i.e., the meaning is felt). In reality, this feeling state is a revelation when it occurs and is a very personal experience. In other words, the seed for contemplation is the "objective principle" contained by the parable.

As with all objective principles, those contained in the parables can be incorporated as values into one's emotional life. For example, when you base your dealings with others on the principle of the Golden Rule—treating them as you would want them to treat you—you don't often consciously think, "I am treating this person as I would like him or her to treat me, if I were in his or her place." In practicing the Golden Rule, you aim for something less calculating and more spontaneous; you simply experience a feeling of delight in being considerate to that person—the same kind of delight you would feel if the transaction were the other way around.

There are three parts, or themes, to the exercises in this section, which, together, form a complete intellectual picture of the principle conveyed by each parable:

- The **philosophical theme** addresses the objective principle revealed by the parable.

- The **existential theme** deals with the applicability of a principle to daily life, exploring how it has surfaced in one's experiences. It poses the question, "With what situation in your life does this parable resonate?"

- The **developmental theme** concerns the lesson to be learned, posing the question, "What virtue do we need to acquire from this parable?"

Exploring these three themes results in a progressive examination of the parable, starting with the intellectual and ending with the practical.

The First Parable—The Sower

Matthew 13:3–9: *A sower went out to sow. And as he sowed, some seeds fell along the path, and the birds came and devoured them. Other seeds fell on rocky ground, where they had not much soil, and immediately they sprang up, since they had no depth of soil, but when the sun rose they were scorched; and since they had no root they withered away. Other seeds fell upon thorns, and the thorns grew up and choked them. Other seeds fell on good soil and brought forth grain, some a hundredfold, some sixty, some thirty. He who has ears, let him hear.*

Philosophical Theme • This parable deals with progressive levels of awakening to the spiritual—awareness, preparedness, commitment, receptivity.

Existential Theme • With what situation out of your life experience does this parable resonate?

Developmental Theme • What virtue do we need to acquire from the lesson of this parable?

HINT: What can you do to ensure that the spiritual seeds that come your way encounter good soil?

Exercise • Trace your steps through these levels and reflect on how you arrived at your current stage of development. How can we ensure that our moments of spiritual clarity and insight lead to tangible spiritual fruits?

Seed of Contemplation • Every moment, every breath, is an opportunity to awaken to the wonder of life.

The Second Parable—Good And Bad Seeds

Matthew 13:24–30: *The Kingdom of Heaven may be compared to a man who sowed good seed in his field; but while men were sleeping, his enemy came and sowed weeds among the wheat, and went away. So when the plants came up and bore grain, then the weeds appeared also. And the servants of the householder came and said to him, 'Sir, did you not sow good seed in your field, how then has it weeds?' He said to them, 'An enemy has done this.' The servants said to him, 'Then do you want us to go and gather them?' But he said, 'No; lest in gathering the weeds you root up the wheat along with them. Let both grow together until the harvest; and at harvest time I will tell the reapers, Gather the weeds first and bind them in bundles to be burned, but gather the wheat into my barn.'*

Philosophical Theme • This parable deals with the principle of navigating competing realities—one based on our moments of clarity and the other arising out of our moments of spiritual sleep (e.g., fears, doubts, lack of faith). What are the ways that we can open ourselves to spiritual reality without at the same time augmenting negativity?

Existential Theme • With what situation in your life experience does this parable resonate?

Developmental Theme • What virtue do we need to acquire from the lesson of this parable?

HINT: Is there a difference between judgment and discernment?

Exercise • Examine the basis upon which you judge events in your life as being good or bad.

Seed of Contemplation • My expectations of life are no guide as to what ought or ought not to happen to me.

The Third Parable—The Mustard Seed

Matthew 13:31–32: *The Kingdom of Heaven is like a grain of mustard seed which a man took and sowed in his field; it is the smallest of all seeds, but when it has grown it is the greatest of shrubs and becomes a tree, so that the birds of the air come and make nests in its branches.*

Philosophical Theme • This parable deals with overcoming and transcending limitations. This principal law of life says that our personal power will grow in proportion to the obligations we have taken on. What objective principle of existence does this parable reveal?

Existential Theme • With what situation in your life experience does this parable resonate?

Developmental Theme • What virtue do we need to acquire from the lesson of this parable?

HINT: What would your life be like if you did not encounter any limitations, and how much authority can we exercise if we do not take on any obligations?

Exercise • Think of a situation in your life where you thought at the time you could not survive or overcome? What determined your assessment of that situation?

Seed of Contemplation • The places of difficulties and obstacles in my life are my growth points.

The Fourth Parable—Leaven

Matthew 13:33: *The Kingdom of Heaven is like leaven which a woman took and hid in three measures of flour, till it was all leavened.*

Philosophical Theme • The philosophical theme of this parable is that of integration—inner and outer, ideal and real. It is only when we put our beliefs into practice that we can be sure that these beliefs are ours and know that we actually understand them.

Existential Theme • With what situation in your life does this parable resonate?

Developmental Theme • What virtue do you need to acquire from the lesson in this parable?

HINT: How comfortable are you in taking your spiritual values with you to your workplace? Would you be comfortable taking your spiritual friends to your place of business?

Exercise • How would your attitude to spiritual exercises (including prayer) change if you were to accept the premise that such exercises are more than strategies to get what you want from life?

Seed of Contemplation • Spiritual exercises are more than strategies to get me what I want from life.

The Fifth Parable—Hidden Treasure

Matthew 13:45: *The Kingdom of Heaven is like treasure hidden in a field, which a man found and covered up, then in his joy he goes and sells all that he has and buys that field.*

Philosophical Theme • This parable deals with the principle of joyous sacrifice. Why did the man sell all that he had, to purchase the field? Couldn't he have sold less of his possessions and paid a lower price for the field?

Existential Theme • With what situation in your life does this parable resonate?

Developmental Theme • What virtue do we need to acquire from the lesson of this parable?

HINT: In what areas of your life do you feel your capacity to serve has been hindered by a lack of qualifications?

Exercise • What do you consider to have been your peak spiritual experience? What would it take to reorganize your life such that this experience is no longer regarded as something extraordinary?

Seed of Contemplation • The Kingdom of Heaven (i.e., the transformation of consciousness) must be received on its terms and not on my own.

The Sixth Parable—The Pearl Of Great Value

Matthew 13:45: *The Kingdom of Heaven is like a merchant in search of fine pearls, who, on finding one pearl of great value, went and sold all that he had and bought it.*

Philosophical Theme • This parable says that each of us must conduct a spiritual search and then face the object of our search when we encounter it. Note that when the merchant found the pearl of great value, he sold all that he had, to enable himself to purchase it.

Existential Theme • With what situation in your life does this parable resonate?

Developmental Theme • What virtue do we need to acquire from the lesson of this parable?

HINT: What things in your life would stand in the way of your realizing your deepest spiritual aspiration, should the opportunity arise? How prepared would you be to give them up to realize this spiritual opportunity?

Exercise • Imagine what you would do if you were suddenly confronted with the object of your spiritual seeking. Can you think of things in your life with which you would not be able to part, even to realize your deepest, most precious spiritual aspiration?

Seed of Contemplation • "Let not the greatness of the ransom turn you aside" (Job 36:18).

The Seventh Parable—The Dragnet of Fish

Matthew 13:47: *The Kingdom of Heaven is like a net which was thrown into the sea and gathered fish of every kind; when it was full, men drew it ashore and sat down and sorted the good into vessels but threw away the bad. So it will be at the close of the age. The angels will come out and separate the evil from the righteous, and throw them into the furnace of fire; there men will weep and gnash their teeth.*

Philosophical Theme • This parable concerns the processes of judgment and assimilation that take place in the human psyche as a here-and-now reality.

Existential Theme • With what situation in your life does this parable resonate?

Developmental Theme • What virtue do we need to acquire from the lesson of this parable?

HINT: Imagine having the opportunity to live your life over again. What personality and character traits would you change? Which ones would you retain for your next life?

Exercise • Can you discern what the message of your life is without judging your life good or bad? How would you approach your next activity if you knew that you would meet your death while engaged in it? How would your life change if you approached all of your activities this way?

Seed of Contemplation • My destiny is shaped by everything that influences me. As I respond to higher motivations, my nature is uplifted and my destiny is changed.

THE LORD'S PRAYER AND THE CHAKRAS:
UTILIZING THE LORD'S PRAYER
FOR SPIRITUAL ATTUNEMENT

Prayer as Spiritual Exercise

All religious practitioners are familiar with the idea of prayer. Although there are many modes of prayer, most constitute some form of address to God, or some higher power, that may include words of contrition, supplication, gratitude, praise, or simply some form of ceremonial address on public occasions.

A less common use of prayer is attunement, in which the occasion of prayer is utilized to access higher energy that can be used to further our goal of transforming consciousness. To better understand this attunement function of prayer, let us consider the following two scenarios:

- The first scenario is that of a man marooned on a deserted island. In his desire to be found, he dispatches bottles into the ocean, with messages offering large financial rewards to anyone who rescues him.

As a prayer model, this is how many of us approach God. We make petitions, supplications, and promises, and the smaller our faith, the more outrageous our promises become.

- The second scenario is that of a prisoner in a dungeon where the only means of escape is by digging a tunnel. He digs a little bit every day, because he knows that failure to dig means that his potential escape is an additional day further away.

As a prayer model, this scenario is the attunement approach to prayer. It treats prayer as an activity of moving closer to the Divine, with the promise that the Divine will also move closer to us.* You might recall the definition of an auto tune-up I shared in chapter 1 that was very evocative for me: *To return a vehicle as closely as possible to the manufacturer's specifications.* A spiritual tune-up is the same idea, except that we're dealing with subtle energy—the way we feel, our overall sense of well-being, of expansiveness, of connectedness.

After every occasion of prayer, we should lose a bit more of ourselves. Prayer should smooth out our edges, just like the action of the ocean on pebbles. That's why we should pray, not to get favors or advantages over our fellow human beings.

The Lord's Prayer

The Lord's Prayer was given by Jesus as a guide to prayer in Matthew 6:5-14:

> [5] "And when you pray, you must not be like the hypocrites. For they love to stand and pray in the synagogues and at the street corners, that they may be seen by others. Truly, I say to you, they have received their reward. [6] But when you pray, go into your room and shut the door and pray to your Father who is in secret. And your Father who sees in secret will reward you.
>
> [7] "And when you pray, do not heap up empty phrases as the Gentiles do, for they think that they will be heard for their many words. [8] Do not be like them, for your Father knows what you need before you ask him. [9] Pray then like this:
>
> [9]"Our Father in heaven,
> hallowed be your name.

---

*James 4:8 "Draw near to God, and he will draw near to you."

[10] Your kingdom come,
your will be done,
on earth as it is in heaven.
[11] Give us this day our daily bread,
[12] and forgive us our debts,
as we also have forgiven our debtors.
[13] And lead us not into temptation,
but deliver us from evil.
[14] For if you forgive others their trespasses, your heavenly
Father will also forgive you, [15] but if you do not forgive others
their trespasses, neither will your Father forgive your trespasses.

There's a temptation that our familiarity with the Lord's Prayer could
lead us to recite it absentmindedly, as if by rote. This would be unfortunate because the main benefit of the prayer is not in the words themselves,
but in the way we utilize them. As a matter of fact, Jesus's recommenda-
tion that we "Pray like this" refers more to the underlying energy dynamic
of the prayer than the actual words used. The prayer is constructed to take
us closer to God, energetically speaking, provided that, as we say its words,
we reflect on their meanings as well as on their implications for how we
conduct ourselves.

Special Feature of the Lord's Prayer

An aspect of the Lord's Prayer that makes it unique is the correlation of its
main clauses and phrases with the seven major chakras, starting with the
seventh and ending with the first. The prayer is designed to draw energy
down into the body, starting with the seventh chakra at the top of the head.

We draw energy "down" when we are able to experience an expanded
awareness while saying the words of the Lord's Prayer. Recall that in chapter 8, energy as it applies to Consciousness was defined as spaciousness
and expansiveness, among other things. The following quotation from Dr.
Richard Moss is excerpted from the larger quote shown in chapter 8:

Higher energy refers to a more inclusive, universal awareness, while lower energy refers to a denser, more personalized consciousness. Higher energy is increased sensitivity. At higher energies, more formlessness and ambiguity can be accommodated in an individual's consciousness, and there is more fluidity between subject and object, less rigidity between what is habitually considered to be self and not-self.*

The words of the prayer are not some sort of magic enchantment. The experiences of an expanded awareness and a larger energy come from the combined effects of our thoughts and attention while saying this prayer. In other words, we think before we speak, and when we speak, we focus our attention on what we are saying.

The best way to derive the benefit of an expanded energy from the Lord's Prayer is to start using it and observing the difference you feel. It also goes without saying that the results you get from this exercise will deepen if you think about the meaning behind the words of the prayer as you say them. Once we deepen our understanding of the words of the prayer, speaking them with intent can have the effect of opening us to a larger energy that can be described as Silence, or Presence. In this state, we can experience a palpable sense of peace and stillness. Some might call this experience the Divine Presence.

It is more important to dwell on the significance of what the words mean than getting to the end of the prayer. And you should not be surprised if at times you are unable to get to the end by reason of being overtaken by the Silence.

I've had very powerful experiences saying this prayer and believe that it should be part of every Christian's toolkit. Of course, the prayer can be used by everyone, as it does not commit anyone to any specific beliefs, other than the expansion of their own consciousness.

---

*Moss, *The Black Butterfly*, 294–5.

To help you in your contemplation, I've provided some commentary on the key phrases and clauses of the prayer that might help you deepen your own thought process.

Contemplating on the Deeper Meaning of the Prayer

We will consider the words of the prayer and their relationship to the seven major chakras at the same time. Since we begin with the seventh chakra, the phrases in the prayer are numbered in reverse order, from seven to one.

vii. Our Father in heaven

The address to "Our Father in heaven" is our way of acknowledging that we share a common source and are connected at all levels of existence. The term "Father" helps us to connect with the idea that a common cause stands as the fountain head of our existence. The term "in heaven" signifies that this unity is still operative, though it may be obscured from our everyday experience. Overall, these words say that we all began as one and are still unity.

vi. Hallowed be your name

The name and the reality are one. The name is hallowed as the reality is hallowed—holy, set apart for holy use. Therefore, we cannot access this reality except through ourselves becoming holy—whole, within and without. The Apostle Paul says: "Strive for peace with everyone, and for the holiness without which no one will see the Lord" (Hebrews 12:14).

v. Your kingdom come

This is an invitation to the Divine to partake of our reality. The Kingdom of God is the "domain of God's rule." It is not of this world, as "the Kingdom of God is within you" (Luke 17:21). This is like saying, "Yes, I'm ready."

iv. Your will be done on earth as it is in heaven

This is a pledge to undertake to let oneself be personally receptive to God's governance. It is a pledge of personal responsibility for anchoring the rule of God in one's life, or in practical terms, to open oneself up to being receptive to objective values.

This also expresses the will to unity—within and amongst ourselves. This is an ordered, dynamic, and organic unity, not a forced unity. This unity is defined by our love of Truth, and openhearted compassion to all.

iii. Give us this day our daily bread

This day—this moment. Daily bread—food for the soul's evolution, namely experiences. Consider that we have never *not* received our daily "bread" from God, from Life.

When we have learned to trust God for our daily existence, we will realize that nothing has ever happened to us that is not in accordance with Divine Will.

The chief cause of anxiety is our sense of aloneness and being cut off. We need to sustain a consciousness of ongoing connectedness.

ii. And forgive us our debts as we also have forgiven our debtors

The key to this petition is reciprocity and our pledge to abide by the law of reciprocity. Under the premise of our unity, to hold enmity is to cut ourselves off from the other, the one that we feel enmity with. To cut ourselves off from each other and to cut ourselves off from God are one and the same thing. When we cut ourselves off from God, we disengage from our possibilities.

How do we forgive? According to Simone Weil, we only truly forgive when we make sure that the person who has done us harm has not lowered us. In her book *Gravity and Grace*, she writes:

> It is impossible to forgive whoever has done us harm if that harm has lowered us. We have to think that it has not lowered us, *but has revealed our true level.*[*]

---

*Weil, *Gravity and Grace*, 5.

If someone does me an injury I must desire that this injury
shall not degrade me. I must desire this out of love for him
who inflicts it, in order that he may not really have done
evil.**

i. Lead us not into temptation but deliver us from evil

Again, the focus is on "us." Temptation arises when we seek completion
and happiness outside of ourselves. The urge to unity can lead to identification and division.

"Deliver us from evil" really applies to the pull of unconsciousness into
sleep. We succumb to evil when we cease to take responsibility for our own
advance—we seek safety in numbers, in a socially sanctioned way of life,
instead of a way of life that our conscience and level of knowledge pre-
scribe for us.

The Chakra Diagram and the Lord's Prayer

Study the diagram below to see which of the phrases of the prayer apply
to which chakra. As you say the words, bring your attention to the respective chakra location on the body. The intensity of your experience will
grow with practice.

**Ibid, 66.

Figure 7: The Lord's Prayer and the Seven Major Chakras

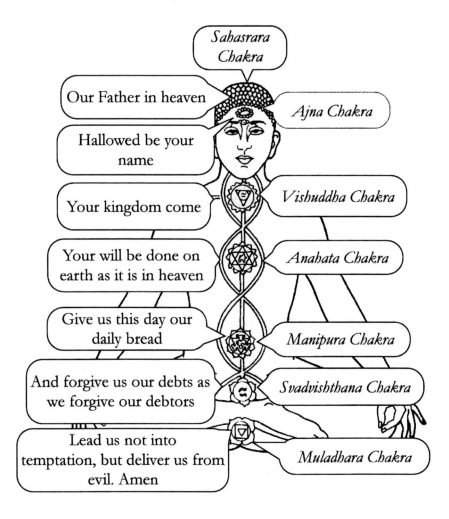

Appendix V

Astrological Symbolism in the Relationship between Jesus and His Twelve Disciples

The relationship between Jesus and his disciples depicts an underlying cosmological principle, with the twelve disciples representing the twelve signs of the zodiac. Evidence for this connection is found in the meanings of the apostles' names, which display affinities with characteristics of the astrological signs.

I was quite surprised to have discovered this relationship on my own in the early 1980s and shared this information in *Meditations on the Apocalypse* (1992)* and *The Meaning of Christ for Our Age* (1984), the predecessor of the present volume. I became aware of a preponderance of astrological and zodiacal motifs in the Book of Revelation while I worked on the manuscript of *Meditations on the Apocalypse*. It was a result of the work I had already undertaken on this topic that prompted my search for further evidence of astrological symbolism lurking elsewhere in the New Testament.

Subsequent to my own research, I became aware of an extensive body of work examining the astrological-zodiacal connection between Jesus and his disciples. This relationship is usually pointed out as evidence of the mythic and nonhistorical nature of the Gospel story of Jesus, in which Jesus is considered the archetypal solar deity and the twelve disciples the twelve zodiacal signs. The alternative and highly improbable explanation would be that Jesus sought out individuals whose names reflected underlying zodiacal characteristics.

---

*Although *The Meaning of Christ for Our Age* was published first (1984), *Meditation on the Apocalypse* (1992) was in manuscript form several years before it.

A listing of the names of the original twelve disciples is found in the tenth chapter of Matthew, verses 2-4:

> The names of the twelve apostles are these: first, Simon, who is called Peter, and Andrew his brother; James the son of Zebedee, and John his brother; [3] Philip and Bartholomew; Thomas and Matthew the tax collector; James the son of Alphaeus, and Thaddaeus; Simon the Cananaean, and Judas Iscariot, who betrayed him.

In the table to follow is a list of the apostles' names and their meanings, together with the astrological signs they represent. The etymology of most of the names is obtained from Bible reference works such as *Dr. Young's Analytical Concordance to the Holy Bible* and *The Interpreter's Dictionary of the Bible,* and is supplemented by characteristics of the apostles as reported in the Gospels.

The association of the twelve disciples with the twelve signs of the zodiac helps to explain the extreme care taken by the writers of the Gospels to list the apostles always in a certain order. The names are given in pairs, but the true significance of their order lies in their arrangement in groups of four, which is done to reflect the zodiac signs according to their quality. Thus, the first four—Peter, James, John, and Andrew—represent the **Fixed Quality** zodiac signs. The second four—Philip, Bartholomew, Thomas, and Matthew—belong to the **Mutable Quality** signs. And the third group—James, the son of Alphaeus; Lebbaeus Thaddaeus; Simon, the Canaanite; and Judas Iscariot—represent the signs of the **Cardinal Quality**.

Mark's Listing of the Twelve Disciples

[14] And he appointed twelve (whom he also named apostles) so that they might be with him and he might send them out to preach [15] and have authority to cast out demons. [16] He appointed the twelve: Simon (to whom he gave the name Peter); [17] James the son of Zebedee and John the brother of James (to whom he gave the name Boanerges, that is, Sons of Thunder); [18] Andrew, and Philip, and Bartholomew, and Matthew, and Thomas, and James the son of Alphaeus, and Thaddaeus, and Simon the Cananaean, [19] and Judas Iscariot, who betrayed him.

Luke's Listing of the Twelve Disciples

[12] In these days he went out to the mountain to pray, and all night he continued in prayer to God. [13] And when day came, he called his disciples and chose from them twelve, whom he named apostles: [14] Simon, whom he named Peter, and Andrew his brother, and James and John, and Philip, and Bartholomew, [15] and Matthew, and Thomas, and James the son of Alphaeus, and Simon who was called the Zealot, [16] and Judas the son of James, and Judas Iscariot, who became a traitor.

The Disciples of the Fixed Signs

It is only after the 12 disciples are each placed on their respective zodiacal sign that we're able to understand the special relationship the four of Peter, Andrew, James, and John seemed to have enjoyed with Jesus. As clearly demonstrated in Figure 8, "The 12 Disciples and the Zodiac," these four disciples represented the four Fixed signs, to form the so-called, Fixed Cross of the zodiac.

Table A-1

THE TWELVE DISCIPLES ACCORDING TO ZODIAC SIGN QUALITY

Grouping by Sign "Quality"	Matthew 10: 2–4	Mark 3:14-19	Luke 6: 13-16
FIXED SIGNS: Taurus, Leo, Scorpio, and Aquarius	Simon, who is called Peter, and Andrew his brother; James the son of Zebedee, and John, his brother	Simon (to whom he gave the name Peter); James the son of Zebedee and John the brother of James (to whom he gave the name Boanerges, that is, Sons of Thunder); Andrew	Simon, whom he named Peter, and Andrew his brother, and James and John
MUTABLE SIGNS: Gemini, Virgo, Sagittarius, and Pisces	Philip and Bartholomew; Thomas and Matthew, the tax collector	Philip, and Bartholomew, and Matthew, and Thomas	Philip, and Bartholomew, and Matthew, and Thomas
CARDINAL SIGNS Aries, Cancer, Libra, and Capricorn	James, the son of Alphaeus, and Thaddaeus; Simon, the Cananaean, and Judas Iscariot, who betrayed him	James, the son of Alphaeus, and Thaddaeus, and Simon, the Cananaean, and Judas Iscariot, who betrayed him	James, the son of Alphaeus, and Simon who was called the Zealot, and Judas the son of James, and Judas Iscariot, who became a traitor

In the Gospels, Peter, James, and John accompanied Jesus on key occasions. Thus, only Peter, James and John were with Jesus at the Transfiguration (Matthew 17:1, Mark 9:2), at Gethsemane (Mark 14:33), and at the healing of Jairus's daughter (Mark 5:37).

Though part of the Fixed sign grouping (as shown in Figure 8), Andrew is usually left out, as his place (Leo, the Lion) is assumed by Jesus, since there can only be four representatives to complete the quaternary. But why was Jesus displacing Andrew and not one of the other three? Because Jesus was also fulfilling his symbolic role of "the lion of the tribe of Judah" (Revelation 5:5) and the Son (or Sun) of God. In astrological lore, the sign of Leo is symbolized by the lion, and the "planetary ruler" of the sign is the sun. There was one occasion when Andrew took up his rightful place with Peter, James, and John, and this was on the Mount of Olives to receive a prophecy from Jesus about the close of the age.

Figure 8: The 12 Disciples and the Zodiac

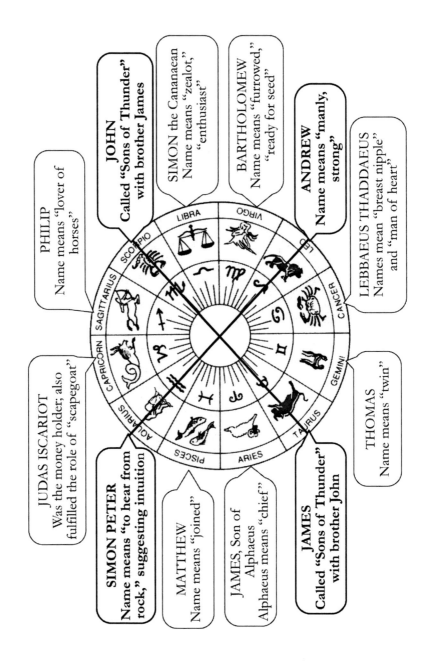

PHILIP
Name means "lover of horses"

JOHN
Called "Sons of Thunder" with brother James

SIMON the Cananaean
Name means "zealot," "enthusiast"

BARTHOLOMEW
Name means "furrowed," "ready for seed"

ANDREW
Name means "manly, strong"

LEBBAEUS THADDAEUS
Names mean "breast nipple" and "man of heart"

THOMAS
Name means "twin"

JUDAS ISCARIOT
Was the money holder; also fulfilled the role of "scapegoat"

SIMON PETER
Name means "to hear from rock," suggesting intuition

MATTHEW
Name means "joined"

JAMES, Son of Alphaeus
Alphaeus means "chief"

JAMES
Called "Sons of Thunder" with brother John

Endnotes

Preface

1. Bhagavad Gita, XIII-28.
2. Ehrman, *Jesus, Interrupted*, and *Misquoting Jesus*.
3. Osman, *The House of the Messiah*.
4. Acharya (a.k.a., D. M. Murdock), *The Christ Conspiracy*.
5. Massey, *The Historical Jesus and the Mythical Christ*.
6. Kuhn, *A Rebirth for Christianity*.
7. Freke and Gandy, *The Jesus Mysteries*.
8. Harpur, *The Pagan Christ*.

Introduction

1. Sugrue, *There Is a River*, A.R.E. Press.

Chapter One

1. Fox, *Meditations with Meister Eckhart*, 28. Matthew Fox describes Meister Eckhart (1260—c.1329) as "a mystic and prophet, feminist and philosopher, preacher and theologian, administrator and poet, a spiritual genius and a declared heretic."
2. *The Passion of the Christ*. Warner Brothers Entertainment, Inc. and Equinoxe Films, Inc. 2004.
3. Aurobindo, "Reason and Religion" in *The Human Cycle*, 122.
4. C. G. Jung describes archetypes as the contents of the collective unconscious. In the glossary of Dr. Jung's autobiography *Memories, Dreams, Reflections*, an archetype is described as "an irrepresentable, unconscious, pre-existent form that seems to be part of the inherited structure of the psyche and can therefore manifest itself spontaneously anywhere, at any time" (p. 392). In the work *Four Archetypes*, from his ninth volume of Jung's collected works, Jung elaborates on this archetype concept: "The term 'archetype' thus … designates only those psychic contents which have not yet been

submitted to conscious elaborations and are therefore an immediate datum of psychic experience... The archetype is essentially an unconscious content that is altered by becoming conscious and by being perceived, and it takes its colour from the individual consciousness in which it happens to appear" (p. 5).

5. As I wrote in my book *The Pilgrim's Companion*, "A fundamental feature of the Life principle is its ability to organize into greater and greater levels of wholeness. We witness this occurring at the level of the human body where various cells organize into tissues, which then organize into organs, and then into systems, then into this wonderful complexity of the human body. From this combined effort, we get something that is more than the sum of the parts, such that each cell, tissue, organ, system, can derive a benefit from the whole that each on its own could not attain. When we speak of the pursuit of spiritual consciousness, we are speaking of consciously extending this process towards increasing organization and wholeness beyond our separate egoic identities" (F. Aster Barnwell, *The Pilgrim's Companion— A Handbook for the Spiritual Path*, Element Books, p.16; 1992.)

Chapter Three

1. The term "collective unconscious" is another expression coined by C. G. Jung in order to place a handle on certain dynamics of the human psyche. Dr. Jung divides the unconscious into "personal" and "collective." Of the personal, he says, "... everything of which I know, but of which I am not at the moment thinking; everything of which I was once conscious but have now forgotten; everything perceived by my senses, but not noted by my conscious mind; everything which, involuntarily and without paying attention to it, I feel, think, remember, want, and do; all the future things that are taking shape in me and will sometime come to consciousness: all this is the content of the unconscious." He adds to this, in another place, by saying, "Besides these we must include all more or less intentional repressions of painful thoughts and feelings. I call the sum of all these contents the 'personal unconscious.' But, over and above that we also find in the unconscious qualities that are not individually acquired but are inherited, e.g., instincts as impulses to carry out actions from necessity without conscious motivation. In this 'deeper' stratum we find also the ... archetypes.... The instincts and archetypes together form the 'collective unconscious.' I call it 'collective,' because, unlike the personal unconscious, it is not made up of individual and more or less unique contents, but of those which are universal and of regular occurrence." Jung, *Memories, Dreams, Reflections*, 401–2.

The idea of attributing a revelation from "the Father in Heaven" to an insight from the collective unconscious is just a way of acknowledging that there are spheres of knowledge to which we may sometimes have access but which may not be the product of our conscious mentation. As such, we cannot take personal credit for such insights when they occur and must acknowledge their provenance as being beyond ourselves. Accordingly, I see the statement that Peter's insight came to him from the Father in Heaven as nothing more than a figure of speech, rather than indicating a specific communication to Peter from "on high." If we were to interpret this term, "Father in Heaven," as indicating a specific, divine point of origin of Peter's idea, we run the risk of localizing the Divine to a point in space. From our three-dimensional perspective then, the "Father in Heaven" is as much a "quality," or aspect, of the Divine Reality, or God, as the Holy Spirit is thought to be. This divine quality that we refer to as "the Father" is the Reality or "Ground" of our common origin and existence, which, as it is not acknowledged and realized in our dimension and our ordinary awareness, remains unmanifest (in Heaven). In this sense, any insight that we may receive which helps us to appreciate, and give validation to our shared existence and destiny, can be said to come from the "Father in Heaven." Since in our conscious existence we are estranged from the fact and the reality that we are one, the shared psychic content that comprises the collective unconscious, to use Jung's terminology, represents a domain, close-to-hand, where that unity is still operative. This is why attributing Peter's insight to the collective unconscious makes sense. For readers who might be uncomfortable with this interpretation, let's consider the case of someone citing "the radio" or "the television" when asked for the source of some information they've just imparted to us. On such an occasion, we would understand that the response of "the radio," or "the television," is given simply to indicate the mode, or the medium through which the information was imparted to them. It's the same idea with the collective unconscious; it's simply a channel through which we can access insight about our commonality.

Chapter Four

1. For example, C.W. Leadbeater, in his book entitled *The Chakras*, described the chakras as "...saucer-like depressions or vortices in its surface" (i.e., the 'etheric double'). He continues in his description: "When quite undeveloped they appear as small circles about two inches in diameter, glowing dully in the ordinary man; but when awakened and vivified they are seen as blazing, coruscating whirlpools, much

increased in size, and resembling miniature suns"; p. 4. *The Chakras* by C. W. Leadbeater, The Theosophical Publishing House, Wheaton, Illinois, 1961.

2. Govinda, *Foundations of Tibetan Mysticism*, 156.
3. Joy, *Joy's Way*, 159.
4. Moss, *The Black Butterfly*, 200.
5. Satprem, *Sri Aurobindo or the Adventure of Consciousness*, 68–69.

Chapter Five

1. Barnwell, *Meditations on the Apocalypse*, 4–5.
2. Carl Jung's distinction between the Self as an intellectual concept and a reality is helpful in this present context. In *Two Essays on Analytical Psychology*, he states: "Intellectually the Self is no more than a psychological concept, a construct that serves to express an unknowable essence which we cannot grasp as such, since by definition it transcends our powers of comprehension. It might equally well be called 'God within'"(p. 238).
3. The term for God used here is Elohim, a plural term. The use of the plural is confirmed by the statement "Let us make man ..." This, more than anything, should help dispel the "Old man in the sky" image many have of the deity. The us relates to a state of being.
4. There have been various interpretations of whether Buddha refused to give an answer in regard to God or the soul. For example, according to Sidney Spencer on page 70 of *Mysticism in World Religion*, the question Buddha was asked was "Is there a self?"
5. The questioner is identified as "Wacchagotta the Wanderer."
6. Aurobindo, *Essays Divine and Human*, 165–66.
7. Lee Sannella in the book *The Kundalini Experience—Psychosis or Transcendence*, op. cit., documents several cases where individuals have suffered symptoms of psychotic disturbances. The same is documented in Gopi Krishna's book, *Kundalini—The Evolutionary Energy In Man* (See Bibliography).
8. These teachings are discussed in P.D. Ouspensky's book, *In Search Of The Miraculous* (Harcourt, Brace & World, Inc., New York, 1949), 220.
9. Gurdjieff, *Beelzebub's Tales To His Grandson*, 107.

Chapter Seven

1. Young, *Analytical Concordance*.

2. The most common interpretation of Tantra is that it deals with the utilization of the sex act to achieve some sort of awakening of the Kundalini energy. According to the Yoga of Sri Aurobindo, Tantra is a general term for a state of equanimity that the spiritual aspirant is to take with him into all aspects of the life.

3. The circle is measured in degrees, minutes, and seconds: 360 degrees to the circle, 60 minutes to the degree, 60 seconds to the minute. At a rate of precession of only 50 seconds a year ($\frac{1}{72}$ of a degree), it would take the Earth 25,920 years to catch up to its original starting point. This period of 25,920 years is called A Great Year. In the meantime, the orientation of the Earth's northern pole would have circumscribed a complete circle and the pole star would have changed several times.

Chapter Eight

1. Moss, *The Black Butterfly*, 294–295.

Chapter Ten

1. A royalty-free electronic text version of John Bunyan's *The Pilgrim's Progress* is available on the Internet as part of the Gutenberg collection at http://www.gutenberg.org/etext/131.

2. The term subconscious is used strictly in the sense of that which is below the threshold of consciousness, namely that which exists at the level of habits, compulsions, etc. The distinction must be made between the subconscious and the superconscious, even though both of these levels lie outside of the sphere of consciousness. As for the superconscious, this relates to the level of moral and spiritual values not subjected to conscious analysis, but that nevertheless play a part in directing the course of life.

Chapter Eleven

1. Here, unconscious includes both sub- and superconscious. To say that there is no split is to say that all actions come under the control of the will. This would imply that the individual takes responsibilities for his own spiritual ideals (i.e., integrates the superconscious) and does not let habits, complexes, traumas, compulsions, etc., run the life.

2. Guillaumount, et al., *The Gospel According to Thomas*, Log. 22, pp. 17–18.

3. Sohl and Carr, eds., *The Gospel According to Zen*, 116.

4. A rather comprehensive and philosophical treatment of the issue of reincarnation, or rebirth, is provided by Sri Aurobindo in his book *The Problem of Rebirth*. In it, Aurobindo puts forward the idea that the individual is a vehicle for the soul, which must experience opportunities in earth life to perfect itself in divine virtues.

5. This interpretation of the sea as the collective unconscious is my own. The implication of this interpretation is that the soul is in the task of harvesting experiences from this collective unconscious for the purpose of refining them further.

Chapter Twelve

1. Campbell, *Occidental Mythology.* op cit. p. 913.
2. From *Man And His Symbols.* by Carl G. Jung, et al., copyright 1964, J.G. Ferguson Publishing, 1964, pp. 153-155.
3. Aurobindo, *The Bases of Yoga*, 110.
4. Avalon, *Serpent Power*, 148–9. Avalon describes these two minor chakras: "The highest of the six centres called Cakra in the Susumna is the Ajna... Close by it is the Cakra called Lalana." He goes on to say, "Above the Lalana are the Ajna Cakra with its two lobes and the Manas Cakra with its six lobes."
5. See endnote 4, preceding.

Chapter Thirteen

1. These other six "bodies" are called, in ascending order, the Etheric, the Astral, the Causal, the Mental, the Soul, and the Spiritual.
2. This list is not meant to exhaust all the different forms of Yoga. These three are mentioned because they are the most "tangible," but there are others, such as Bhakti (the Yoga of devotion), Gyana (the Yoga of concentration), Laya (the Yoga of mastery over nature), and more.
3. Aurobindo, *The Life Divine*, 3.
4. Satprem, *Sri Aurobindo or the Adventure of Consciousness*, 299.
5. Ibid., 344.

BIBLIOGRAPHY

Bibles, Bible Aids, and Other Holy Books

The Bhagavad Gita.

The Holy Bible, English Standard Version® (ESV®).Crossway, a publishing ministry of Good News Publishers, 2001.

The Holy Bible, The King James Version. Nashville and New York: Thomas Nelson Inc., 1970.

The Holy Bible, The New Oxford Annotated Bible, Revised Standard Version. Oxford University Press, 1977.

Interpreter's Dictionary of the Bible: An Illustrated Encyclopedia. Nashville: Abingdon Press, 1962 (Supplementary volume, 1976).

Guillaumount, A. et al. *The Gospel According to Thomas.* New York: Harper & Row; 1959.

Rieu, E. V. *The Four Gospels:* A New Translation from the Greek. Penguin Books, 1961.

Young, Robert. *Analytical Concordance to the Holy Bible.* London: United Society for Christian Literature, Lutterworth Press; revised edition, 1939; eighth printing, 1966.

Chakras, Kundalini, and the Psychology of Consciousness

Avalon, Arthur (a.k.a., Sir John Woodroffe). *The Serpent Power.* Madras, India: Ganesh & Co.; twelfth edition, 1981.

Barnwell, F. Aster. *The Pilgrim's Companion: A Handbook for the Spiritual Path.* Element Books. 1992 (out-of-print).

Fox, Matthew, *Meditations with Meister Eckhart.* Santa Fe, New Mexico: Bear & Co. Inc., 1983.

Gopi, Krishna. *Kundalini: The Evolutionary Energy in Man.* Boulder and London: Shambhala, 1971.

Govinda, Anagarika. *Foundations of Tibetan Mysticism.* York Beach, Maine: Samuel Weiser, 1969.

Joy, W. Brugh, MD. *Joy's Way: A Map for the Transformational Journey.* Los Angeles: J. P. Tarcher, 1979.

Lansky, Philip. "Neurochemistry and the Awakening of Kundalini" from *Kundalini, Evolution, and Enlightenment.* Anchor Books, Doubleday & Co., 1979.

Leadbeater, C. W. *The Chakras.* Wheaton, Illinois: The Theosophical Publishing House, 1974.

Moss, Richard, MD. *The Black Butterfly: An Invitation to Radical Aliveness.* Berkeley, California: Celestial Arts, 1986.

Ornstein, Robert E. *The Psychology of Consciousness.* Pelican Books, 1975.

Sannella, Lee, MD. Kundalini*: Psychosis or Transcendence?* San Fransisco: H. S. Dakin Company; 1977.

Satprem. *Sri Aurobindo, or The Adventure of Consciousness.* France and Mirra Aditi, Mysore, India: Institut de Recherches Evolutives, fifth revised edition, 2008.

Tansley, David V., DC. *Radionics and the Subtle Anatomy of Man.* Essex, England: The C. W. Daniel Co., Ltd., 1980.

Symbology, Mythology

Barnwell, F. Aster. *Meditations on the Apocalypse.* Element Books, 1992: 2011 Authors Guild Backinprint.com reprint edition. iUniverse.com.

Campbell, Joseph. *The Masks of God, Vol. 1: Primitive Mythology.* Copyright 1964 by Joseph Campbell. Reprinted by permission of Viking Penguin Inc., and Russell & Volkening

_____ *The Masks of God, Vol. 2: Oriental Mythology.* Copyright 1964 by Joseph Campbell. Reprinted by permission of Viking Penguin Inc., and Russell & Volkening.

_____*The Masks of God, Vol. 3: Occidental Mythology.* Copyright 1964 by Joseph Campbell. Reprinted by permission of Viking Penguin Inc., and Russell & Volkening.

_____*The Masks of God, Vol. 4: Creative Mythology.* Copyright 1964 by Joseph Campbell. Reprinted by permission of Viking Penguin Inc., and Russell & Volkening

Hamilton, Edith. *Mythology: Timeless Tales of Gods and Heroes.* New American Library (Mentor Books), 1969.

Hull, R. F. C., trans. "Four Archetypes: Mother; Rebirth, Spirit, Trickster" from *The Collected Works of C. G. Jung, Vol. 9.* Princeton University Press, 1969.

Hull, R. F. C., trans. "Four Archetypes: Mother; Rebirth, Spirit, Trickster" from *The Collected Works of C. G. Jung, Vol. 9.* Princeton University Press, 1969.

Hull, R. F. C., trans. "Psychology and Religion: West and East" from *The Collected Works of C. G. Jung, Vol. 11,* Princeton University Press, 1969.

Jung, C. G. et al. *Man and His Symbols.* l. G. Ferguson Publishing, 1964.

Jung, C. G. *Memories, Dreams, Reflections.* Recorded and edited by Aniela Jaffe, translated by Richard and Clara Winston. New York: Pantheon Books, a division of Random House Inc., 1965.

Philosophy

Aurobindo, Sri. *The Life Divine.* Pondicherry, India: Sri Aurobindo Ashram, Publications Department, tenth edition, 1977.

_____ *The Bases Of Yoga.* Pondicherry, India: Sri Aurobindo Ashram, Publications Department, 1973.

_____ *The Problem Of Rebirth.* Pondicherry, India: Sri Aurobindo Ashram, third edition, 1973.

_____ "Reason and Religion," *The Human Cycle.* Pondicherry, India: Sri Aurobindo Ashram Trust, second edition, 1977.

Bennett, John G. *The Masters of Wisdom.* U. K.: Turnstone Books, 1977.

Gurdjieff, G. I. *Beelzebub's Tales to His Grandson: All and Everything.* London: First Book, Routledge & Kegan Paul, 1976.

Lao-tzu. *The Way of Life.* American version by Witter Bynner. New York: Capricorn Books, 1962.

Ouspensky, P. D. *In Search of the Miraculous.* New York: Harcourt, Brace & World Inc, 1949.

Schuon, Frithiof. *Stations of Wisdom.* Pates Manor, Bedfont, Middlesex, U.K.: Perennial Books, Ltd., 1980.

Sohl, Robert and Carr, Audrey, eds. *The Gospel According to Zen.* New American Library (A Mentor Book), 1970.

Spencer, Sidney. *Mysticism in World Religion.* Penguin Books, 1963.

Sugrue, Thomas. *There is a River.* New York, New York: Dell Publishing, 1974 (nineteenth printing). This book is currently available from A.R.E. Press, Virginia Beach, Virginia, USA, 1979.

Weil, Simone. *Gravity and Grace.* Ark Paperbacks (An imprint of Routledge & Kegan Paul), 1987.

Yogi, Ramacharaka. *Mystic Christianity, or the Inner Teachings of the Master.* Chicago: Yogi Publication Society, 1907.

History, Origins of Christianity

Acharya S. (a.k.a., D. M. Murdock). *Suns of God.* Kempton, Illinois: Adventures Unlimited Press, 2004.

_____ *The Christ Conspiracy.* Kempton, Illinois: Adventures Unlimited Press, 1999.

Burleigh, John. H. S., ed. *Augustine: Early Writings.* The Westminster Press. (This title can be browsed at Google Books.)

Ehrman, Bart D. *Jesus, Interrupted: Revealing the Hidden Contradictions in the Bible (and Why We Don't Know About Them).* New York, New York: Harper Collins Publishers, 2009.

Freke, Timothy and Peter Gandy, *The Jesus Mysteries,* Thorsons, 1999.

Handford, S. A., trans. *Fables of Aesop.* Penguin Books, 1977.

Harpur, Tom. *The Pagan Christ.* Toronto, Canada: Thomas Allen Publishers, 2004.

Kuhn, Alvin Boyd. *A Rebirth for Christianity.* Wheaton, Illinois: Quest Books, The Theosophical Publishing House, 1970.

_____ *Shadow of the Third Century: A Revaluation of Christianity.* Filquarian Publishing, 1949 (2007 reprint).

Massey, Gerald. *The Historical Jesus and the Mythical Christ.* Kessinger Publishing's Rare Reprints (no date).

_____ *Ancient Egypt: The Light of the World, Part 1.* Kessinger Publishing's Rare Reprints (no date).

_____ *Ancient Egypt: The Light of the World, Part 2.* Kessinger Publishing's Rare Reprints (no date).

Osman, Ahmed. *The House of the Messiah:* Controversial Revelations on the Historical Jesus. London: HarperCollins Publishers, 1992.

Allegorical Fiction

Bunyan, John. *The Pilgrim's Progress.* A royalty-free, electronic text version of this title is available on the Internet as part of the Gutenberg collection at: http://www.gutenberg.org/etext/131

Radice, Betty, ed. "Treasure Trove" (Story No. 172) from *Fables of Aesop.* Penguin Classics, Penguin Books, 1977.

CPSIA information can be obtained at www.ICGtesting.com
Printed in the USA
LVOW040646171111

255312LV00001B/86/P